Breaking Barriers to Learning in Primary Schools

Breaking Barriers to Learning in Primary Schools takes an expert and informative look at the Integrated Children's Services agenda in practice in today's primary schools and examines the ways in which an increasing number of different professionals help to improve children's life chances. The author examines the roles of those employed directly by the schools themselves, for instance learning mentors, teaching assistants and those employed in health or social work and other agencies, such as school nurses, educational social workers, study support workers, school attendance workers and educational psychologists. A final section looks at the work of volunteers and consultants.

Through an exploration of how each individual helps break down barriers to children's learning, this book:

- Examines the growth and development of the children's workforce
- Provides a broad and integrated view of the wider school network
- Explores the roles of individuals within the school workforce
- Makes links to Every Child Matters and Extended Schools initiatives
- Provides evidence of breaking down barriers, through interviews and studies with those working at the heart of integrated schools
- Presents an analysis of recent statistics relating to children's lives
- Gives practical advice for good practice throughout.

An essential text for all those working in education and in training to become part of this wider school network, this book takes into account the findings of the recent Primary Reviews, government data and original research to fully explain how to build, maintain and successfully work with today's primary children. It is an excellent text for Foundation Degree students, as well as those studying education studies and those training to be teachers.

Pat Hughes is Senior Lecturer at Liverpool Hope University, teaching on undergraduate and postgraduate initial teacher training courses, as well as more generic undergraduate and postgraduate Education Studies courses. She is a course leader for a Master's Level Course in Integrated Children's Services and is also a Non-Executive Director of a Primary Care Trust (NHS), which operates in a local authority where both health and social care share budgets. The authority is recognised nationally as a leader in this field of partnership.

Breaking Barriers to Learning in Primary Schools

An integrated approach to children's services

Pat Hughes

Routledge
Taylor & Francis Group

LONDON AND NEW YORK

First published 2010
by Routledge
2 Park Square, Milton Park, Abingdon, Oxon OX14 4RN

Simultaneously published in the USA and Canada
by Routledge
270 Madison Avenue, New York, NY 10016

Routledge is an imprint of the Taylor & Francis Group, an informa business

© 2010 Pat Hughes

Typeset in Bembo by Prepress Projects Ltd, Perth, UK
Printed and bound in Great Britain by TJ International Ltd, Padstow, Cornwall

British Library Cataloguing in Publication Data
A catalogue record for this book is available from the British Library

Library of Congress Cataloging-in-Publication Data
Hughes, Pat, 1933–
Breaking barriers to learning in primary schools : an integrated approach to children's
services / Pat Hughes.
p. cm.
1. Children with social disabilities—Education (Elementary)—Great Britain. 2.
Children with social disabilities—Services for—Great Britain. I. Title.
LC4096.G7H83 2010
372.170941—dc22   2009020472

ISBN 10: 0-415-47944-4 (pbk)
ISBN 10: 0-415-47943-6 (hbk)
ISBN 10: 0-203-86544-8 (ebk)

ISBN 13: 978-0-415-47943-1 (hbk)
ISBN 13: 978-0-415-47944-8 (pbk)
ISBN 13: 978-0-203-86544-6 (ebk)

Contents

Illustrations

Figures

Tables

Boxes

Acknowledgements

The following individuals provided advice, notes and inspiration:
Matt and Julia Barlow
Lynne Berry
Paula Cain
Anita Challender
Adam Chamberlain
John Clare
Steve Clarke
Kath Cox
Paul Checkley
Angela Crummer
Ann Edwards
Cath Fairhurst
Angela Fullerton
Joe Gazdula
Steve George
Gillian Goddard
Barbara Gowans
Ann Grindrod
Philip Hallman
Kelly Hardy
Chris Head
Kate Lee
Yvonne Jameson
Norman Jones
Sam and Suzanne Kerr
Annie Kirby
Kate Lee
Hilary Letts
Paul Lock
Sabba Mann
Lynn McCann
Anita Marsland
Keith McDougal

Ila, Doug and Rachel Miller
Dawn Molloy
Pat O'Brian
Chris O'Hare
Keith Hughes
Liz Priest
Jean Robb
Mike Ronald
Jan Rowe
Sherbana Sari
Mahnaz Siddiqui
Mike Shankland
Julie Sheriff
Keith Skinner
Maggie Smith
Meena Visawanathan
Marian Walsh
Gill Walton
Jane Watts
Elaine Whitby
Paula Worthington
AnnMarie Young

Also Jordan and Stephan, who gave me pictures about barriers to learning

Educational professional undergraduate students, full- and part-time primary PGCE students, Master's students on the Integrated Children's Services Module

The following agencies provided critical documentation, advice and support:
Bridge Street CP
Cheetham Hill CP
CAST
Eccleston Lane Ends
English Martyrs
Longview CP
Mount Carmel
Overdale CP
Prescot CP
St. Joseph the Worker
St. Lawrences
St. Martins
St. Patricks
St. Williams
Sacred Heart
Successful Learning
Three Lane Ends CP
Woodhouse Junior.

Abbreviations

A&E	Accident and Emergency
ACPC	Area Child Protection Committees
ADD/ADHD	Attention Deficit (Hyperactivity) Disorder
AfL	Assessment for Learning
AFL	Assessment for Literacy
ALPS/alps	Accelerated Learning in Primary Schools
ALS	Additional Literacy Strategy
APP	assessment for pupil progress
ARCH	Action Rights for Children
ASB	Anti-social Behaviour
ASD	autism spectrum disorder
BECTA	British Educational Communications Technology Agency
BEST	Behaviour and Education Support Team
BIP	Behaviour Improvement Project
BIP	Behaviour Intervention Plan
BSF	Building Schools for the Future
BST	Behaviour Support Teacher
CACE	Central Advisory Council for Education (England)
CAF	Common Assessment Framework
CAMHS	Child and Adolescent Mental Health Service
CAST	Central Agency Support Team
CEOP	Child Exploitation and Online Protection Centre
CoRT	Cognitive Research Trust
CP	County Primary or Community Primary
CPAG	Child Poverty Action Group
CPD	continuing professional development
CRB	Criminal Records Bureau
CSI	Crime Scene Investigation
CVA	Contextual Value Added
CWDC	Children's Workforce Development Council
CWN	Children's Workforce Network
CYPAN	Children and Young People's Area Network
CYPP	Children and Young People's Plan
DCSF	Department for Children, Schools and Families from 2007 (replacing DfES Department for Education and Skills)

DH	Department of Health
DT	Design Technology
EAL	English as an additional language
EALSEN	children with EAL who also have SEN
ECM	Every Child Matters
EEG	Electroencephalography
EiC	Excellence in Cities
ELLI	Effective Lifelong Learning Inventory
ELS	Early Literacy Support
ELW	extended link worker
EMAS	Ethnic Minority Achievement Service
ESW	educational social worker
EWO	education welfare officer
EYS	Early Years
FACE	Family and Community Education
FE	further education
FGM	Family Group Meetings
FLP	Family Learning Programme
FLS	Further Literacy Strategy
FMRI	Functional Magnetic Resonance Imagining
FSM	Free School Meals
FSW	family support worker
GNP	Gross National Product
HE	Higher Education
HLTA	higher level teaching assistant
HO	Home Office
IT	information technology
ICS	Integrated Children's Service
ICT	Information and Communications Technology
IEP	Individual Education Plan
IQ	Intelligence Quotient
IQF	Integrated Qualifications Framework
ISP	Improving Schools Programme
ISSP	Intensive Surveillance and Supervision Programme
ITS	Intermediate Treatment Scheme
ITT	Initial Teacher Training
JAR	Joint Area Review
L2L	Learning to Learn
LA	local authority
LAA	Local Authority Agreement
LAC	looked-after children
LDSS	Learning Development and Support Service
LEAP	Leap confronting conflict
LINC	Learning in Neighbourhood Centres
LM	learning mentor
LS	Learning Support

LSA	Learning Support Assistant
LSCB	Local Safeguarding Children Boards
MAARF	multi-agency assessment and referral form
MEG	Magnetoencephalography
MEND	Mind, Exercise, Nutrition . . . Do it!
NCSL	National College for School Leadership
NHS	National Health Service
NLS	National Literacy Strategy
NNEB	National Nursery Examination Board
NNF	National Numeracy Framework
NOF	New Opportunities Funding
NOS	National Occupational Standards
NQF	National Qualifications Framework
NS-SEC	National Statistics Socio-economic Classification
NSPCC	National Society for Prevention of Cruelty to Children
NUT	National Union of Teachers
NVQ	National Vocational Qualification
PA	Persistent Absence
PCSO	police community support officer
PCR	Primary Curriculum Review
PCT	Personal Construct Theory
PCT	Primary Care Trust
PE	Physical Education
PET	Positron Emission Tomography
PFI	Private Finance Initiative
PG/PGCE	post-graduate certificate in education
PLSU	Primary Learning Support Units
PLT	Primary Link Teacher
PLTS	personal, learning and thinking skills
PPA	Planning, Preparation, Assessment
PPO	police protection order
PPP	Positive Parenting Programme
PRU	personal response unit
PRU	pupil referral unit
PSHE	personal, social and health education
PSLO	primary school liaison officer
PTFA	Parents, Teachers, Friends Association
QA	Quality Assurance
QCA	Qualifications and Curriculum Authority (from 2009 known as the QCDA: Qualifications and Curriculum Development Agency)
QTS	qualified teacher status
RE	Religious Education
ROA	record of achievement
SAIO	School Attendance Improvement Officer
SAO	senior attendance officer
SATs	Standard Assessment Tasks/Tests

SEAL	Social and Emotional Aspects of Learning
SEN	special educational needs
SENCO	Special Educational Needs Coordinator
SEP	School Evaluation Form
SIP	School Improvement Partners
SLA	Service Level Agreement
SLO	school liaison officer
SMSCP	Spiritual, Moral, Social, Cultural and Physical Growth
SOW	schemes of work
SPAA	Sport Physical Activity Alliance
SRE	Sex and Relationship Education
SSCO	School Sports Coordinators
SST	specialist support teacher
STA	special teaching assistant
TA	Teaching Assistant
TDA	Training and Development Agency (replaced TTA – Teacher Training Agency)
TED	Technology, Education and Design
TES	*Times Educational Supplement*
UNCRE	United Nations Convention on the Rights of the Child
Unicef	United Nations Children's Fund
VFM	value for money
WALT	We are Learning to . . .
WIIFM	What's In It For Me
WILF	What I'm Looking For
YIP	Youth Inclusion Programme
YOT	Youth Offending Teams

Introduction

Helpers make learning easier.

(Year 4 child when asked to identify what made learning easier)

Part 1

This book aims to look at the wider primary school workforce in terms of the ways in which different members of this workforce identify and break down barriers to learning. The Children's Plans and the 'Every Child Matters' (ECM) agenda are closely linked to this concept of a wider school workforce, within an Integrated Children's Services (ICS) framework. Currently, this is bureaucratically alive and well, but the operational complexities, i.e. the aspects that actually influence children's day-to-day lives, are still being worked out. The second part of the book provides some of the stories about how this is happening.

Breaking Barriers to Learning is intended to help all members of this wider school workforce to identify its enormity and examine the sort of work that is being done in our primary schools. It is also about opening an information portal in thinking about different ways of working with children for those who are currently on courses from which they will gain some qualification that identifies them as likely to work with children and young people – indeed, some of the people you might meet working in a school. It helps to provide a broader view of the school workforce if you are aware of who may be working in schools – what they do and how they do it, what barriers they feel they are lifting and how they are doing it.

The initial impetus for this book came from a day's attendance at a course on updating legislation and practice on Safeguarding Children. This was in liaison with a primary school where I had taught and at which I am now a governor. I walked into the Local Authority (LA) Conference Centre and looked at the 50 or so people sitting at tables, wandering around with coffee, chatting and networking. I assumed at first glance that we were being given the input as part of a local cluster of schools and those in this conference hall represented three or four different schools in our local cluster. When I sat down, I quickly realised that I knew a lot of people. Moreover, they worked at the school. This turned out to be not three or four primary schools, but just one school. They were all educational professionals in the school workforce. Each had different roles and responsibilities in the school, but, ultimately, their work involved making a difference to the lives of the primary children with whom they worked. This was a school that I knew very well. I knew, at one level, that it employed far more people than when I had worked there. However, the visual impact was quite staggering, as the presenter herself commented.

About 3 months later, I interviewed the headteacher and Table 0.1 represents just some of the people who were there that day. Some of the people were employed directly by the school, some of them were part funded by the school and some of us were volunteers. The headteacher and I then discussed other professionals, who came into the school, but who had not been present at the Safeguarding Children day. For this particular school they included:

- *Generic health professionals* – the school nurse, Healthy School Programme workers
- *Sensory Impaired Team* – speech and language worker, educational psychologist, behaviour support, educational social worker
- *Social Services* – family workers
- *Environmental services* – eco-schools project, including eco-play project, recycling
- *Subject specialists* – sports coaches
- *Technology* – computer system support, including safeguarding package
- *Whole-school support systems* – Intensive Support Programme (ISP) (comes into action if school SATs fall below 60%); numeracy and literacy consultants; Education Change Partner (ECP); School Improvement Partner (SIP);

TABLE 0.1 Attendees at a safeguarding conference

ROLE	EMPLOYED BY
16 teachers plus headteacher, deputy headteacher	School
8 TAs	6 employed by the school, 2 funded by both school and LA
1 HLTA	School
1 LM	School – partly funded by LA
3 administrative workers	School
1 site manager	School
1 parent mentor	School – partly funded by LA
9 welfare assistants – some with dual roles as cleaners and servers of food	School
5 governors	Volunteers: two local authority representatives, one a community representative and two parent governors
1 vicar	Volunteer and also a governor

external consultants, employed by the school but advised by the LA; Behaviour Improvement Team (BIP); Behaviour and Education Support Team (BEST); Minority Ethnic Group (MEG).

Note that this list is by no means definitive. LAs are given central statutory obligations, but choose to implement them in ways that best fit their own circumstances – political and social. There is also a growth in the numbers of those contracted in for short periods of time.

Some of those employed by the local authority and other agencies also provide services to the schools (Table 0.2). Sometimes, this may be on a very regular basis, for example the private companies and charities who run extended schools services in many areas. Sometimes, it may be as part of school or local/central government authority projects; for example the fire officer interviewed in Part 2 was called into primary schools with colleagues to look at the work of the fire service.

TABLE 0.2 Other educational professionals providing services to children in primary schools

Generic LA (integrated services, leisure, libraries, etc.)	Emergency duty team (safeguarding)	Youth offending team
CAFASS (Court and Family Court Advisory Support Service)	Primary Care Trust (NHS), e.g. school dentists	Child and adolescent mental health services
Work experience – some of whom are paid	Substance misuse such as anti-smoking – LA and charities	Children's welfare charities such as the NSPCC, The Children's Society, Barnardo's, Save the Children, Children in Need
Charities directed to the child e.g. ChildLine, Rainbows. May include professionally trained play workers	Charities linked with academic need, e.g. volunteer reading	Professionals working with children in museums, galleries, visitor centres, outdoor centres
Before- and after-school clubs – private companies and charities	Local authority initiatives linked to specific strategies, such as literacy, numeracy and citizenship	Play and holiday schemes
Theatre in education	Author/artist in residence schemes	Creative Partnerships
Police/road and/or rail safety/fire prevention – Safety for Schools programme workers	Faith workers	Specialist curricular support from private companies – modern foreign languages (MFL), sports, drama, dance, music, arts workshops

Extended from Hughes (2008).

Book overview

This book looks at how and why in the years since I worked in that school there has been an increase in the number of those working in the school. Ironically, or paradoxically, there has also been a decrease in the number of teachers employed. It has been a gradual process, largely led by different central government policy changes and initiatives, which have required a broader and more specialist workforce in schools. There have also been pressures by outside agencies, including LA health and social care departments, to have a greater direct input in schools.

This is reflected elsewhere, as other organisations such as the police and fire services reach out to primary pupils. In the past many of these services, who are now quite heavily involved in primary schools, would have left any educational work they did to the secondary sector, for example sports coaches. Now, the far-seeing ones are reaching out into both primary and preschool settings.

Part 1

Chapter 1 looks at this growth of what is now known as the Children's Workforce and some of the opportunities and challenges it presents to our primary schools. This first chapter also looks for a definition of an educational professional, particularly for organisations and agencies who do not necessarily see themselves as working as part of the school-based element of a wider Children's Workforce or who do not see themselves as educational professionals.

Chapters 2–6 provide a framework for work in primary schools today. This looks beyond the more usual texts directed generally at the teacher and may improve their practice. These chapters look at specific challenges for primary pupils as effective learners from a number of different research disciplines.

Chapter 2 looks directly, and critically, at how data collection is being used to identify differential performance in primary schools. This, in turn, raises important questions about the data collection and the political agenda that drives the huge statistical public databases for school performance. It is important because primary school Standard Assessment Tasks/Tests (SATs) results have been in the public domain for several years, and judgements made about school effectiveness are based on these scores.

Chapter 3 acknowledges that child poverty is still seen, by policy-makers, as a major determinant of school performance. Often this is known as the postcode lottery. This chapter provides a useful guide to the historical, political and sociological background to ways in which child poverty has been defined and challenged over the years.

Chapter 4 acknowledges that in order to look at ways in which barriers to learning can be addressed by educational professionals, we need greater knowledge about the learning process. Much of current educational provision takes a fairly traditional approach to how children learn and this does provide some sort of starting point for looking at how children are identified as learners. The chapter also looks at differing constructs of the child as a learner over a period of time, and enables the reader to question and reflect on how current constructs of childhood may be influencing how schools and pupils see themselves. The interviews in the second part of the book show how many of those working with children to raise barriers to learning hold different constructs to childhood and families than those hidden within the Qualified Teacher Status (QTS) standards for teachers.

Chapter 5 moves into looking beneath the surface of schools at learning and teaching practices and the general school environment. It explores ways in which to identify some hidden curriculum barriers for primary children.

The following chapter looks at some of the challenges and changes for primary schools. Some of these arise directly from the previous chapters, but some are linked to more general changes in society, technology and the growing scientific base for learning.

All of the chapters in Part 1 have suggested activities and tasks throughout, which work to support understanding of the ideas. In Part 2, this is replaced by the general suggestion that the best way of gaining further understanding is for the reader to interview educational professionals themselves. This can be done by using the semistructured format used for this book or developing an alternative approach. Certainly, for working in one school, or in one setting, for example health, it would be necessary to change the format, as there are likely to be sensitive issues raised by some questions.

Part 2

In the second part of the book, those who work in schools tell their stories. These are the operational workers who carry out the day-to-day, year-on-year practical tasks of working with primary children to make a difference to their lives. Some, such as TAs, are directly involved in conventional teaching. Others are in more diverse, and often more dynamic, areas of children's lives, such as family support workers (FSWs). The missing element in this second part of the book is the primary class teacher. This is because its purpose is to highlight the work of the more invisible members of the primary school community. The increase in the number of support workers is clearly changing the role of the primary class teacher and books such as *Principles of Primary Education* (Hughes 2008) illustrate some elements of this change.

We look first, in Chapter 7, at the work of the TAs, who spend the majority of their working life working in classrooms. Chapter 8 contains interviews with five primary mentors and looks with them at their roles of the learning mentor, behaviour mentor and parent mentor. Chapter 9 provides a primary case study, drawn from an Ofsted report, that described the team as 'An Exceptional Pastoral Care Team'. Two members of this team, a counsellor and a family support worker, were interviewed, as was the headteacher, and it was a genuine privilege to be able to attend one of their meetings, which is also recorded in this chapter.

Chapter 10 looks at the work of five professionals working in different local authority attendance, health and study support teams. These were just a number of professionals, who work either directly or indirectly with primary children, who, in four instances, had trained as teachers and were using that expertise to inform and support different professionalisms.

Chapter 11 examines an example of how one local authority started to plan for improved integrated working in relation to its schools services. This work had been well on its way prior to the ECM agenda, but has developed and continues to develop.

This is also the case for the professionals interviewed in Chapter 12, who were employed by the police and fire service. Their role is changing in relation to primary schools and, in some cases, older police officers recognised a pattern from the past which had disappeared but appears to be returning. The final interview chapter looks at the work of those who work in charities, consultants and volunteers.

Searching for a wider academic base

This book is not a traditional academic text, but the first section in particular is informed by academic research in various fields, which I have loosely described as social science perspectives, in particular sociology, psychology, social history, philosophy, politics and economics. Table 0.3 provides a simple overview of this. As many of those I have chosen to define as educational professionals come from different professional backgrounds, some of the theoretical and practical strands of their training have important implications for those whose training is heavily school based and vice versa.

The book is also informed by the two reviews of primary education, which reported early in 2009.

The Primary Review and the Primary Curriculum Review

In 2006, the government set up a review of primary schools under the stewardship of Robin Alexander of the University of Cambridge. Its purpose was to draw together data from a variety of sources to make recommendations for future national policy related to primary schools and other relevant agencies. Section 6 of this Primary Review has several papers that provide an overview of the research in this area of multi-agency work. The Review papers do provide some excellent research evidence for both what has happened in the past, and what is likely to happen in the future for a much wider school agenda. Many covered good literature reviews of much of the action-based research that has been carried out in recent years.

The following year, the government set up a review of the primary curriculum under Sir James Rose. This was far more limited in terms of its remit and was told not to look at key issues such as assessment and testing. In the Alexander Review this had proved very politically controversial, with clear conclusions about testing practices and procedures in primary schools. The Rose Review, as it came to be called, looked at how the primary curriculum should change to ensure all children gain a good grounding in reading, writing, speaking, literacy and numeracy. Both reported in 2009.

The Rose curriculum review was a political document that captured the political middle ground on what should happen in primary schools. From its initial creation it was obvious that it was much more likely to influence what happened in the schools over the next few years and certainly take up those most important media sound bites.

TABLE 0.3 Research areas that inform professionals working with primary pupils

RESEARCH AREA	RELEVANT INFLUENCES ON PUPILS IN TODAY'S SCHOOLS
Historical	Tradition of schooling in this country; oral history of schooling within a child's family, their own experience of schooling, both in the UK and elsewhere
Sociological	Life chances; labelling; distinct groups, communities and family patterns identified as 'problematic'; these include race, gender, class, faith, special needs, inclusion and equality issues
Psychological	Learning theories, developmental and personal psychology; social psychology, including the social construction of childhood
Economic	Poverty – in a community and/or family; built-in limits on central/local government and family funding, poverty dynamics
Political	Political ideologies related to education resulting in legislation and guidelines (local and national) covering nearly all of school provision, rights of the individual, role of the state, inspection procedures the national Ofsted report for 2002 identified underperformance in disproportional numbers in minority ethnic and faith groups, travellers, asylum seekers and refugees; pupils with English as an additional language; pupils with special educational needs; looked-after children; gifted and talented children; other children, such as sick children, young carers, families under stress, pregnant girls, teenage mothers; disaffected and excluded pupils; inequalities issues
Geographical	Demographic factors; economic, social, political and regional factors; international relations
Legal	International, European and national rights of the child; statutory obligations related to attendance, behaviour towards children, etc.
Educational	Educational policy, technology, teaching methods, training of teachers and other educators plus all of the above
Health and social care	Physical and social development from birth onwards, holistic child development, diet and nutrition, health and community care, hygiene, safeguarding
Social administration	Welfare, public services, delivery, social policy
Management	Management theories, systems processes, planning for change, operational and strategic management, financial management, budgets, inspection
Generic and developing areas	Such as childhood studies, inclusion, disability, family learning, education studies, family and identity programmes

This book is also informed by my own and colleagues' experiences of visiting many primary schools all over the country, talking and working with both children and staff and interviewing many of the workers involved directly about their work in relation to breaking barriers to learning.

Defining and expanding the current definition of 'barriers to learning'

The expression 'barriers to learning' comes from the initial documentation related to the creation, training and employment of school-based learning mentors in inner city schools (DfES 1999a). This initiative was originally aimed at improving inclusion and the definition was further refined by different local authorities and schools to provide a workable job specification, such as the following: 'to overcome barriers to learning in whatever form they may take to assist pupils to reach their individual potential'. This definition is the one most commonly used and covers the work of many of those working in our primary schools.

It does, however, need expanding, because the 'barriers' in this definition are seen very much on the child's side. It implies that it is the child who holds the barriers to learning within themselves, which a trained educational professional can help to break down. This book, and certainly many of those interviewed for it, felt that there are also other barriers that are created in the minds and structures of our society. The first few chapters of this book look at these in more detail. In Chapter 2, for example, we look at the way in which research evidence has been gathered to give hard data about the performance of different social and economic groups. This can – and often does – lend itself to stereotyping and stigmatising children who fit into specific groups. These sort of barriers are very much harder to identify because they are deeply embedded in our society and in our own minds.

Barriers to learning for some children may be a direct result of the institution of school itself and its place in our society. International comparisons are useful here. One of the comparisons most questioned is the very early age our UK children come to school; in many European countries, entry to school can be 1–2 years later. This enables children to spend more time in kindergarten, where the focus is on a much more holistic, play-related curriculum; it may be that for many young children in the UK this practice could prevent barriers being raised at a very early age. Certainly, there has been much media, as well as research, attention to the Foundation Stage profiling that takes place when children reach the end of the Foundation Stage. This identifies what 5-year-olds should be able to do when they enter Key Stage 1. A prominent argument is that this can place too heavy a pressure on some children who may not be ready for the sort of direct teaching some of the learning outcomes may require. After all, a child born in June, July or August of an academic school year is very much younger than those in the same class born in September, October and November.

Finally, the very word 'barriers' has a negative feel about it; rather like the word 'problems', which, when I was a social worker many years ago, was used as a pejorative adjective to describe many of the families with whom we worked. It is more positive to think of 'problems' and 'barriers' as challenges and opportunities. Certainly, many of those involved with this book have seen their tasks as challenges and worked hard at the strategies to break the 'barriers' to learning. When strategies have not worked as expected, they have been ready to try and find out why not and what can be learnt from their own 'informal' data collection.

Conclusion

In this introduction, we have noted the increasing numbers of adults working in our primary schools today. We have described these as educational professionals and roughly classified them as those employed by the school, those employed by the local authority, those whose work includes supplying services to the school and those who work as volunteers in school. The introduction has defined what is meant in this book by 'breaking barriers to learning' and broaden the term 'educational professionals' to move beyond the school gates.

Part 2

The children

But before we go further to look at this school workforce, we should look at what the main school workforce think; those who so often get ignored – the children. They work hard, often in quite crowded and uncomfortable conditions with no pay and little control over what they do. They often have to ask permission to move or to go to the toilet and only in the last few years have they been allowed to have something to drink during their working hours. Most of them work from 9.00 am to about 3.15 pm, with time for one or two short breaks and a lunch-time of up to 1 hour. Others start at 8.00 am and finish at 6.00 pm.

Two classes (Year 2 and Year 4) were asked what they found easy to learn and what they found difficult. One class recorded what was easy to learn and then what was difficult and the other identified difficulties/challenges/barriers first and then compared these with when they found learning easier. Table 0.4 shows their views in the 'adultspeak' of this book, organised into categories. An important element of the first part of *Barriers to Learning* is to demonstrate how very much more complex this is.

The teachers

Teachers can supply nearly all the strategies to address those issues raised by the children in Table 0.4. However, there are still many children whose needs will not be reached. I have deliberately not included teachers within this book, because so many other books address these issues. *Barriers to Learning* is intended to look beyond that and look at the voices and influence of some of the other members of this wider school workforce, as well as those with an Integrated Services brief.

TABLE 0.4 Pupils' voice: barriers to learning

BARRIERS TO LEARNING	WHAT MAKES LEARNING EASIER
Curriculum ■ Times table ■ Science and spelling ■ Tests ■ Some subjects I don't like ■ I don't really like reading ■ Homework ■ Maths ■ My dragon picture ■ Having to explain things	*Curriculum* ■ Liking the subject ■ ICT – like PowerPoints ■ ICT – Apple Macs ■ Presenting work in different ways ■ Puzzles and games ■ Having a fun way of learning ■ Key facts ■ Dinosaurs ■ PE, football ■ Having stories ■ Art and painting ■ Creative writing
Resources ■ No fingers (for doing mental maths) ■ No helpers ■ No TV ■ Nothing to use ■ No number square ■ Untidy writing ■ No equipment ■ Not wearing my glasses	*Resources* ■ Helpers ■ Having a whiteboard ■ Spelling with a word book ■ Using a dictionary ■ Number line ■ Playstation (the school has one as part of its IT provision) ■ Cameras ■ Seeing things on the walls ■ 'Pretty teachers' (Year 6 boy)
Learning ethos ■ Loud voices ■ Just talking at you and telling you what you can't do all the time ■ Not letting kids talk ■ Boring teachers who say the same things all the time, anyway so what's the point ■ When you have to do so many questions and read them clearly ■ When I can't draw pictures and colour things that will help me ■ Long date on the board to copy ■ Not repeating things ■ Not getting enough time to finish	*Learning ethos* ■ Having time to do the work ■ Practising things ■ Explanations ■ Working in a group or pairs ■ Making things ■ Working outside ■ Doing things in an artistic way ■ Trips out ■ Discussions when the whole table discusses something ■ When everyone joins in and makes it fun ■ Not waiting a lot ■ Different ways of writing ■ Not writing a lot ■ Seeing things ■ Using syllables ■ Hearing it ■ Being shown ■ Music

BARRIERS TO LEARNING	WHAT MAKES LEARNING EASIER
Other children	*Other children*
▪ When people talk	▪ Sitting next to a good person
▪ Distractions	
▪ Nudging me because they are left handed	
▪ No friends	
Myself	*Myself*
▪ Get distracted	▪ Reading is easy
▪ Rushing to get out to play	▪ Answer is in front of you
▪ Forgetting things and no time to go over	▪ Nothing is difficult
▪ Hard to read, not understanding some words	
▪ Not listening because I don't know what to do	
▪ Reading tests too hard for me	
▪ Fidgeting on the carpet and then don't know what to do when I go to my own place	
▪ I don't really like reading	
▪ 'Mack's my wock hard is I am dilecso'	

1

The Wider Children's Workforce in Primary Schools

The government considers the children's workforce to mean everyone who works with children and young people and their families, or who is responsible for improving their outcomes.

Building Brighter Futures: *Next Steps for the Children's Workforce* (Department for Children, Schools and Families 2008)

Chapter overview

- Identify what is currently meant by the term 'wider school workforce'

- Define the meaning of 'educational professionals' in the context of this book

- Evaluate the value, to those in the wider school workforce, of two models for managing change.

The changing nature of primary school personnel

Figure 1.1 provides an overview of the Core and Wider Children's Workforce and is adapted from the Department for Children, Schools and Families (DCSF) 2008 document *Building Brighter Futures*. It was later extended in a further DCSF publication *2020 Children and Young People's Workforce Strategy*. At present, the DCSF separates out a Core Children's Workforce and a Wider Children's Workforce. It defines the core as those professionals who work or volunteer with children, young people and their families, or who are responsible for their outcomes all the time. The Wider Children's Workforce is defined as those who work or volunteer with children, young people and/or their families part of the time, or who are responsible for their outcomes as part of their jobs. Interviews in the second part of this book cover both.

I have narrowed the focus to children of compulsory school age in primary schools, i.e. from 5 to 11 years. One reason for this is because the Foundation Stage, birth to 5

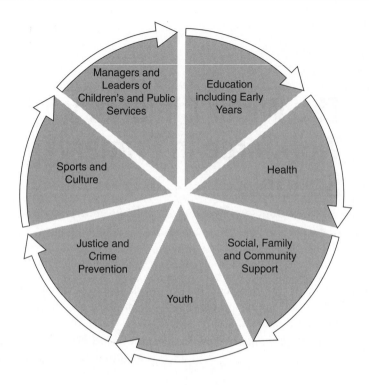

FIGURE 1.1 The core and wider children's workforce. Adapted from DFCS (2008)

years, in its widest sense, deserves a book of its own, as do the secondary and special needs sectors, although there are many overlapping features.

I have also tried to limit the focus to those members of the wider school workforce who come into primary school to work directly with children, but have also provided some examples of professionals who work with primary children outside schools, for example the Study Support coordinator. This distinction is disappearing slightly, as more and more schools house multi-agency workers; for example children's centres attached to a primary school may have rooms on site for 'travelling' educational professionals, such as speech therapists and educational psychologists. Primary Care Trusts (PCTs) share and build new multipurpose health clinics alongside primary schools, so primary carers can take themselves and their children to the GP, nurse practitioner or dentist on their way to and from school.

Sometimes you might hear the terms 'paraprofessional' or 'allied professionals' used to describe school-based professionals, such as teaching assistants, but this is a rather demeaning term that denies the specific professional skills they require in order to fulfil their responsibilities.

The Training and Development Agency (TDA) refers to 'learning support staff', and this covers teaching assistants (TAs), Higher Level Teaching Assistants (HLTAs), nursery nurses, cover supervisors, pupil support workers, administrative staff, specialist and technical staff, site staff and school business managers. The website, at the time of writing, covered a section on support staff roles, career development, national occupational standards, training and qualification. However, there is surprisingly little information on many other support roles, or on the much wider aspects of support staff roles in relation to the Integrated Children's Workforce.

Ofsted and the wider school workforce

Interestingly enough, Ofsted, in their 2008 report on the wider school workforce, made this a specific recommendation for the TDA. They visited 23 primary and secondary schools to evaluate how effectively the reforms to the workforce had been implemented. They looked at deployment, training and development of the wider workforce, and the impact on the quality of teaching and learning and on the lives of the pupils and their families. This overambitious remit resulted in a report of just 23 A4 pages but it did recommend that the TDA should help the wider workforce and their managers to gain a 'secure knowledge and understanding of the national occupational standards and the career development framework by providing accessible information and guidance'.

None of the 28 people whom I interviewed mentioned or seemed to know about the national occupational standards or the career development framework, although several did mention professional development. This perhaps links with another of Ofsted's 2008 recommendations that schools need 'to improve their detailed knowledge and understanding of the role of the TDA and make full use of the national occupational standards and the career development framework to develop the wider workforce'.

Meanwhile, Ofsted will continue to monitor the effectiveness of the reforms to the school workforce and this book will, hopefully, contribute to the knowledge base for that workforce in any one primary school.

Defining the educational professional in primary schools

Many of those attending the safeguarding conference, mentioned earlier in the introduction, would not have defined themselves as either members of the wider school workforce or educational professionals – the governors and the vicar for example. The role of the educational professional in this book, however, is defined very widely to include all of those whose role and responsibilities include working with children in school. It is recognised that they are multiprofessional, as well as being multi-agency workers.

By defining them as being 'educational professionals' when working with primary school children we acknowledge that there is a specific educational expertise that is needed to do this work effectively. There is a knowledge and skills base that enhance children's learning and which those working with children either have or need to develop.

There is an acknowledgement within the current documentation that a children's workforce 'encompasses a diverse range of professions and occupations'. This includes people with a wide range of professional identities. It also includes people with very different levels of qualification, training, employment arrangements, and terms and conditions under which they work. Educational professionals may also work in the public, private and/or third sector, or they may be volunteers, as the interviews in the second part of this book demonstrate. Even here it is sometimes difficult to identify whether a 'professional' is that part of their role for which they are paid or their volunteer role. For example, one of the parent volunteers interviewed was also a paid welfare assistant in the same school and both she and the school had difficulty distinguishing some of the different aspects of what she did.

There are specific issues here that are related to professional identities and terms and conditions of work, which lead to some specific challenges, and, operationally, we should be thankful that so many educational professionals seek to make a difference in children's lives and prioritise that.

Here in this book we also look at some people who work mainly with adults, such as the parent mentor and the healthy schools manager, but whose work is also related to improving children's lives and breaking down barriers to learning.

Professional identity

Health workers, such as school nurses, who come into school and work with children, are specifically trained in their own profession, for example health. So their 'professional identity' is health, and their work in schools makes them a specific sort of 'educational professional'. The interview with the school nurse in Chapter 10, however, challenges this assumption that the school nurse is regularly in primary schools. Increasingly, training for 'professional identity' will involve more practice in other settings and training with people from other disciplines. This has already led to the creation of new forms of posts, for which individuals are trained more generically and professionals become, in theory, less defined by their initial and more specific professional identities. In this particular case, the school nurse was no longer responsible, at an operational level, for doing the screening; this job was now undertaken by specially trained workers who were paid at a much lower rate than the nurse. The nurse's role was to oversee the results of the screening and organise any follow-up if required.

School workforce reform also challenges the traditional view of a *professional* as 'an occupation that controls its own work, organized by a special set of institutions sustained in part by a particular ideology of expertise and service' (Friedson 1994) or *dual professionalism* as 'an ideology of expertise and service which is drawn from two occupations, which are organised by two special sets of institutions'.

In the past, considerable research has been carried out into 'professional identity' and how it can be developed initially and then changed as required. A summary of this research by Brott and Kajs (2001) suggests some key points for success in developing a professional identity. They include career development, professional socialization and development, and working alliances.

1. *Professional identity* – This includes having good mentors who can develop new professional and personal development by acting in the role of parent figure, scaffolder, guide and counsellor. This takes place on two levels – externally and internally.

2. *Professional socialization and development* – This involves the acquisition of specific knowledge and skills in such areas as critical thinking, interpersonal skills and conflict resolution, as well as the ability to use computer technology and alternative assessment techniques. There also has to be a person–environment fit to ensure job involvement, satisfaction and tenure, organisational commitment, individual health and adaptation, and correct work attitudes.

3. *Working alliances* – This involves being in a workplace that is a good forum for continued learning. Among other things, this will include good communication skills, such as attending and listening, reflecting and clarifying, and challenging and confronting. These are often seen as generic skills, which, of course, they are, but for workers in primary schools they need to be built into good primary practice, which moves out from narrow classroom structures.

This all sounds very reasonable, but the ideas are largely based on a very traditional view of career progression and development. Indeed, it looks remarkably similar to the apprentice approach of medieval England and the sort of apprenticeship that many of our great-grandparents experienced. It ignores, for example, the facts that much training now takes place in the form of distance learning, which is often isolated, and that information technology (IT) plays a key role in training, much of which is a one-way system of information-giving. This is changing gradually; for example MirandaNet discuss 'braided learning' as being when people working in online communities 'combine to answer a question or research issue posed'. However, both of these sorts of development significantly change the way in which professional development is likely to develop in the future. It is more likely to be on an informal basis, rather than formally developed through training schemes. It has implications for the wider school workforce because professional identity, socialization, development and working alliances have an important role to play in effective training and development.

Both the educational social worker (ESW) and the educational psychologist in Chapter 12 mentioned concerns with professional identity in terms of their ability to keep up to date in their own areas, and both had developed a networking strategy to manage this.

Deskilling

1. *Working outside initial professional training.* This can be really exciting and transformational, but it can also raises issues about personal identity, linked with a specific expertise and the ability of those not trained in a specific discipline to recognise limitations to their expertise when drawn into unknown areas for themselves. At the time of writing, many so-called 'generic courses' often draw on a relatively narrow range of social science disciplines and many of those undertaking them may be unaware of this bias. For example, a childhood studies course may have programmes that have a particular focus on early years' pedagogy and policy-making, or modules on inclusion studies that focus on special educational needs (SEN), rather than the wider political, philosophical

and sociological aspects of inclusion.

2. *More generic, less qualified.* Also, undoubtedly, there are issues concerned with the creation of professional roles that are more generic, but less well qualified. This can have the effect of a professional feeling unsure of their professional identity, particularly if they are significantly less well paid than another professional with the same focus discipline.

3. *Salary.* Another key point related to salary is the saving of money by employing fewer well-trained people. This can be an important point if vacancies can be filled by cheaper personnel. Channel 4 looked recently at vacancies in social work and found that where trained social workers existed 80 per cent of their time was spent on 'desk work', much of which was related to meeting targets. There was also a high levels of vacancies: two quoted were 27 per cent and 31 per cent, both in very challenging local authorities (LAs), a fact so sadly brought out by most reviews and enquiries when a failure of safeguarding procedures results in a child's death. It is doubtful whether anyone could justify that highly trained, and often relatively highly paid, professionals should be spending 80 per cent of their time at a computer screen and meetings, rather than in practice.

Several of the people who were interviewed for this book described themselves, in one way and another, as sometimes being 'out of their comfort zone' when working with children in school, yet their knowledge and expertise of their key training and experience brought in a completely new dimension for primary pupils and other educational professionals working in schools. For example, one worker pointed out that he was being asked to use teaching, presentation and interpersonal strategies to inform young children about his work and what they could do to keep safe. He had received limited training in these techniques, and felt that this was a barrier to his effectiveness. Another worker in a similar field felt that her ability to work in primary schools was greatly aided by the fact that her mother and several other members of her family worked in the education sector. This meant that she had access to their professional knowledge and was using it.

All educational professionals in this much wider sense are on a steep learning curve in an area that is still very new and changing all of the time.

Managing change

The ongoing agenda for the wider school workforce will involve change for all of those working with children. This includes the requirement for:

- Working as part of a multi-agency team (Chapters 9 and 11 provide case study exemplars of this)

- Using, developing and maintaining Common Assessment Framework (the CAF is looked at in more detail in Chapter 11)

- Building up a common core of skills and knowledge, including an understanding of the national occupations standards (see below)

- Information sharing, which may involve some complex technological skills and a good understanding of data protection
- Identifying and working with lead professionals outside key specialisms
- Continuous workforce reform and professional development.

Two models of change

Most of us feel concerned about some sorts of change and the theoretical model, like that shown in Figure 1.2, can actually help us to understand our responses to change and help us to manage it.

Model 1: learning to cope with change

This model obviously applies not only in our working lives, but also in our daily lives. When we are in our comfort zone, things feel familiar and certain – work is controllable and predictable, you feel comfortable and competent, there is no threat to self-esteem or identity and there is a sense of belonging. *But* in the comfort zone you generally do not need to learn new things and therefore do not change.

Moving to the outer circle is when we feel stress and panic, and it generally comes when people are confronted with a change with which they do not agree or do not feel they have a place within the new change model that is being presented to them. Most of us have been there and it results in feeling stressed, worried and fearful. It can also make you feel angry, irritated and annoyed, or it may make you feel sad and depressed. Sometimes when people are stressed they feel guilty, inadequate and frustrated. It also results in people freezing and finding it impossible to change and unable to learn how to change. Several of those people whom I interviewed said that they had felt this at some point about specific aspects of new work they were undertaking, and certainly union websites reflect this concern. There is also a reluctance to mention concern to more senior managers who are recognised as being under stress themselves and unable to cope with genuine concerns about proposed change. The 2009 National Union of Teachers Annual Conference identified some 'Stepford heads' in this category, who bullied staff because they felt bullied and stressed themselves.

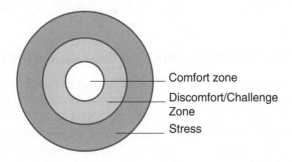

Comfort zone

Discomfort/Challenge Zone

Stress

FIGURE 1.2 Change related to learning to cope with learning challenges. From Hughes (2008)

Activity/task 1

1. Use the model from Figure 1.2 to identify a particular situation in which you have had to go from a feeling of comfortable stability into a feeling of panic, i.e. you moved from the comfort zone to the panic/stress zone.

2. Now think of an example for someone you know and how you helped them to move from their 'safe' zone. This could be a child with whom you have worked.

This leads us into the all-important question of how people change from one role to another, and in the case of many educational professionals that can be several times during a day. The model makes it clear that they need to move from comfort zone to discomfort/challenge zone, where they are most likely to change and learn how to do things differently.

The leadership literature and current philosophy about successful leaders suggests that the leaders and managers of change should:

- Create the right learning environment and culture
- Create a vision of how things could be
- Provide access to appropriate training and positive role models
- Provide feedback and support groups
- Ensure that systems and structures are consistent.

Again, this too can be interpreted very simplistically; certainly the National Council for School Leadership (NCSL) work hard to broaden the idea of a sole charismatic school leader who can supply the answer to all problems/challenges.

Activity/task 2

Can you think of two scenarios (either professional or in your private life) – one when the move from comfort to challenge zone was successful and one where it was not?

Model 2: dealing with confusion, anxiety, resistance and frustration

In his book on the brain, Alistair Smith (2002) suggests that there are four easy ways to spot how children respond to the anxiety that can accompany learning in schools. I think his observations can just as easily be linked to adult responses to change which are not well managed. He calls these different possible responses the four Fs – flocking, freezing, flight and fight. The four explanations given by Smith have been adapted for looking at change:

1. *Flocking* involves adopting 'the norms, values and behaviours of the herd' – in this case, the peer group/working colleagues. This peer group will police, and in some cases collectively suppress, change. This makes it 'difficult to be different'.
2. *Freezing* is a temporary paralysis. It happens when you get stuck or someone suddenly asks you a question out of the blue and you can't think of an answer. If you work with children this is most easy to see when someone is pouncing questions at them. I can still remember oral tables tests when I was about 10. The teacher would shout out a question while pointing to a member of the class. I just froze, and even while I write about it now my stomach is churning at the memory – and it is a long time ago.
3. *Flight* is an avoidance tactic we have all used. I had an appalling statistics lecturer at university. I was in a large group of about 180 of whom about 30 were women. And boy, did he pick on us. I spent three terms at the back of the lecture theatre, every two hours on a Monday morning, with my head hung down. This avoided him seeing me or at least making eye contact; I 'fled' and how I passed the course, I just do not know – certainly 'no thanks' were due to Professor Smith. Other avoidance tactics include doing the minimum. This hides the inability to understand or carry out the activity required. It seems that many children, and I suspect adults as well, would rather be labelled lazy, than have attention drawn to their inability to do something that everyone else seems to be able to do, or is expected to do, as part of their changing role. Several of those people interviewed, who worked in classrooms, identified this particular strategy among the children with whom they worked. In the workplace other tactics include looking for another post, taking time out for stress, living and planning for holidays and weekends.
4. *Fight* is any form of tantrum, rebelliousness or bad behaviour.

Activity/task 3

It is worth thinking about a time when you were faced with change and reacted in 'survival mode' by using one or more of the strategies suggested by Smith – flock, freeze, flight and fight. How successful was it, both for you and for the organisation? What happened eventually?

Most of us in our working lives have been witness to this sort of behaviour and certainly in my earlier working life I was often guilty of it. This is probably why I am sceptical about all theories of change, because they assume that change is always a good thing. Sometimes, it is not, when proposed changes are not implemented or they are changed almost as soon as they are implemented. The separation between operational managers and leaders and strategic managers and leaders is often unhelpful in practice. When the strategic leaders are politicians with their own agenda, proposed changes in areas they know little about can be positively dangerous. A couple of those interviewed in Part 2 mentioned this.

Government strategies

The Children's Workforce Strategy: a background

In 2003, the government published a green paper entitled 'Every Child Matters' (ECM). This was a direct result of the murder of Victoria Climbie and was designed to set the goal of improving outcomes for all children in terms of health, safety, enjoyment and achieving, making a positive contribution and achieving economic well-being. Politicians tend to forget what has gone before and in many ways this green paper followed strategies to improve lives which had already been in place. In Chapter 2, we look at the Beveridge Report. This was one of the most important post-Second World War strategies that was also aimed at reducing the level of poverty. It also had five clear outcomes.

Activity/task 4

Visit the ECM website, which is part of the Department for Children, Schools and Families (DCSF), and consider the current position of this agenda. The website and strategies have been modified/developed almost continually and much of the original guidance on it has not only disappeared, but also been forgotten.

The five outcomes were seen as possible only if the existing professional silos were dismantled and a united children's workforce established. In 2005, the government published their first, post-ECM, Children's Workforce Strategy.

This made it quite clear that the only way in which the five ECM outcomes could be achieved was to have a children's workforce that was 'skilled, well-led and supported by effective, shared systems and processes' (DfES 2005). People in different parts of the workforce would need to be able to work well together across institutional and professional boundaries, so that they could focus around the needs of the child and young person.

At central government guidance level this resulted in a Children's Workforce Strategy that set out action to be taken nationally and locally to ensure that there were the skills, ways of working and capacity in the children's workforce to deliver change for children. This has frequently been updated, particularly through the Children's Plans, as have the other four elements:

1. Practical guidance on multi-agency working

2. A Common Assessment Framework (CAF)

3. A common core of skills and knowledge for the children's workforce

4. Attempts to provide a better infrastructure for employer-led reform through the Children's Workforce Development Council (CWDC), which is part of the Skills for Care and Development Sector Skills Council.

This, of course, is all government speak and only gradually are the actual workings of this strategy coming into place. This varies from agency to agency and can be confused by the multiplicity of the large numbers of agencies working with children and the complexity of the different professional competences and standards already in place.

Integrated Qualifications Framework (IQF)

The initial document for the common core of skills and knowledge for the Children's Workforce focused on the non-controversial and obvious features that professionals would need to know and be able to do:

1.   Engage in effective communication and engagement with children, young people, their families and carers

2.   Have knowledge of child and young person development

3.   Have knowledge of safeguarding and promoting the welfare of the child

4.   Be skilled in supporting transitions

5.   Have knowledge and skills in multi-agency working; and

6.   Share information.

Interestingly enough many of these features do not currently appear within the Standards for Qualified Teacher Status (QTS) and certainly the 9-month primary post-graduate certificate in education (PGCE) course requires potential candidates to have already had experience and expertise in these areas.

These six features are linked with what the government described as common values that promote equality, respect diversity and challenge stereotypes. They were intended to help to improve the life chances of all children and young people and provide more effective and integrated services. Service managers are seen, in government documentation, as the key personnel to (a) design induction, in-service and interagency training, (b) identify and support individual development and (c) provide a practical tool for workforce planning. The non-statutory guidance also recognises that qualifications for work with children, young people and families will include appropriately differentiated common core skills and knowledge.

Training and Development Agency (TDA) and the Children's Wider Workforce in primary schools

The TDA took over responsibility for support staff in 2004, when it changed its name from the Teacher Training Agency (TTA). This marked a commitment to take over responsibility for training both teachers *and* support staff, such as TAs. Initially, it looked towards what was available in the IQF for the Children's Workforce in relation to school support staff. In 2004 there was not much training available and the

ECM agenda supplied a generic overview of what training for the Wider Children's Workforce was expected to cover. This had the aim to support development 'of a children's workforce that is competent in its own specialist areas, able to work effectively with others across the sector and able to transfer more easily from one sector to another'.

Initially, it looked at the less complex area of higher qualifications with the Higher Education (HE) section and expected that this sector would use the qualifications for frameworks that already existed. This included Foundation Degrees, Honours Degrees, PG Certificates, Diplomas and Taught Master's Degrees. The TDA itself provided a framework for the design, delivery and assessment for the Foundation Degree and advised accredited agencies to base their programmes on that framework. It is now in the process of doing the same for the Taught Master's degree.

The TDA linked its provision at another level to looking at relevant National Vocational Qualifications (NVQs) and the materials being produced by the CWDC. The CWDC was set up in 2005 to support the implementation of 'Every Child Matters', and worked, in turn, with the Children's Workforce Network (CWN). In 2009, the CWDC produced a functional map for the CWN for the foundation of a 'coherent workforce'. The key purpose for this was to 'plan, manage and provide comprehensive, coherent, integrated services that improve the lives and outcomes for children and young people and support their families and carers'. The 'functions' covered six areas:

- *Function A.* Develop and implement responsive strategic and operational plans and systems that are outcomes focused and provide integrated services and support for children, young people, their families and carers

- *Function B.* Promote equality, participation and the rights of children and young people

- *Function C.* Communicate and maintain effective relationships with groups and individuals

- *Function D.* Safeguard children and young people

- *Function E.* Work in partnership with other agencies, service providers and individuals to ensure that policies, services and systems are outcomes focused and structured to facilitate integrated working

- *Function F.* Promote the well-being of children and young people to help them to achieve their potential

The TDA has a much more practical approach that provides fairly detailed standards, which, personally, I find easier to comprehend, even although I may disagree with some of the focus. It recognises that the pace of change has led to a diversity of job roles and wider range of demands on school support staff, and that initiatives, such as extended schools, as well as the developments in the ECM agenda, will require continuous development of materials.

Hilary Burgess, in the *Primary Education Review*, provides an overview of the government's workforce reform strategy and the impact it has had, so far, upon primary teachers, headteachers and schools. This comes over as a very limited review because, like the TDA, it effectively concentrated on the teaching force in schools, including the teaching assistants. This makes both procedures and outcomes comparatively neat, but ignores the much Wider Children's Workforce, which is also involved with schools. It highlights the huge challenge of action-based research, which looks at knowledge, skills and competencies in fields relatively unknown by those researching them. The same is also true for those evaluating practice, both in terms of its outcomes but also looking at value for money (VFM).

The interviews in the second part of the book highlight the experiences of those who are part of the children's workforce in primary schools. In some cases, the Wider Children's Workforce is scarcely an issue for the professional; in others it constitutes the move from comfort zone to challenge.

2

Setting the Scene: Differential Performance in Primary Schools

Christine Gilbert, the head of Ofsted in 2008, said it was unacceptable that 20 per cent of pupils still failed to master basic English and maths when they left primary school, while 10 per cent of 16 to 18-year-olds who dropped out of education were not in work.

(*TES*, May 2008)

In this chapter we look at ways in which data have been shown to identify specific groups within our communities who are underperforming, and we discuss the challenges of ensuring that such labelling does not result in a self-fulfilling prophecy in which the 'have-nots' have been identified, stereotyped and sometimes stigmatised. And if you should question why this matters then Table 2.1 shows just one of the alarming outcomes when children do not learn to read adequately, have poor numeracy skills, regularly play truant and leave school with no qualifications. The cost of each of these school failures is, at the time of writing, just under £50,000 per year.

Chapter overview

- To look and evaluate historical and current sociological theories in relation to performance

- To examine economic and political, audit and inspection findings that identify under performance patterns in primary school settings

- Explore how factors identified with underperformance overlap to provide challenges in breaking down barriers to learning

- Recognise the need to understand more about changing ideas on under-performance in order prevent labelling/stereotyping of specific pupils.

TABLE 2.1 Profile of prison offenders

CATEGORY	GENERAL POPULATION (%)	PRISON POPULATION (%)
Regular truant	3	30
Excluded from school	2	49
Adult numeracy at or below Level 1	23	65
Adult reading at or below Level 1	23	48
No qualifications	15	52
Unemployed	5	67

Introduction

In this second chapter we take first a traditional sociological perspective to equality issues in education. Traditional generic sociology texts have tended to take social mobility as a long-term outcome of measuring inequality in educational outcomes.

The traditional sociological research has used methods of identifying inequalities in education through narrowly defined examination and test results. In the primary sector this was the 11-plus, until it was virtually replaced by SATs at the ages of 7 and 11 years. The educational measurement in the secondary sector tended to be GCSE, A Level, and entry to university results. Traditional sociologists then looked at specific social factors in measured educational attainment, such as class, race and gender. Reasons for the differences were then extrapolated.

Second, the chapter looks at how Ofsted data, collected from Ofsted general school inspection and special surveys, identified specific vulnerable groups within schools. This expanded initial work done by sociologists on class, race and gender, and provided a more complex pattern of measured underperformance. Nationally, the focus has changed to inclusion and current Ofsted commentaries reflect this.

The third area looks more closely at complex data collection, linked with academic analysis and undertaken through commissioning experienced researchers from several different social studies fields. Recently, this work has come under specific fields, such as 'poverty studies' and mobility studies. It includes data collection from specific research findings and census data. This makes it possible to look at a number of different determinants for any neighbourhood and show, through fairly simple diagrams and charts, how these factors work together to produce areas of high risk to those seeking effective outcomes from the schooling system.

The fourth section looks at questioning the whole approach of seeing barriers to learning simply as performance outcomes, and links most obviously to questioning exactly what is seen as the purpose of schooling.

Finally, the chapter acknowledges that the concept of 'barriers for learning' has moved from being seen as strictly class related to a more complex relationship between different forms of determinants. This resulted in showing identifiable underperforming social groups and resulted in political initiatives to 'narrow the gap' and 'improve social mobility'. There is some degree of political consensus among politicians about these underachieving groups. Media attention tends to focus on particularly easy messages to convey, such as white boys' underachievement, and this makes it easy for desk-based journalists to make links with other media-preferred areas, such as crime and alcohol abuse.

Sadly, whichever collection approach has been taken, performance seems always to result, almost entirely, in terms of what has been measured easily through tests and examinations.

Traditional sociological research findings

Sociology is traditionally seen as the study of human social life, groups and societies. It often challenges personal views about the family, institutions and communities in which we ourselves live. It still provides a useful evaluative tool for looking at any organisation. In this chapter we are using sociology to reflect and evaluate the performance of different social and cultural groups in primary schools and, more importantly, to examine strategies to reduce this.

The Victorians

The Victorians were quite clear about why education produced differing outcomes for different groups of people. The hymn 'All Things Bright and Beautiful' used to contain the wonderful verse: 'The rich man in his castle, The poor man at the gate, God made them high and lowly, And ordered their estate'.

This certainly puts most of us in our place at the gate. It was a form of social determinism that can still be found in parts of the world today; basically, you are born wealthy because it is God's will and born poor for the same reason and there is nothing you can – or should – do about it. Indeed the history of free public education shows us that until the 1988 National Curriculum was introduced, there was no requirement to provide the same curriculum for all children. Social determinism is still alive and well in England today and often children believe that however hard they try, they just do not have the intelligence to do any better academically – therefore why bother to try? Many of those interviewed in Part 2 made this point, often linking it to reasons for misbehaviour – it's better to be seen to be 'naughty' than stupid.

Towards the end of the nineteenth century, the Victorian perspective in the UK changed into a more scientific, biological determinism. Evidence was gathered to show how intelligence (or 'brain power' as it is often popularly called today) could be measured, and from these measurements it was believed possible to draw up some form of hierarchy of intelligence. The book *Not in Our Genes* (Rose *et al.* 1987) makes a particularly useful record of the type of experiments and techniques that were used in the late nineteenth century and early twentieth century to demonstrate why the most intelligent people 'just happened' to be white, wealthy, Anglo-Saxon men; indeed, the very same people who were devising and writing up the findings. Early intelligence testing provided a 'seemingly logical explanation of social inequality':

■ It identified differences in Intelligence Quotient (IQ) according to status, wealth and power

- These differences were seen as products of different intrinsic ability, which could be easily measured by an 'intelligence test'
- Differences in intelligence were largely a result of genetic differences between individuals, which meant that they were fixed and unchangeable.

Sadly, we still find views like this offered today as explanations for inequalities in schooling outcomes and they always need to be challenged. The 'learn to learn' movement (Claxton 2002) shows primary children that there are effective strategies to improve their learning.

Twentieth century

War has often provided an impetus for social policy changes. Legislation that was drafted during the Second World War included a white paper on 'Education Reconstruction'. It focused on inequalities of provision in secondary schooling.

Before the war, most state elementary/primary schools provided free education. If you went to a state secondary school, however, some payment was generally involved. This was recognised by many as dividing the secondary school population by ability to pay. Children from poorer backgrounds were almost entirely confined to elementary schools and only two per cent of the population went to university. The 1944 Education Act introduced free secondary education for all, and most local authorities used this as a means of providing different sorts of schools for pupils with different needs. It was assumed that different types of children would need different forms of education. A test at 11, known as the '11-plus', divided pupils up into two or three groups. The academic ones went to the grammar school for an academically based education; the others went to the 'modern' school for a craft-based education. In some authorities a third group went to a technical school, although this was often at the age of 12 or 13 years, rather than 11.

Activity/task 1

The 11-plus examination and grammar schools still exist in some parts of the UK and most people over 55 can remember the days of the 11-plus. Speak to someone who went through primary school between 1944 and 1965 or who lives in an area which still has the 11-plus. What issues arise from their primary school experience as well as their secondary schooling? What comparisons can be made with primary schools today?

By the mid-1960s, data gathered by sociologists made it obvious that these different forms of secondary schooling were not working in terms of equality of outcomes. Competition for grammar school plans was fierce and the grammar schools contained largely the children of the growing ranks of professional and semi-professional workers. The secondary modern schools took those who failed the 11 plus, who just happened to be mainly the children in families of semi-skilled and unskilled workers. Girls in some areas were disadvantaged because more girls 'passed' the 11-plus, but it was considered unfair if more girls went to grammar school than boys or, alternatively, there were fewer grammar school places for girls. Technical schools were still underdeveloped.

This period was probably the heyday of sociological research, accompanied by a political consensus about the purposes of education. By 1965, this resulted in a drive to abolish the 11-plus and provide local comprehensive schools, which were seen as a means of providing a neighbourhood solution to the inequalities in schooling produced by the 11-plus.

Barriers linked to class, race and gender

Class as a determinant of school performance

Definition by occupation

Class has always been a partly difficult form of classification and is often used extremely vaguely, including its use in some of the research outlined below. A more formal definition of class was determined initially by the use of the Social Registrar General's positioning of different occupations within six different bands. This was a descriptive scheme, based on occupational categories. An extended version of this can be found on the government's statistics site.

1. Class 1: Professional

2. Class 2: Intermediate

3. Class 3 NM: Non-manual Skilled

4. Class 3 M: Skilled Manual

5. Class 4: Semi-skilled

6. Class 5: Unskilled Manual.

By 2000, this had been largely replaced by the National Statistics Socio-economic Classification (NS-SEC).

Activity/task 2

What sort of limitations does this mean for categorising people in terms of class? For example:

■ Those who are not working in paid employment e.g. unemployed, pensioners and children

- Those who have great wealth as a result of their work including celebrities
- Those with inherited wealth and windfall wealth such as lottery wins
- women who traditionally have taken the class status of men such as their father and, when married/partnered, with their partner.

Identifying class through occupation was just a starting point and sociologists investigated and extrapolated on how class influenced inequalities in educational outcomes.

Definition by father's occupation and family size

One of the best known studies in relation to class and performance was that done by Douglas in 1964. The comprehensive, longitudinal study showed that differences in pupils' literacy and numeracy were associated with family size and father's occupation. The evidence also showed that this difference was from a very early age and continued throughout schooling. A later study from Douglas (1964) continued to show that factors of social class and family size were linked with pupil attainment at the ages of seven and 11 years. At least one of those people interviewed in Part 2 identified large family size as a barrier to learning, based on her experience over 16 years in the same school.

The DfES Youth Cohort study published in 2002 (DfES 2003a, b) showed that things have not changed much. The chance of gaining five or more GCSE grades at A* to C, by parents occupational groups, was as follows:

- *Higher professional* – defined as doctors, lawyers, dentists – 75 per cent
- *Lower professional* – defined as teachers, journalists, nurses, actors – 64 per cent
- *Intermediate* – (secretaries, airline cabin crew, photographers, firemen) – 52 per cent
- *Lower supervisory* – (train drivers, plumbers, foremen) – 35 per cent
- *Routine* – (bus drivers, waitresses, cleaners) – 32 per cent
- Other – 32 per cent.

Those working in primary schools know well that the seeds of success at secondary, further and higher education level are nurtured in nurseries and primary schools. These figures from the 2002 survey clearly pinpoint an equality gap between the children of different occupational groups.

Definition by occupation and language

Bernstein (1975) suggested that children from different backgrounds/classes developed different language codes (forms of speech) in their homes as they grew older. This affected their learning in school because some forms of speech were more useful and acceptable in the school situation. Children from wealthier homes appeared to develop a speech code that supported their school learning. Initially, the language of working-class children was identified as being a 'restricted code', which was tied into its own cultural setting. Middle-class children, on the other hand, developed an 'elaborate' language code, which made it easier for them to generalise and express abstract ideas.

A discussion paper entitled 'Why do many young children lack basic language skills?' to accompany the launch of the 2005 'Talk to Your Baby' National Literacy initiative drew on American research to suggest that class is an additional factor in children's performance (www.literacytrust.org.uk/talktoyourbaby/about.html).

Class defining the type of education children receive through the hidden curriculum

Illich (1995), in his most popular work, *Deschooling Society*, argued that schools had a hidden curriculum to teach children their role in life – 'to know their place and to sit still'. He saw the development of schools as a means in which children were socialised into what was needed for the economic growth of the country.

Class and cultural reproduction

Bourdieu (1984) also looked at this argument and linked it with the idea of schools being responsible for cultural reproduction through the hidden curriculum. Schools reinforced the values of the society in which their pupils were growing up and their own position in it. This resulted in limiting opportunities for those children whose families were in a particularly weak position in society and enhanced the opportunities of the more powerful and wealthy.

GENDER AS A DETERMINANT OF PERFORMANCE

Victorian elementary schools had different formal curriculums for boys and girls, based on the perceived different lifestyles for which they were being 'prepared'; woodwork for the boys and needlework for the girls, for example. This may have been toned down by the mid-1960s but it certainly continued until the introduction of a National Curriculum in 1988. This established, for the first time, a common formal curriculum for boys and girls.

The reasons suggested for differences in performance of boys and girls in school vary considerably. What is known is that girls outperform boys in school, although a quick look at the employment market shows that this better performance is not reflected there. Evolutionary biologists claim that gender differences are innate and many cultures take this view as well by providing a different education for boys and girls. Hopefully no one working in our primary schools believes this today.

Sociologists would suggest that gender difference is a social construct, created by the cultural patterns of the society in which we live. Blakemore and Frith (2006) demonstrated this very clearly by looking at international gender differences in relation to mathematics. They identified variations in the size of the gender effect between cultures. For example, although boys outperformed girls in both China and the USA, girls in China performed better than boys in the USA. However, when Chinese girls were taught in the USA their mathematical ability declined to the level of US girls.

The growth in neuroscience has shown some subtle differences between male and female brains, but many of the results are still equivocal with little agreement about what the differences mean.

ETHNICITY

The first major government report on educational outcomes for the rising numbers of ethnic minorities in the UK was *Education for All*, produced by the Swann Committee in 1985, largely as a result of concern by ethnic minority communities, who saw the underperformance of their children in school. The Swann Report found significant differences in terms of levels of academic achievement among groups of children from different ethnic backgrounds and called for a change in the behaviour and attitudes throughout the country towards these children, their families and communities.

Over 25 years later, this is still evident and the following figures illustrate that Level 4 results in English show different percentage scores for different ethnic groups. These figures are taken from the 2007 Standard Assessment Tasks/Tests (SATs) results:

- Chinese and Indian – 85 per cent
- White – 81 per cent
- Bangladeshi – 77 per cent
- Black Caribbean – 74 per cent
- Black African and Pakistan – 72 per cent.

SUMMARY OF TRADITIONAL SOCIOLOGICAL RESEARCH

For some considerable time there has been concern about the differing outcomes of schooling for different groups. The focus was initially on inequalities relating to class, but later on inequalities that could be linked with a child's gender and/or race. We have already seen that many of the findings were based on data which, today, would have been questioned more closely. The very word 'class' continues to be used vaguely by politicians, the media and academics.

Current data collection on determinants for children's performance are far more sophisticated, as are the software programmes that are used to analyse it. This has resulted in many different groups being identified as having barriers to learning, and this has created a sort of hierarchy in which particular factors play the greater role in determining a child's educational success.

In the next few sections of this chapter, we look at summary findings from Ofsted reports and from two major charities that are involved in improving children's lives in the widest sense – the Rowntree and Sutton Trusts. However, what has not been touched upon yet is the need to identify another sociological theory – 'labelling' – and the danger that it poses to the very children whom we are most concerned about helping.

Labelling theory

This theory suggests that there is a danger in labelling specific groups as being less likely to perform well at school. It results in all individuals who 'fit' the group characteristics being labelled and stigmatised as poor performers. Labelling theory suggests that they are therefore more likely to become deviant learners and fit the image of their group as a deficit performing group. Their own expectations, and those of others, influence performance itself through self-image, group image and a deviant/deficit model of behaviour that fits with the stereotype, along with the lower performance expectations from those working with them.

Children's self-theories of intelligence influence their response to schools and their motivation to learn. Dweck (1999) showed that children who believe their intelligence is fixed are less likely to make much effort to learn, whereas those who believe their intelligence can grow will try harder when faced with a learning challenge. She suggested that if effort was praised rather than performance, children's intrinsic theories can be altered and children's motivation to learn can increase. Personally, I am not so sure about indiscriminate praise for effort, as it can result in some very ineffective working strategies where length of time spent is equated with effort.

A more recent example of this labelling theory is the term 'English as an Additional Language (EAL)', which is used to describe the 12.5 per cent of primary children who have English as an additional language. They are frequently presented as having achievement that is lower than that of native speakers. However, the figures show that those EAL children who are behind in reading at the age of 7 years have no gap by the time they reach 16. Research for the *Primary Education Review* (Ainscow *et al*. 2008) argued that the very term 'EAL' creates its own problems. For many years it has assigned children into a category of special educational needs; it did not value multilingualism – rather it lowered teachers' expectations and led to missed opportunities for the children concerned to use their native language to help them learn English. A 2005 study on Key Stage 2 English SATs showed that the gap between teachers' expectations and Key Stage test results was a 5 per cent difference for EAL pupils at Key Stage 2, rather than the 2 per cent for non-EAL pupils.

Government bodies are also guilty of this deficit labelling for specific groups, often because they simplify what are extremely complex ideas. This simplification is fed to the press and, in turn, may feed into the expectations that educational professionals have of specific groups. In a school I visited the other day, the teachers, on government advice, divided the two reception classes into three ability groups for literacy. The work was clearly defined between the groups. I wondered, as I often do in these circumstances, what messages those four- and five-year-olds were receiving about their ability; in particular, those whose birthdays were at the end of the academic year and who were almost a year younger than the children who were born in September and October.

One of the great challenges in breaking down barriers to learning is having a good understanding of data collection, as well as the complexity of the variables to which it is subject. Labelling theory should provide a useful deterrent to ability grouping at a very early age and contrasts strongly with early childhood education in many European countries (Hughes 2008).

Ofsted and vulnerable groups

Ofsted identified fourteen vulnerable groups in the 1990s, when its first inspections and surveys took place: minority and faith groups; travellers; asylum seekers; English as an additional language (EAL); special educational needs (SEN); looked-after children (LAC); gifted and talented; sick children; young carers; families under stress; boys; pregnant girls; teenage mothers; disaffected and excluded children.

Activity/task 3

First identify why each of these groups might have specific barriers to learning and, second, what strategies can be offered in schools to support achievement and avoid labelling. In our concern about performance, particularly in the SATs, it is often difficult to remember that all of these individuals do bring positive things to schools if their knowledge, skills and experience can be drawn on effectively.

Later Ofsted surveys identified other groups who were underperforming. For example, the 2006/7 Annual Report identified barriers to learning linked with pupils who:

- Had poor attendance – Ofsted cited a clear link between low attendance and deprivation
- Were of Black Caribbean and mixed White/Black Caribbean heritage – surveys have shown that these pupils were excluded in disproportionate numbers
- Were in pupil referral units (PRUs)
- Were in secure accommodation.

In their 2007 report *Raising Standards, Improving Lives*, they identified children in the following groups as being in vulnerable circumstances:

- Living away from home
- Disabilities (mental or physical)
- Subject to abuse or bullying
- Race and racism
- Child abuse
- Domestic violence
- Drugs – misusing parents/family members
- Families living in temporary accommodation
- Living as migrants, victims of trafficking or unaccompanied asylum-seeking children or young people
- Being young carers.

One of the factors that many of these children have in common is that they live in families and communities that are among the most impoverished in the UK. Poverty, however defined, has been seen as a major factor in educational performance.

Inclusion groups that are currently recognised nationally

These groups are as follows: children with physical disability; looked-after children; ethnic minority; English as an additional language; faith groups; sick children; attendance; young carers; children who frequently take holidays; visual/hearing impaired; children living in poverty; children frequently changing schools; gifted and talented; specific learning difficulty; moderate learning difficulty; severe learning difficulty; behavioural/emotional/social; speech, language and communication; autistic spectrum disorder; child protection register; gender; asylum seekers/refugees; victims of domestic violence; travellers; drug abusers – parents/children; bullying – victims and perpetrators; mental health; bereaved children; excluded children; and disaffected children at risk of exclusion.

Academic and poverty studies

This section looks at the work of two trusts that provide important data on poverty and education, which is often used to inform political agendas and policy-making.

Joseph Rowntree Trust

This trust has a long charitable history, dating back to the Victoria era when it was established. It is important for us, as educational professionals, to recognise that it sought not only to relieve poverty, but also to look at the causes of poverty and effect change. In the words of its Quaker founder Joseph Rowntree, the Trust was established 'to search out the under-lying causes of weakness or evil in the community, rather than of remedying their more superficial manifestations'.

One of the ways in which this has been done over the years has been by massive surveys of the population. These have defined and identified groups in or near poverty levels and led the way in establishing some of the key features of poverty dynamics that appear on many websites. The Trust's work is comprehensive and covers research and development work on communities, poverty, homes, families, care and disability.

Data on poverty have shown that it is dynamic and changeable – people move in and out of poverty and this movement is difficult to measure. Work done for the Trust on poverty dynamics research in the UK shows that:

1. Over an 8-year period, one-third of the population experience poverty at least once – twice as much as the poverty rate at any one point in time

2. Research highlights different types of poverty – transient, persistent and recurrent

3. Most people who enter poverty leave quickly, but a minority experience persistent poverty

4.   Some people experience recurrent episodes of poverty because income mobility tends to be short range

5.   Poverty in one generation increases the chances of poverty in the next. Educational attainment is the best way of mediating the risk of poverty over the life course

The Trust's findings are used to inform not only the Trust, but also national policy-making, although the complexity of the findings often makes it difficult to translate directly into action.

The summarised findings outlined below are from the Trust's 2007 Education and Poverty Programme, which looked into the experiences and attitudes of children from different backgrounds, and show that socio-economic differences are associated with a wide range of influences on children's learning.

Findings from the Joseph Rowntree Foundation's 2007 Education and Poverty Programme

Key points:

1.   Low income is a strong predictor of low educational performance

2.   White children in poverty have, on average, lower educational achievement and are more likely to continue to underachieve; boys are more likely to have low results than girls, especially those of Bangladeshi, Pakistani and black African origin

3.   Just 14 per cent of variation in individuals' performances is accounted for by school quality; most variation is explained by other factors, underlining the need to look at the range of children's experiences, inside and outside school, when seeking to raise achievement

4.   Children from different backgrounds have contrasting experiences in school: less advantaged children are more likely to feel a lack of control over their learning and to become reluctant recipients of the taught curriculum, which influences the development of different attitudes to education in primary school that help shape their future

5.   Children from all backgrounds see the advantages of school, but deprived children are more likely to feel anxious and unconfident about school

6.   Out-of-school activities can help build self-confidence; children from advantaged backgrounds experience more structured and supervised out-of-school activities

7.   Many children and young people who become disaffected with school develop strong resentments about mistreatment (such as perceived racial discrimination) – work with disaffected young people is most effective when it makes them feel more involved in their own futures, and equality of educational opportunity must address multiple aspects of disadvantaged children's lives

8. These factors are at the heart of the social divide in educational outcomes, but have not been central in solutions so far – measures to improve the extent to which disadvantaged children engage in education are elusive but cannot be neglected.

I find these findings quite optimistic. There are clear strategies that can be adopted to support disadvantaged pupils and break down barriers to learning, and we see some of these in many primary schools. The extended school services movement, including Study Support, is a particular example of this, although I would always add the cautionary note, that the provision has to be excellent.

The Sutton Trust

This was established much more recently than the Rowntree Trust, by Sir Peter Lampl in 1997. Its main objective, in its founder's words, is to 'support innovative projects that provide educational opportunities for young people from non-privileged backgrounds'. Lampl describes the Trust as a 'do tank' rather than a 'think tank', which exists to challenge educational inequality and stop the resulting waste of talent.

The Trust's own website provides a good record of its work. The particular area we are touching on here is its most recent findings about the continuing lack of mobility in terms of educational performance. Work by Blanden *et al.* (2005), commissioned by the Trust, found that:

1. Intergenerational income mobility for children born in the period 1970–2000 has stabilised, following the sharp decline that occurred for children born in 1970 compared with those born in 1958

2. The UK remains very low on the international rankings of social mobility compared with other advanced nations

3. Parental background continues to exert a very powerful influence on the academic progress of children

4. Those from the poorest fifth of households but in the brightest group drop from the 88th percentile on cognitive tests at the age of 3 years to the 65th percentile at the age of 5. Those from the richest households who are least able at the age of 3 years move up from the 15th percentile to the 45th percentile by the age of 5. If this trend were to continue, the children from affluent backgrounds would be likely to overtake the poorer children in test scores by the age of 7

5. Inequalities in obtaining a degree persist across different income groups. While 44 per cent of young people from the richest 20 per cent of households acquired a degree in 2002, only 10 per cent from the poorest 20 per cent of households did so.

The reports from both the Trusts make challenging reading. And it is continuing data like these which have led to the central government funding of programmes such as *Narrowing the Gap*.

Central government: neighbourhood statistics

Activity/task 4

Figure 2.1 looks at the neighbourhood statistics for a school that I visit. It is clearly in an area where the determinants used to define deprivation are almost universally high. These determinants cover income, employment, health, education, barriers to housing and services, crime, living environment and deprivation. You might like to suggest why 'housing and services' does so well in the ranking in comparison with the other areas.

Now use the neighbourhood statistics website yourself to look at your own postcode and then to a school you know using the following website – http://neighbourhood. statistics.gov.uk/

Measurement of achievement and breaking barriers to learning to improve standards in primary schools

The quick political and expedient answer to measurement of success about raising barriers to learning is that we must raise standards in our schools and these can be measured by the SATs in primary schools. It is often even narrower than this because standards are seen, almost universally, as being levels of attainment in mathematics and literacy. When comparisons are made internationally the literacy element often shrinks to reading. Results internationally have not been good and James Bartholomew (2006) in his book on the welfare state provides some fairly damning evidence to support this.

Breaking barriers to learning as a holistic approach to raising standards and the quality of education in primary schools

We would all recognise that the standards of learning in primary schools are reflected by more than the SATs scores. A more complete structure might be one suggested by the Primary Curriculum Review (PCR), which would cover a number of different aspects that influence the quality of learning:

- Affective (e.g. attitudes, aspirations, quality of life)
- Behavioural (e.g. skills, cooperation, initiative)
- Cognitive (e.g. academic achievement)
- Demographic (e.g. gender, socio-economic status)
- Expenditure (e.g. financial, temporal)
- Flow (e.g. who is taught what for how long, curriculum balance)
- Growth (e.g. physical, motor and health development).

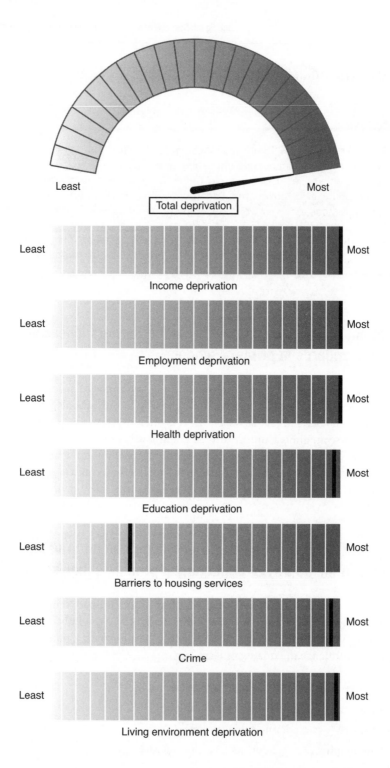

FIGURE 2.1 Postcode rating for a primary school in the north-west. All 32,482 neighbourhoods in England have been ranked on a range of topics, together with a 'total deprivation' ranking. The most deprived neighbourhood in England has a rank of 1 – the further to the right a marker is for a particular topic, the more deprived the area

These areas are the very ones that are often drawn on by educational professionals who are trying to identify strategies to improve pupil learning. Sadly, the PCR acknowledges that there are few national significant data that would provide a fuller picture of educational standards relating to at least four of these categories – behavioural, demographic, expenditure and growth.

Identifying the purposes of education

An essential element of devising a more holistic approach to standards and quality in primary education is to examine exactly what its purpose is. If primary education is to be more than SATs results then what do we want children to get from schooling? What else could be measured? What might not be so easily measured?

Activity/task 5

It is worth stopping at this point and looking at what you feel are the purposes of primary education. What do you feel are its aims and values? Four very common responses to this question are outlined in the text below.

Education for economic growth

All of those people working in primary schools know that schooling and education, in its widest sense, is something very much more than SATs results. All of the political parties share a consensus, at the moment, that the vast amount of the Gross National Product (GNP) spent on education is to promote economic growth. Our children represent our future. We all benefit if they work hard through school and later in paid employment. Those 5-year-olds in reception class today will be paying our pension and health bills long after we have finished working.

The emphasis on SATs results and general assessment and testing today fits into this philosophy exactly. But it is not the only possible aim and value in education.

Education for fairness and equality

Equality issues have always played a part in primary schools and education is seen as a measure to ensure that equality of provision. One of the earliest questions was how this 'equality' could be most effectively achieved. There is equality of input – compulsory schooling from 1890 was linked closely to this form of equality. Then there is equality of outcome. The effectiveness of schooling in terms of equality can be measured in terms of formal results at its end. The move towards comprehensive secondary education in the 1960s was certainly linked closely to measuring school outcomes in terms of improved access to higher education. It can be seen in terms of resources and support, so that those identified as needing more support to achieve equality of outcome can be provided with this during their time at school. Certainly many of the current strategies to 'narrow the gap' are linked to this understanding of equality. However, sadly, there is a lengthy history of data collection showing that achieving fairness and equality is a far more complex undertaking than it appears initially.

Education for good citizenship – nationally and locally

The 1999 version of the National Curriculum included, for the first time, a philosophy about promoting children's spiritual, moral, social, cultural and physical growth (SMSCP). It also stated schools' responsibility for preparing pupils for the opportunities, responsibilities and experiences of life. As Shuayb and O'Donnell (2008) pointed out, this explicit statement of values focused on the self, relationships, society and the environment.

The emphasis on this element increased over the next 10 years as education was seen as a means of combating some of the deficit behaviours reported in the media. I have used Bartholomew's headings below as a guideline. As a lead writer for the *Daily Mail* when he wrote the book, he can be seen to represent the 'Middle England' concerns that so often hit the headlines in the media.

- Increased immorality, drunkenness and crime
- The need for a healthy population, whose excesses, such as smoking and eating, can be controlled, so that they do not form a heavy burden for the NHS
- Improved economic growth
- Creating and maintaining order
- Raising rates of functional literacy – Bartholomew identifies approximately one-quarter of the population as being functionally illiterate.

And to be fair to what is a heavily critical chapter by Bartholomew on the state system of education, these concerns reflect those of most of us. They also feed directly into a final aim.

Education for personal achievement and enjoyment

The Plowden Report (CACE 1967) had coined the expression 'child-centred' education to describe their philosophy. This focused on a holistic and rounded education, which was concerned about children's varied needs and individualisation. It proved challenging to implement and by the late 1970s and 1980s the child-centred education philosophy had fallen into disrepute.

In recent years, there has been an increased emphasis on the need to look more closely at this holistic approach and what it would look like in practice. David Miliband, a senior government minister at the time, effectively reintroduced it in a 2004 speech to the North of England Education Conference. He called it 'personalised learning' and defined it as something in which all schools must invest.

This resulted in 'personalised learning' being seen as a 'new' idea that required significant changes in how the primary school curriculum was organised.

Later this 'personalised learning approach' was linked to guidance for schools on changing their assessment procedures. This introduced new acronyms, such as Assessment for Learning (AfL) and Assessing Pupil Progress (APP).

Education for personal achievement and enjoyment, linked closely to a 'personalised learning' curriculum was, however, an important ideological acknowledgement that children were not all the same. They have different learning needs and the communities and homes from which they come have an important bearing on their achievement in school. This was not a new philosophy, but the political and media climate made it possible to acknowledge the need, once again, for a more child-centred approach to learning. Most of those interviewed in the second part of the book welcomed this more child-centred approach.

2004 Education Act and Children's Plans

This gave a statutory outcomes framework to a more holistic approach to the ways in which we support our children. It provided five outcomes drawing from the highly publicised ECM agenda. They applied to all children and young people in every area of their lives and covered promoting a healthy lifestyle; safeguarding children in its widest sense; achieving economic well-being; helping children to make a positive contribution; and, finally, encouraging children to enjoy and achieve.

This broadened the remit of schools considerably and represented a distinct philosophy about the purposes of education. It also identifies the power of the media in determining educational purpose. A glance at any media coverage shows that when children and young people are seen as threats, for example knife crime, there are recommended strategies that involve schools.

The Children's Plans of 2007 onwards took a strategic view of the ECM agenda. An analysis by the National Foundation for Educational Research found that at a local level:

- The importance of developing local partnerships and responding to local needs is recognised across the plans
- There is a marked diversity in the coverage of the different themes across the plans
- The ECM outcomes framework is used in a variety of ways, suggesting that local authorities work with it as a conceptual tool rather than adhering to it as a blueprint formula
- Many local authorities produced additional material written specifically for children and young people, reflecting an intention to be accessible and to engage young people
- There is scope for future guidance on identification and allocation of resources, performance management arrangements and commissioning strategies.

Activity/task 6

Look at the website for your own local authority (LA) and see how easy it is to find the LA Plan. How much sense do you feel it makes? How much publicity has it had to inform the general public about what the LA intends to do?

Narrowing the gap: a political response

In 2006, the DfES set up a programme to 'narrow the gap' in outcomes between 'vulnerable children' and the rest. The language of the programme marked a distinct change from the sociological labelling that had taken place before. The word 'inclusion' has largely replaced the words 'disadvantaged' and 'vulnerable', almost as an acknowledgement that aiming strategies at specific groups provided an all-too-simplistic approach. However, a quick look at the Ofsted website certainly demonstrates that this more traditional approach continues to give rise to many reports over the years, as do figures taken up by the media and political groups.

Research for the programme has also criticised the tendency to assume that underperformance can be automatically attributed to poor leadership and teaching in schools. Evidence over a period of time shows that the idea of a charismatic leader is ultimately a simplistic as well as a flawed one. It assumes a surplus of such leaders and ignores the fact that many experiments using this model have failed in the long term when the charismatic leader has moved on to new horizons. It may be that new forms of leadership are needed, based on the principle of shared responsibility and distributive leadership (National Council for School Leadership 2008).

Ainscow, a co-author of a report on *Equity in Education: Responding to Context* (Ainscow *et al.* 2008), told the TES (30 May 2008) that 'for schools in disadvantaged areas, the solutions lie beyond the school gates'. Many of those people interviewed in the second part of this book record this as one of the many barriers to children's learning. Among other things this represents a challenge to national strategies that have blocked innovation and closed minds. More optimistically, Ainscow also suggested that the system does have untapped capacity to improve itself.

Educational issues could and should be linked to broader social and economic agendas, such as those illustrated by the Neighbourhood Statistics website – income, employment, health, housing, crime living environment, transport. These of course cut across local authority boundaries, across different agencies and across age ranges. Even without the Children's Workforce Reform initiative, it has long been recognised that there needs to be greater collaboration between workers involved in them.

Summary

This chapter provides an overview of observations, data and conjecture about differential performance in primary schools. It places warnings about the measurement of performance, labelling, stereotyping, stigmatising and using a deficit model to explain contrasting educational outcomes. Many of the areas in this chapter have been identified by the educational professionals working in primary schools, although the language used is often different. In the next chapter, we start by looking at a brief history of the establishment of the welfare state after the Second World War in order to provide some lessons in the complexity of changing social dynamics through legislation.

3

Tackling Poverty: From Beveridge to 'Every Child Matters'

> Low income is a strong predictor of low educational performance.
> (Joseph Rowntree Foundation's Education and Poverty Programme, Cassen and Kingdome 2007)

Chapter overview

- Skill in identifying parallels between the past and the present in relation to a more holistic approach to breaking barriers in learning.

- Identifying initiatives regarding barriers to learning, which have their own history and lessons to be learnt from it.

Introduction

In the previous chapter we looked at how government and other research data identified specific groups who were more vulnerable to inequality life chances through the education system. There is nothing very new in this and in this chapter we look at the formal establishment of the welfare state in the UK to show how tackling poverty is not a simply a current concern, but a continuing one, which has a long history from which lessons should be learnt. Sadly, the media and politicians have an agenda that often needs to show their own new and original ideas and there is a failure to recognise parallels from the past and learn from them.

Educational professionals working with primary children, who work either directly or indirectly to break down barriers to learning, tend to see part of the picture of poverty. This chapter provides an opportunity to gain a more informed knowledge of the debate about poverty, in particular child poverty and current/past strategies to tackle it. The previous chapter provided a rather depressing view of educational underachievement. This chapter provides a more optimistic view of strategies to support changes in provision and ways in which standards of living and educational life chances can be improved. It also suggests there is a danger in looking back at the past with nostalgia as if we had some sort of golden age, with much less political interference.

The chapter starts with looking at the Beveridge Report of 1942 and the similarities and differences between its proposed outcomes and those of the Every Child Matters (ECM) agenda. This is being covered in order to demonstrate how visions within the ECM, the 2004 Education Act and the Children's Plans are not new, but have been visualised in the past. Sometimes the language may be different, but many of the determinants are the same.

The current focus for educational underachievement and breaking down barriers for learning is on children in poverty that is linked with social exclusion. This makes a change from identifying specific vulnerable and disadvantaged children. This particular political focus may also reflect a rather negative view, reflected in the media, of feckless people who have far too many children and who live off state benefits. These viewpoints fall nicely into that Victorian and pre-Victorian category of the undeserving poor. Information from such sources as the Child Poverty Action Group and the Barnardo's website provides a very different perspective.

This brief historical review also demonstrates that solutions to very complex social issues, such as child poverty, are not easy. There is no quick political, social or economic fix, and practical strategies need to be looked at over a period of time.

Second, the chapter takes a historical perspective to the ECM agenda and 2004 Education Act. Third, we look at how changing philosophies about education informed the way in which children have been taught at different points in time, and perhaps celebrate the fact that at the time of writing a more holistic approach to learning is becoming a more accepted philosophy.

In 1942, as well as today, poverty was seen as a major fact in social inequality and although the term 'barriers to learning' may not have been used then, poverty was certainly seen as influencing children's life chances. Finally, the chapter will examine what lessons, if any, can be drawn from history to help with strategies today to support children's learning.

Defining poverty

I have chosen to go back to 1942 simply because it does mark the formal development of the welfare state. Those interested in reading more widely about this will find Robert Lowe's *The Welfare State in Britain since 1945* useful (2005). Bartholomew provides a very readable critique in *The Welfare State We're In* (2006). Those interested in primary source material will find some wonderful evidence in old school log books that recorded poverty in both urban and rural schools in the Victorian era. The link with this to legislation, which was introduced to alleviate this, can be found in any social history of the UK.

As the researchers from the Joseph Rowntree Trust found when they were asking practitioners, definitions of poverty were very different; practitioners tend to avoid using the word poverty and certainly did not share a common concept of it. Instead they use 'softer' language, such as 'needy' or 'deprived'. It is worth taking a moment to think how you would define poverty before reading any further.

Poverty is a difficult concept to define, but there are three main ways of doing it.

1. *Absolute poverty.* This is based on the minimum needed for survival – food, water, clothing, warmth and shelter. Those without these minimum requirements die. The problem with this sort of definition is that it is subjective; it does not recognise that standards of acceptable food, water, clothing, warmth and shelter change over time and that we need other things for mental health (Figure 3.1). Absolute poverty can be found at the very base of Maslow's hierarchy: 'physiological needs'. However, we also know that we ourselves can learn more purposefully only when we feel safe and secure, when we are in a setting in which we feel we belong and when we have some belief in ourselves as successful learners.

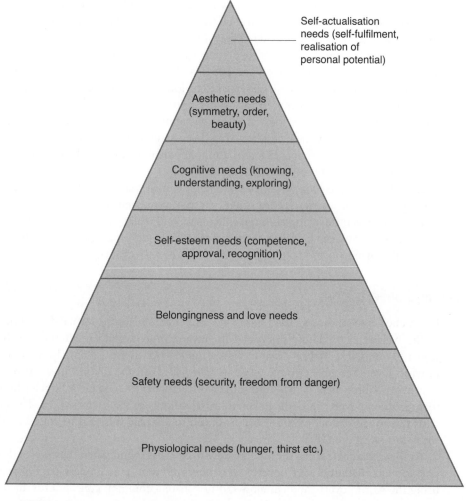

FIGURE 3.1 Maslow's hierarchy of basic needs

2. *Relative poverty*. When people are compared with those around them, this can include educational opportunity, material possessions, health care, good-quality housing, civil rights and social opportunity. The Neighbourhood Census in the previous chapter covers several of these areas (see Figure 2.1). Relative definitions tend to measure inequalities, rather than poverty.

3. *Subjective poverty*. This is based on how individuals feel and it is probably used more by most of us about our own situation than many of us realise. You can feel poor if those around you have more than you do. In our multimedia world today, we are offered daily images of other lives which probably make many of us feel poor by comparison. We are of course offered daily images of those in absolute poverty. Individuals tend to vary about which images have the most relevance to their own lives.

One of the most commonly used definitions of poverty is that it covers those who have less than 50 per cent of the average national income. Twenty per cent of the population in the UK has an income below this definition and the number of children affected is higher than that, as poverty is often greater in families with children and those on pensions. As we saw in the previous chapter, these figures change as people move in and out of poverty during the course of their lives.

Activity/task 1

It is sometimes said that there is no absolute poverty in the UK today. What evidence is there for this statement? And how might you argue against it, particularly in terms of children in school?

There is a considerable quantity of free literature related to poverty studies, some of which is given in the bibliography for this chapter. Readability varies considerably and it is important to check critically whether you are looking at a very verbose sound bite or a piece of genuine research. Even then, it is useful to know who has carried out the research and who has commissioned and paid for it. The 'whois.com' website is also useful for establishing site ownership.

Social exclusion

This expression is often used by the government in place of the word poverty.

Social exclusion is something that can happen to anyone. But some people are significantly more at risk than others. Research has found that people with certain backgrounds and experiences are disproportionately likely to suffer social exclusion. The key risk-factors include: low income; family conflict; being in care; school problems; being an ex-prisoner; being from an ethnic minority; living in a deprived neighbourhood in urban and rural areas; mental health problems, age and disability.

(Social Exclusion Unit 2001)

The Beveridge Report

Back in the early 1940s, these differing concepts of poverty were not a particular issue. Poverty was seen in absolute terms, although there were differences about what this actually meant in practice.

War has always been recognised as having a huge impact on the development of services. The Boer War, for example, at the start of the twentieth century, alerted the nation's attention to the fact that many of the potential British recruits had such poor physical health that they were too unfit to serve. Several authorities, such as that in Manchester in 1879, had already introduced school meals for 'destitute and badly nourished children' in order to improve the health of their school population. It took another 40 years to introduce a National School Meals policy in 1940, when rationing was implemented in the Second World War.

There were probably three major reasons for the political consensus about the need to tackle poverty during the Second World War:

1. To provide a vision for those fighting that conditions at home after the war would improve. Many of those on the home and the war front had bitter memories of the 1930s depression.

2. An acknowledgement that many children who were evacuated to the countryside from major cities had been living in abject poverty in the cities and urban sprawls from which they came. This is not to deny the rural poverty which existed at the time, but it did draw the attention of the more affluent in the shires to the living conditions from which so many evacuees had come.

3. To create a feeling of social solidarity when the country was under threat.

In 1942, the wartime coalition government published a report entitled 'Social Insurance and Allied Services'. The committee that produced it was headed by a Liberal economist called William Beveridge, and their report became known as the Beveridge Report. Much to everyone's surprise, it became the blueprint for the establishment of the British welfare state. At the time it was published, people queued in the streets for a copy. It is hard to image a government report doing that today. Its attraction was that it sold a believable vision of a better economic future, with the promise of legislation that would improve people's lives.

Beveridge identified five evils of British society – want, disease, squalor, ignorance and idleness. Figure 3.2 provides a very brief summary of some of the key areas of the Beveridge Report.

It is easy to see how the resulting legislation to relieve poverty and improve housing, employment, health and education would have had important implications for the lives of children. And with hindsight it is possible to see how very comprehensive it was. This makes a contrast to the more ad hoc policy-making to which we are more accustomed today. It may also explain why even welfare state critics such as Bartholomew still go back to this framework.

The 1944 Education Act is mainly remembered for its introduction of free secondary education for all but it also covered the development of the youth service

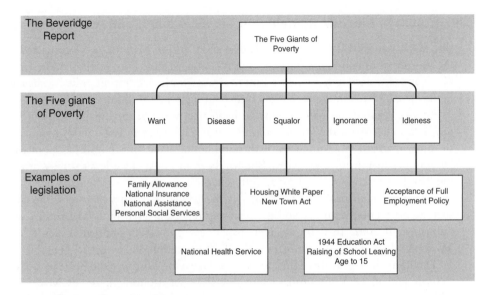

FIGURE 3.2 The Beveridge Report

and a child care service for children and young people in care. Children were still seen as having different types of aptitudes and the new secondary system was to accommodate this by having three different types of school – grammar (for those 11-year-olds who were seen as being academic), technical (for those with technical skills) and modern (for the rest).

Activity/task 2

The Beveridge Report was intended as a fivefold attack on poverty 'from cradle to the grave'. The interests of children in poverty were seen very much as part of an overall approach to poverty. (a) Compare this with the five outcomes of the ECM agenda. (b) Now try mapping some current legislation on to the Beveridge outcomes. It is surprisingly simple, although I doubt politicians today would get away with having a heading 'idleness'.

'Every Child Matters'

Although this report, the legislation and guidelines that followed it were not visualised in exactly the same way as the Beveridge Report, there are marked similarities. The Beveridge report was driven by the need to improve society generally, particularly after the depression of the 1930s. The ECM agenda was driven by different forces but, as can be seen from the comparison of the 'five evils' of society, it did incorporate many of the basic ideas of the 1942 Beveridge Report.

Background to the ECM agenda and the 2004 Education Act

On 21 January 2001, Marie-Therese Kouao and Carl Jon Manning were convicted of the murder of Kouao's great-niece Victoria Climbie, a child born in 1991 in the Ivory Coast and entrusted to her father's aunt to arrange for her education. Initially, she and her great-aunt lived in France for 5 months but then moved to England.

Anyone reading this will know what happened next and the horrific story of her death. 'She has spent the last few months of her life (winter 1999–2000) living and sleeping in a bath in an unheated bathroom, bound hand and foot inside a bin bag, lying in her own urine and faeces.' She had been in England for less than a year and the 'family' was known to at least 12 different public service departments.

Like other high-profile child deaths at the hands of parents or carers, this also sparked off a public enquiry and the resulting report, chaired by Lord Laming, was published in 2002. In 2003, a green paper was published, entitled 'Every Child Matters', which resulted eventually in the 2004 Education Act.

The immediate priority of this Act was to change the existing child protection laws to try to prevent anything similar happening. The Act also took up the ECM agenda, which took a much more holistic approach to children, as the outcomes framework illustrates.

Nearly all child protection and safeguarding legislation has been triggered by the appalling death of a child, which shocked a much wider population through high media coverage. Most of the legislation in the past has appeared to be aimed at those working in social services and health. The education service was often seen as an 'add on' in terms of integrated services in relation to child protection. However, by 2000, all schools had a named child protection officer. This was often the headteacher in primary schools, indicating the importance schools placed on their responsibilities to safeguard their pupils. The vision of the ECM agenda was intended to draw in education and other related public and private services to provide a truly integrated service.

Looking back to well before the ECM green paper, those working in schools have always been involved directly in helping to 'prevent' legislation being needed to protect the children in their care. What has changed is a recognition that many of those employed in today's schools have a direct legal responsibility because they work with specific individuals or groups of vulnerable children who are now identified by the school, if not by other agencies. Another key factor is the massive increase in paperwork involved, which several of those I interviewed attributed to fear of their service/agency/school being held responsible for a child's death and individuals who worked for it being pilloried in the press.

Any vision for education involves 'making a difference' to children's and young people's lives. Therefore all of those working in schools are part of this 'integrating children's services' movement.

Activity/task 3

Teachers in training often have very limited experience of school-based child safeguarding training. Educational professionals, such as LMs, have a great deal more, and receive regular updates. Look at a school you know and identify the provision there for safeguarding training.

Figure 3.3 shows how much work still must be done. It comes from the 2004 ECM document and, sadly, was an understatement of the issue even then. The numbers of looked-after children (LAC), for example, is steadily rising. In 2007 it was up to about 80,000, but, by March 2009, care proceedings had increased by nearly 38 per cent from 2008, largely as a result of the Baby P case. Local authorities are required to produce an Annual Report for LAC. The report and related figures are useful to look at as they provide a more immediate view of what is happening at local level.

It is also important to note that from April 2008 the Child Protection Registers were replaced by the List of Children Subject of a Child Protection Plan. This was in line with the government guidance *Working Together to Safeguard Children* (DfES *et al.*

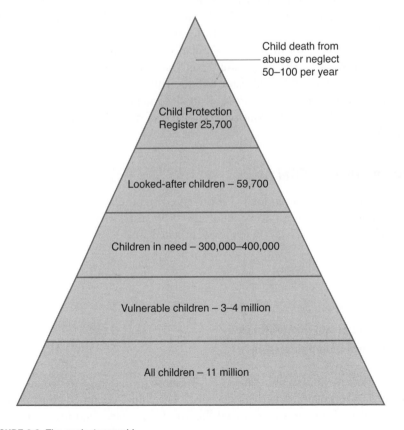

FIGURE 3.3 The neglect pyramid

2006). It was intended to emphasise the importance of the multi-agency plan, rather than the act of registration.

Indeed compulsory education has always played an important role in providing formal educational and pastoral services for children and young people. By the very nature of schooling, teachers were often the only individuals who maintained substantial contact with individual children, apart from their parents and carers. Logbooks from Victorian schools show that, despite their harsh reputation, teachers have always felt this duty of care (Hughes 2008). This care might have been demonstrated in different ways from that done today, but it was nevertheless an integral part of the teacher's role. Today's schools, of course, employ a much more extensive number of staff, who have varying parts to play in providing children's services.

'Change for Children'

As a direct result of the Laming Report into Victoria's death, the government introduced its policy *Every Child Matters: Change for Children*. This was presented as a new approach 'to the well-being of children and young people from birth to age 19.' Certainly, taking 19 years as the cut-off point, it created an image of childhood that was much longer than it has been in the past. It was also a much more holistic approach to child protection than the legislation that it replaced. It gave the government a much greater involvement in the lives of children and those working with children. There is considerable concern about this and the fear that safeguarding children, like terrorism, provides a rationale for increased surveillance by government agencies on the whole population. Work by the King's Fund has found that in other areas, such as healthy living, the general public did want the government to be 'bolder and take action'. The King's Fund provides some useful articles and publications on the health system, which address many of the issues educational professionals identify about local health support.

Documentation for ECM

The initial documentation for ECM presented an outcomes framework that showed a vision of entitlement for every child, aged 0–19 years, whatever their background or their circumstances. These outcomes were stated as:

- Be healthy
- Stay safe
- Enjoy and achieve
- Make a positive contribution
- Achieve economic well-being.

The documentation also carried a commitment that support would be put into the system to ensure that this happened. The initial documentation presented an overall view of how it was proposed this would take place and many of these initial fundamental points have remained. These included systemic change at both local and national level and an integrated children's workforce.

Systemic change was needed in order to:

- Build services around children, young people and their families
- Support parents and carers
- Develop a skilled children's workforce with changing culture and practice embedded.

At a national level this would involve:

- The appointment of a Children's Commissioner
- Provision for indexes or databases to enable better sharing of information
- A Joint Inspection Framework/Joint Area Reviews (JARs)
- Single statutory Children and Young People's Plan (CYPP).

At local level:

- Universal and targeted services
- Services across the age range 0–19 years
- Duty to cooperate (April 2005 and revised in 2008)
- Duty to safeguard and promote welfare of children
- Duty to set up Local Safeguarding Children Boards (LSCBs)
- Provision for indexes or databases to enable better sharing of information
- Director for Children's Services
- Lead Member (councillor) for Children's Services
- CYPP
- Provisions on foster care and private fostering
- Duty to promote educational achievement of looked-after children (LAC).

In many ways it recognised what many local authorities were already piloting, such as senior appointments across health, education and social services. Once these senior posts were in position, others at more operational levels were introduced (see Figure 11.1 for an example).

Educational professionals in schools are all part of this children's workforce, even if sometimes they may not be recognised as such. Every member of the workforce has to be committed to break down barriers, so that all the outcomes of the ECM framework can be reached. This requires a children's workforce, which, in the words of the government:

- Has high quality
- Is retained by offering better development and career progression
- Is strengthened through interagency and multidisciplinary working

■ Promotes stronger leadership and management.

The promise was that at an operational level integrated children's services would be enhanced through:

1. Multi-agency working – panels, teams, services

2. Sharing a Common Assessment Framework (CAF)

3. Sharing a Common Core of Skills and Knowledge

4. Using technology and networking to ensure effective information sharing

5. Protecting children at risk through the creation of lead professionals, who would act as the named person

6. Continuous workforce reform and professional development.

The Children's Workforce Development Council website provides useful and readable worksheets on features such as the CAF and schools.

The Children's Workforce

The creation of a Children's Workforce was a direct result of the ECM agenda. It was, and indeed remains, a huge and complex commitment and was examined in more detail in Chapter 1. It pulled in and extended many services, whose work with children formed only a comparatively small part of their overall work. This was true both for the services themselves and for the people who worked for them. We shall see some operational/practical examples of this later in the book.

The Children's Workforce in schools

Another thing that the Act did was to remind and/or inform people that there were important links between services for children which might not have been seen as relevant to children's education. Taking health as an example: health is an overarching area of children's lives; breaking down barriers for learning includes having a good understanding of factors that may influence how healthy our learners are.

Figure 3.4, on health determinants, shows this very clearly. We have already seen some of these health determinants in Chapter 2 when we looked at neighbourhood statistics, for which health of the community was measured on a levels of deprivation chart. This figure enables us to look at it in terms of individual children, whose health may be preventing them from making the most of their schooling and also failing to prepare them for a healthy adult life.

Very young children have little influence on most of these health determinants, but are certainly subject to their results, either as children or when they grow up. Their physical, emotional, social, moral and spiritual welfare is largely determined by their carers. The power children hold, or are allowed to hold, is also determined by carers; the large number of very fussy eaters have often been trained and allowed to be fussy, so that a diet of sausages and chips is seen as much easier than having a battle over

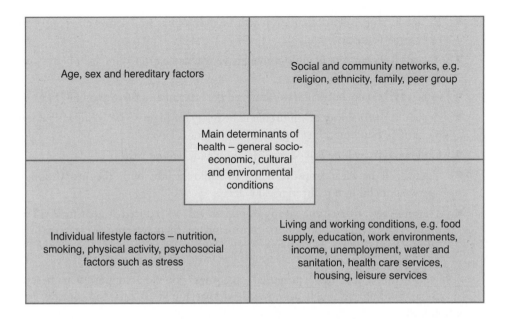

FIGURE 3.4 Determinants of health. Adapted from Naidoo and Wills (2009)

broccoli. One of the things that successful healthy schools programmes have been able to show is that children can be taught to initially question and perhaps change lifestyles, both of themselves and of their families. Pester power can be used in more than one way.

The Children's Plan and its updates

One key element about operational political practice is that it never stays still. Updates on the ECM agenda continued to roll out, until another major political initiative was drawn up. This was largely in response to the growing concern at that time, when there was a strong economy, that there were still many issues about children's safety, their health, their ability to enjoy and achieve, their economic achievement and their being able to make a positive contribution to society (SHEEP).

In 2005, the Labour government drew up a Children's Plan outlining a 10-year vision to make 'this country (England) a better place for children and young people'. Part of this was also a political response to the Unicef international findings (see Chapter 4) that showed UK children being at the bottom of a well-being league of 21 countries (see Table 4.4). The plan aimed to 'raise attainment and aspirations for this and future generations, closing gaps in educational achievement and ensuring standards of educational excellence for everyone' (DCSF 2005).

The initial plan was built on the fact that young people spend only one-fifth of their childhood at school, and the philosophy that they learn best when their families support and encourage them and when they are experiencing positive activities outside the school day. It set out a series of ambitions for all areas of children's lives:

- By age 5, 90 per cent of children will be developing well across all areas of the early years foundation stages
- At age 11, 95 per cent of children will have reached expected levels in literacy and numeracy
- At age 19, 90 per cent will have achieved the equivalent of five good GCSEs
- At age 19, the majority of children will be ready for higher education, with at least 6 out of 10 children achieving the equivalent of A Levels
- Child poverty will be halved by 2010 and eradicated by 2020
- There will be clear improvements in child health, with the proportion of overweight children reduced to 2000 levels
- The number of first-time young offenders will be reduced so that by 2020 the number receiving a conviction, reprimand or final warning for a recordable offence has fallen by one-quarter.

It was claimed that these proposed outcomes would be supported with some additional funding, although acknowledged that much of this had already been announced.

Activity/task 4

What are some of the issues for measuring outcomes from some of these proposals, for example the halving of child poverty and the specific measurement educational measurement of outcomes at 19?

The 2007 update moved the goal posts slightly again. It was based, yet again, on five principles:

1. First, it acknowledged that the government does not bring up children, parents do. The government therefore needs to do more to back parents and families.

2. A repetition of the ECM outcomes that all children have the potential to succeed and should go as far as their talents can take them.

3. Children and young people need to enjoy their childhood as well as grow up prepared for adult life.

4. Services need to be shaped by and responsive to children, young people and families, not designed around professional boundaries.

5. It is always better to prevent failure than tackle a crisis later.

Again, nothing very much anyone could disagree with. It is then quite interesting, that the focus in this and later updates moved more directly on to education, in particular schools, which were identified as central to their success. This resulted in the update identifying initiatives, such as the introduction of the Early Years Foundation Stage, reform of the secondary curriculum, the introduction of diplomas and increasing the school-leaving age. It also claimed to introduce policies on:

- Personalised teaching, learning and testing
- The introduction by 2010 of a learning guide for each pupil, helping them work to their full potential
- A wide-ranging review of the primary-level curriculum to help smooth the transitions from early years, free up space in the school day and enhance focus on literacy, numeracy and languages
- Implementation of the foundation learning tier
- Schools to increasingly work in partnership with other agencies to actively contribute to all aspects of children's lives, such as health and well-being, safety and care
- Greater priority to be placed on raising expectations for children with special educational needs
- More advice, information and guidance to parents and families about their child's development
- All new teachers to be able to study for a Master's degree.

Schools, further education and higher education had all been well aware of all this before the publication of the Children's Plan and its 2007 update. It simply repeated previous guidance and ministerial statements. It then went through each of the five ECM outcomes outlining some specific operational initiatives, which again it could be argued were already being put in place. It also resulted in more formal legislation being put in place.

2009 Children and Young People's Plan Guidance 2009

In this the government introduced yet more non-statutory guidance to replace the previous guidance on the 2005 and 2007 Children's Plans. There was an increased focus on 'young people', which may easily have been linked with the increased media coverage on gangs of youths, street and knife crime and, in particular, the murder of Rhys Jones (aged 10) in Liverpool, by a group of 16- and 17-year-olds. It looked more closely at performance management agreements and Local Area Agreements (LAAs) and announced that there would be more legislative changes in the future. The intention was to ensure that regulations set out clearly how local authorities would be inspected in terms of their CYPPs. It is of course possible to read much more visionary outcomes of this and other updates, but it was clear from the informal comments in many of the interviews that it was often the stick, rather than the carrot, which was driving specific local changes. This was often a direct result of funding difficulties, resulting in money being moved from one sector to another.

Summary

History shows us that there are no easy solutions to tackling poverty. The definitions of poverty have changed over the years and the consensus has gone about what constitutes poverty and how much individuals may be responsible for their own poverty. As a recent newspaper report commented, we are spending more on alcohol and cigarettes than on food.

The chapter looks at one particular attempt to combat poverty in the early post-Second World War years, which resulted in a stream of welfare legislation. Lowe's book *The Welfare State in Britain since 1945* (2005) provides a particularly readable extension of this up to 2005. It is complex, as is the relationship between poverty and school success. The drawing up of the ECM agenda is very briefly looked at in relation to this. The ECM agenda is not the sole solution and, as frequent adaptations and post-2004 postings on its website show, we are still far from even getting an agency holistic approach to child poverty as it is seen today. The CYPP then became the means of revitalising and updating guidance and regulations to improve children's lives. Indeed, in mid-2009, the ECM website had no details or links about the latest Children's Plan update. ECM had become history and the death of Baby P in 2008 reinforced this.

4

Learning and Concepts of Childhood

Free the child's potential, and you will transform him [sic] into the world.

(Maria Montessori)

Chapter overview

- Examine traditional psychological theories about how children learn in order to identify some of the factors which may act as barriers to learning

- Develop this to look at some of the different concepts this implies of children as learners (construct of the pupil)

- Explore implications and strategies for Educational Professionals seeking to break down barriers to learning.

Introduction

In this chapter we look at traditional theories about learning, which have come largely from findings in the field of psychology and, second, explore what these findings imply about the child as a learner, i.e. the social construction of the child as a learner. We limit, as much as possible, the review to what goes on in relation to learning in primary school; but recognise that it is much wider than this. There is also no apology for calling this chapter 'traditional theories' because, as Chapter 6 shows, these theories have been heavily challenged by the growth of scientific evidence regarding the brain and learning.

Starting points

Towards the end of the seventeenth century, well before there was any such discipline as psychology, an English philosopher called John Locke wrote the equivalent to an academic bestseller called *Some Thoughts Concerning Education*. Today there are hundreds of such books, blogs, videos and computer forums addressing both parents and teachers on how children learn or they should be taught to learn. So it is quite difficult to imagine a situation in which one individual's advice was so powerful.

Locke outlined a theory of learning which said that the child's mind was a 'blank slate' and this blank slate needed educating in three ways. These were (a) the development of a healthy body; (b) the formation of a 'virtuous' character; and (c) an appropriate academic curriculum. This sounds surprisingly familiar and we can draw parallels with healthy schools; personal, social, health and emotional education; and the Primary Strategy. What is hopefully different is the image of the child learner as a blank slate. However, it is sometimes possible to listen to government initiatives on what schools should do in order to effect change in the wider society and suspect that optimistic writers are assuming that what is taught is what is automatically learnt.

In the eighteenth century, another philosopher, Jean-Jacques Rousseau, challenged this image of the child. He believed that all children went through a specific development process and learnt mainly through their innate curiosity: the child could not be seen as a 'blank slate' but actively sought to make sense of the world in which he – and it was just a male world – lived. Learning took place, through what we would today describe as 'scaffolding'. Later major educational philosophers, such as Vygotsky and Bruner, provided more informed views on this scaffolding. It involved the adult observing the child and recognising the stage of learning they were at and then providing help to reach the next stage (in Bruce and Meggitt 2005). The current assessment for pupil progress (APP) follows this as well. This philosophy was later taken up by the 1967 Plowden Report on primary schools and determined the philosophy of 'child-centred' education. The construct of a child in this report was that the pupil was 'active, engaged in exploration or discovery, interacting both with the teacher and with each other. Each child operates as an individual, although groups are formed and reformed related to those activities which are not normally subject-differentiated'. This may not be the image that you and I probably have of all primary pupils, although it may be held more often of children in early-years settings.

Activity/task 1

It is easy to see how the ideas of both Locke and Rousseau about how a child learns will influence the learning that takes place. What sort of challenges are presented by the view of the child as some sort of sponge who soaks up what is taught? What other sorts of challenges are presented by a view of the child as innately curious, who learns through structured problem-solving activities that feed into his/her innate curiosity?

Traditional psychological theories

The word 'psychology' comes from the combination of two Greek words; *psyche* meaning 'mind' and *logos* meaning 'study'. Like all sciences, its goals are to describe, explain, predict and, ultimately, in this case, control 'the study of the mind'. This is a huge topic and it has expanded far beyond the initial and traditional findings of the work of the first psychologists whose work informed those who worked in schools.

In *Principles of Primary Education*, I suggested that for those working in classrooms there are three possible ways of organising these theories, by looking at the areas of:

1. Child development
2. Theories of learning
3. Learning styles.

Of course all three areas can be subdivided. Education is no different from other disciplines and this means that there are alternative theories and views, which are contested not only by fellow theorists, but also by practitioners, politicians and the media. Different language or discourse is used and many words have both day-to-day meanings as well as a technical meaning. Well-being, for example, has a dictionary meaning, a philosophical meaning, an academic one and a political one. Yet it is discussed as if we all share the same understanding. After 5 years of research, the Economic Social Research Council group defined it as an academic concept: 'Well being is a state of being with others, where human needs are met, where one can act meaningfully to pursue goals and where one enjoys a satisfactory quality of life'. This is a significantly different meaning from that of the government in the 2004 Children's Act: 'Arrangements are to be made with a view to improving the well-being of children in the authority's area so far as relating to (a) physical and mental health and emotional well-being (b) protection from harm and neglect (c) education, training and recreation (d) the contribution made by them to society (e) social and economic well-being'.

Child development theories

It is generally recognised that there are three theory groups within child development theory – maturationists, environmentalists and constructivists.

Maturationists

Maturationists, such as Arnold Gesell (Fetsco and McClure 2004), believed that child development was a natural biological process that occurred automatically in stages over time.

Environmentalists

Environmentalists, such as Albert Bandura, challenged the maturationist approach. They argued that the child's environment shaped their learning and behaviour.

This meant the human behaviour, development and learning were reactions to the child's environment. In a school context this assumed that young children developed and acquired new knowledge by reacting to their environment. This enhanced the importance of ensuring a positive learning ethos for all children.

Constructivists

This is perhaps the best-known group in child development. It includes figures such as Jean Piaget, Lev Vygotsky and Jerome Bruner. At its most simple level they all believed that a child's cognitive development was a natural process and that young children learnt through interacting with the environment and the people around them. This belief and philosophy has major implications for strategies to support effective learning. These included the need to supply small, attractive learning spaces that were conducive to learning and teaching. This has implications for educational professionals today. Large hall teaching spaces, when needed for briefings, such as road safety, need good screens, so everyone can see and hear. Opportunities need to be provided for children to discuss their learning with others, while it is taking place. Some of the most exciting designs for the Building Schools for the Future (BSF) have incorporated these ideas. The growth of 'nurture groups' in many primary schools, targeted at vulnerable pupils, are often supported by taking place in small, attractive areas.

Theories of learning

These can be divided into four theory groups (Fetsco and McClure 2004):

1. Behavioural
2. Cognitive
3. Social cognitive
4. Cognitive development.

Behavioural view of learning

The behavioural view of learning is a very basic theory and is used by many schools as a means of breaking down barriers to learning, in particular behaviour management. Indeed it is often used to manage a child's behaviour so that some learning can take place. Schools using 'assertive discipline' have adopted a behavioural approach to behaviour management. And it is frequently used on a one-to-one basis with children who have challenging behaviour.

Behaviourism in the school setting implies that (a) the educational professional is the most important force in the classroom; (b) modification of a child's behaviour is possible; and (c) changes in behaviour may eventually be followed by changes in attitude, for example racist name-calling.

Activity/task 2

Here are four different sorts of behavioural reinforcers that are used in schools and early learning centres to enhance learning:

(a) Social reinforcers – demonstrated by adult approval (such as a smile/frown)

(b) Activity reinforcers – behaviour or privilege earned ('golden time')

(c) Tangible reinforcers – physical object earned through behaviour (good work sticker)

(d) Natural reinforcers – behaviours that contain their own reinforcement (intrinsic motivation).

Think of some other examples you have seen either inside or outside schools. What disadvantages are there in total dependency on the first three reinforcers?

Learning is seen here as being supported by rewards and sanctions. Most classroom practice has plenty of evidence of this – stickers, house points, raffle tickets, etc. When this fails, sanctions seem to be the main force behind the inducement for children to sit still and learn. Encouraging extrinsic motivation can often produce challenges for educational professionals, particularly those who are less regular visitors to school, who do not have access to the same whole-school system. Schools with strong behaviour management sanctions are not always so good at providing alternative strategies for visiting professionals working in different, and often quite creative, circumstances, such as arts specialist teams.

Educational professionals, such as LMs, on the other hand, who work with individual children and small groups outside the classroom and are often relatively independent of the class teacher, usually develop their own specific and individual strategies, which can be adapted quickly and easily to changing circumstances in children's lives. Several of those people interviewed in Part 2 spoke about the need to have effective rewards for learners who were poorly motivated, for example the promise of, or withdrawal of, the right to take part in a sports activity.

Cognitive learning theory

There are four main principles behind this learning theory: (a) prior knowledge; (b) organisation of knowledge; (c) appropriate matching of new knowledge and skills with working memory; and (d) acknowledgement of learning as an active process.

■ *Prior knowledge.* This involves linking new knowledge and skills to the learners' existing knowledge and skills. Learning occurs when the learner can add to and modify existing knowledge. This is often the reason why student teachers and other educational professionals are advised to include prior knowledge in their planning sheets. It is also one of the areas in which educational professionals who live in the local community can really enhance learning. I observed a lesson in a Year 5 class the other day on recycling. The student teacher had prepared well, but lived about 9 miles from the school in another local authority. The teaching assistant (TA) was able to enrich the session by getting the children to identify the colours and purposes of their own refuse bins at home. She provided photographs of the recycling sites at the local supermarket and the local authority wastage depot. Some of the children from outside this particular authority were able to contribute by identifying different colours and materials in their own back gardens. The local knowledge made the learning personalised and relevant in a way which enhanced both content and understanding. It built on and developed prior knowledge.

- *Organisation of knowledge.* This is needed in order to encourage learners to organise their learning. This is often done through a process of 'scaffolding' and is carried out in a number of ways. Some of these are specific: we do this and then we do that. Many pupils are asked to write or describe the learning outcomes prior to undertaking an activity. In many primary schools this organisation of knowledge is further linked to Assessment for Learning (AfL) and Assessing Pupil Progress (APP). Other techniques include WILF (What I'm Looking For . . .) and WALT (We Are Learning To . . .). Both of these are characters: WILF is used when children are asked to write how the educational professional will know that they have achieved their learning objective, whereas WALT, the other character, is displayed on a board in each class with a speech bubble for the teacher to write in the learning objective. The cognitive learning theory supports this by suggesting that learning is helped because the children are being asked to identify and record what they hope to gain from doing the activity. It organises their learning into required outcomes. Of course it is sometimes more exciting with very practical activities to identify what the children feel they have learnt after the activity. Primary science and investigative history and geography lend themselves to this particularly well when planned as skills-based themes.

- *Working memory.* Knowledge about this is necessary in order to ensure learners are not required to learn more than their working memory can cope with at any particular time. This forms part of a theory about how information is processed and involves different forms of models that describe thinking and memory. Working memory is seen as a memory store in which information is temporarily maintained before it is stored in long-term memory. As we all know from our own learning experiences, the efficiency of working memory tends to vary according to a number of variables, such as how we feel, the task itself, the time of day, the weather, and so on. This makes it very difficult to plan for.

- *Learning as an active process.* This principle recognises that learning is an active process and needs to be goal directed. These goals need to be personal. Today this is often known as the What's In It For Me (WIIFM) factor.

Cognitive learning theory is a much more personal, individualist approach to learning than behaviourism. It signifies the difference between extrinsic and intrinsic motivation, which we look at later in this chapter. Behaviourism encourages the desired learning through external factors such as rewards (extrinsic). Cognitive theory encourages the learner to make the learning meaningful for themselves by linking it with what they already know and identifying what they need to get out of it.

Social cognitive theory

Current social cognitive theory is heavily based on the work of Albert Bandura. He suggested three main features that learners need to have:

1. Models of learning from which they can acquire knowledge and behaviours about how to learn. One example you may observe in classrooms or nurseries is the teacher, or other relevant adult, 'thinking aloud'. There might be a mathematical problem on the board and the teacher models the process by which the problem can be solved. The 'thinking aloud' can test out a hypothesis, and reject it, as well as finding a hypothesis that works. Puppets and soft toys are often used to model learning with younger children.

2. Learners need to have belief in themselves as effective learners and their potential to control their own learning process. Many of us can identify strengths and weaknesses in our own learning. These are not always accurate or realistic of course, and a great deal of work has to be done with some children to raise their expectations about their ability to learn. A less obvious challenge are children whose self-esteem is quite high, but who are actually failing to acknowledge the amount of work that they will need to do in order to succeed at a task. Most of us recognise this in adults, who seem to know a great deal about something and then you find out that they know a lot less than they think they do.

3. Learners need to have the opportunities and abilities to regulate their own learning processes. This is fairly obvious: we learn better when we want to learn something and can create the best conditions in which to do this. In the real world, many learning activities are determined for children by others and there is little choice about what and how to learn. In essence, self-regulation of learning is challenging.

Cognitive development theory

This theory suggests that learning is more effective if:

1. Learners actively construct their own understandings
2. Those who work with learners take into account their cognitive development levels – in primary schools this is often interpreted as age related
3. Learning is assisted by the nature of the interaction with people and objects in their environment.

Key constructivists for cognitive development theory are Piaget, Vygotsky and Bruner.

Activity/task 3

Use an educational psychology text to find out more about the ideas of Piaget, Vygotsky and Bruner. Most educational psychology texts will also provide you with practical examples of how their findings can be exemplified in schools and early-years settings. You will find plenty of critiques about their work, but note that much of their work that you do recognise takes place in good practice.

Learning style theorists

I expect everyone who is reading this has completed at least one questionnaire to identify their preferred learning style. These exist online as well as in psychology and general educational texts. They are available for children as well as adults, but do need to be treated with care and be evaluated. This section outlines three different learning style theories, but there are many more; however, they do not all necessarily adapt easily to work in primary schools or to help you identify how barriers to learning may be linked to inappropriate learning styles that are being promoted either in school or by local/central government. What is certainly true is that the educational professional needs to know more about what is meant by a learning style than a tabloid newspaper version.

Howard Gardner

Howard Gardner devised a fairly non-scientific theory of learning, based on the idea of 'multiple intelligences'. He himself has acknowledged that he has moved on from his original thinking: he has extended his theory of seven intelligences (linguistic, mathematical, visual, musical, bodily, interpersonal, intrapersonal) to nine intelligences, including 'naturalistic' and 'existential', and has speculated on including another two – 'spiritual' and 'moral'. Whatever Gardner may now feel, the idea of multiple intelligences has certainly taken on a life of its own, although there is very little scientific evidence for it. Measurements of different types of intelligences, however attractive, have failed to produce valid results.

The sense of what is covered by most of these intelligences is fairly self-evident, although the latest four – existential, naturalistic, spiritual and moral – are more difficult to identify. The inability to measure any of them is less important than the acknowledgement that we are made up of more than one single intelligence. Yet many learning situations do not reflect this much broader approach to intelligence and in classrooms, including reception classes, children are often set into groups based on their reading ability. This seems to make sense when activities are linked to reading worksheets in any subject area, but may hide the fact that some weaker readers have much to offer in other areas. There are also issues of equality of access to the whole curriculum.

Activity/task 4

- Which of Gardener's intelligences are measured by Standard Assessment Tasks/Tests (SATs)?
- What are the implications of this in terms of measurement of school achievement for primary children?
- What are the implications in terms of children's own learning identity?

David Kolb

Kolb's learning style model identified four different learning styles. This theory sorted learners into four types, who at the extreme ends of the model were:

- *Divergers.* These are learners who prefer to learn by concrete experiences and reflective observation. The initial school attachment experiences, which generally start all teacher training courses, play very much to this learning style. The student teacher can be part of a school and have plenty of time to learn through concrete experience of and working with groups of children. They observe and then reflect on their observations.

- *Assimilators.* These also learn by reflective observation, but this reflection is informed by abstract rather than concrete experiences. I actually have problems recognising this learning style in the schools in which I have worked and visited. However, I have met adults who quietly observe and then seem to have grasped and understood things that I have missed.

- *Convergers.* These learners prefer to learn by active, physical experimentation and abstract conceptualisation. I meet a lot of these learners in schools and it is surprisingly easy to find this abstract conceptualisation in very young children (National Research Council 2001). The idea of the sun going down at night, through the globe to Australia, was the concept verbalised by one Year 4 child. An 18-month-old child, who tripped over a pram strap that her father then hung back over the pram handle, could be seen looking at the strap and her father. She then walked back, put the strap on the floor again and repeated her initial walk. This second time, she carefully stepped over the strap.

- *Accommodators.* This learning style prefers active experimentation and concrete learning experiences. The recent growth in seeing the teacher as an action-based researcher fits into this learning model. It involves being willing to try/experiment with new ideas, resources, curriculum designs, etc. In order to be successful, it does have to involve reflection.

Kolb acknowledged that although almost everyone makes use of all these learning models – diverger, accommodator, converger and assimilator – each one of us has a preferred learning style.

Dunn and Dunn

These researchers looked at how learning was influenced by 'instructional preference'. This might seem very obvious to us, but if you have an image of the child as a blank slate, the idea of instructional preference challenges this. Dunn and Dunn identified five basic stimuli that affected an individual's ability to perceive, interact with and respond to the learning environment. This was out of a learning model that identified more than twenty stimuli. The basic five were environmental, emotional, sociological, physiological and psychological.

Implications of traditional learning theories for breaking barriers to learning

See Table 4.1 for a summary. The table also shows how different views about how children learn are a product of beliefs or philosophies about the child as a learner. These 'constructs' are often not made explicit but inform the way in which central and local government recommend strategies for school improvement. The table illustrates how different theories present the learner in different ways, for example the child as a:

1. Blank slate

2. Active learner

3. Learner who develops their own learning through general mental and physical development and/or environmental factors

4. Learner who needs rewards and sanctions to be motivated

5. Learner who is intrinsically motivated to learn

6. Learner who learns in their own way and this can vary with changes in both learning conditions and the learner themselves – subject matter, method of presentation, how the learner feels, what is happening in the learner's life outside school; this results in learning needs to be personalised – current schooling cannot of course do this on a day-to-day basis.

TABLE 4.1 Some implications of traditional learning theories for breaking barriers to learning

CONSTRUCT OF CHILD AS A LEARNER	STRATEGIES FOR IMPROVING LEARNING
Child as a blank slate (Locke)	What is taught can be learnt. If learning is not effective then the teaching must be at fault and needs to be adapted and modified. Early Ofsted reports were heavily into this idea, pointing out if results were low that this meant that teaching was unsatisfactory. Inspectors – and I was one – had to argue hard if they found teaching was good, but SATs results were low compared to national averages.

TABLE 4.1 (continued)

CONSTRUCT OF CHILD AS A LEARNER	STRATEGIES FOR IMPROVING LEARNING
Child as active learner (Rousseau)	Children are naturally curious, therefore the adult's role was to provide problem-solving situations. The solutions would be driven by the child's innate curiosity. The 1967 Plowden Report (Central Advisory Council for Education) constructed a view of the pupil as 'active, engaged in exploration or discovery, interacting both with the teacher and with each other. Each child operates as an individual, though groups are formed and re-formed related to those activities which are not normally subject differentiated.'
Child as a developing learner through general mental and physical development and/or environmental factors	These developmental theories are on a continuum. At the extreme end, children develop in a series of stages, give or take a couple of years. Pre-readiness tests might be administered to see if the child is ready for the next stage. This is based on the assumption that children will acquire knowledge naturally and automatically as they grow physically and become older. Certainly the 'Readiness for Reading' tests I administered in the late 1970s would have resulted in some children as never being ready for their first reading scheme book. Aspects of this approach are useful: the visiting educational professional talking about road safety can quickly gain some understanding of children's understanding by asking a few pertinent questions. Modern technology makes this much easier, with individual personal response units (PRUs), so that a hall with 180 children in it, each with their own unit, can respond quickly to questions related to prior knowledge about road safety issues, for example. The professional providing the input then gets a quick idea of prior knowledge from the majority of the audience. The developmental approach that links children's environment to their natural development includes both their physical and emotional environment. A 5-year-old child living on a dairy farm will have a much great understanding of milk quotas, artificial insemination and milking technology than urban adults like me. Like Rousseau, constructivists saw young children as active participants in the learning process. They also had the very optimistic belief that young children initiate most of the activities required for learning and development. Thus educational professionals need to be proactive in providing a positive ethos for learning. Small rooms that are set aside for educational professionals to work with small groups or individual children need to be attractive and conducive to learning. Large hall teaching spaces need good screens and acoustics so that everyone can see and hear and there are comfortable seating arrangements. Opportunities need to be provided for children to discuss their learning with others, while it is taking place, and they should not expected to be stationary and silent for periods of time.

TABLE 4.1 (continued)

CONSTRUCT OF CHILD AS A LEARNER	STRATEGIES FOR IMPROVING LEARNING
Child needs extrinsic motivation through behaviour modification	Behavioural reinforcers for learning need to be developed, e.g. non-verbal and verbal communication, rewards and punishments, and making it clear that it is particular behaviours that are unacceptable, not the child. These need to be comprehensive.
Child as a cognitive learner, with intrinsic motivation if learning is personalised	Cognitive learning theory implies that those working with children must have some knowledge of what the child already knows, so that they can draw on prior knowledge and skills; support children in organising existing learning and new learning; be realistic about working memory and develop strategies – often games and puzzles – to improve it; personalise goals for children, so that they have a vested interest in learning; and model themselves as good learners and encourage children to believe themselves to be good learners and have control over learning. Cognitive development: providing opportunities for discovery learning, so that pupils can use problem-solving techniques to create new knowledge; ensuring children have comprehensive learning experiences that enable knowledge to be integrated and viewed from different perspectives; giving opportunities for thinking and working collaboratively with their peers and other educational professionals; providing the means whereby pupils can self-regulate their learning and design their own learning experiences; and trying to ensure authentic learning experiences.
Child with an individual/ personalised learning style	Identify children's own learning style preferences and plan for this; enhance other styles of learning that might consolidate and extend preferred styles. This preferred learning style may have preferred instructional styles and these also need to be identified.

Activity task 5

Think of yourself as an adult learning about new ideas or skills. Which type of learner construct best fits yourself? I think I vary. On occasions, with some new piece of technology, I have been an active learner, for example when I bought a dishwasher and had to learn (and be taught) how to use it. Of course it is easy to see that there was learning taking place, which was extrinsically motivated by the reward of a machine doing the work for me. But the poor souls who taught me certainly had to personalise the learning – several times! However, I have had to sit through many a technical or 'informative' briefing about which I have had minimal interest, or indeed involvement, and learnt nothing; I started as a blank slate and finished as one, albeit more bored, discontented and restless than I was 2 hours before it started. What is exciting is when, with low expectations and a low skills level, I attend an event and get lifted as a result of the high-quality presentation, involvement and teaching. However, none of us can expect others to be super-performer/teacher all of the time and many times I have learnt more through discussion, collaborative tasks, practising something, trying it out myself, making mistakes and going back.

Good schools ensure that learning is as personalised as is possible for individuals, although obviously personalising learning for 30 individual children is a challenge. This is one reason why many schools have learning and teaching policies and ensure that community needs are recognised in these. There is at the very basic level an acknowledgement by educational professionals – if not by the media and politicians – that schooling has to be driven by the community needs as well as the statutory guidance.

Other concepts of a child that influence learning

In this section we examine other constructs of childhood that have implications on what goes on in school and what barriers this may raise for learners and the educational professionals who are working with them. Those who have read widely in the general area of childhood studies will be very familiar with this broader view of pupils, but, interestingly, it forms very little part of the professional discourse of those training to be teachers or indeed of what goes on in schools, despite the fact that many decisions are made on the basis of such constructs.

The history of childhood in the UK is a fascinating one. Hugh Cunningham's *The Invention of Childhood* provides a very readable introduction to a surprisingly unfamiliar area of history. Looking at the history reminds us that the construct of childhood has changed in the UK over the years and it is different from that in other countries. In the following section we look at four different constructs and speculate on the implications for those working with pupils in the primary school.

These constructs are children's rights, children as victims, children as threats and children as investment for the future. The section also recognises the need to see how these constructs of childhood need to inform professionals in order to support the child's positive self-image as a learner as well as a child.

The United Nations Convention on the Rights of the Child (UNCRC)

The most important document in relation to children's rights is the 1989 UNCRC. The UK ratified this 2 years later and thereby committed itself to embedding it into UK law. It implies that 'children's rights' are in some ways different from the rights of the rest of the population. Our television screens feed us with many images of how children elsewhere in the world are seen as simply part of their own community, with no additional rights as a child, for example child workers making cheap clothes for us, but it is more complex than this. The tight monitoring of children in the UK today does influence their rights. This monitoring is often actively encouraged by commercial concerns who sell items such as mobile tracking devices so that children have no personal freedom from parental scrutiny.

The convention contained 51 articles, 41 of which can be put, rather tidily, into three main groups: the '3 Ps'. They are:

1. *Provision* – welfare rights to ensure children's survival and development
2. *Protection* – welfare rights to ensure children's protection from abuse and exploitation
3. *Participation* – liberty rights to ensure children's participation in decision-making.

There is, of course, a key difference between provision and protection, which in the school setting come under the very broad remit of safeguarding. Participation is a very different right: it implies that the child has the option to participate or not, but schools are actively encouraged to empower children to participate through activities, such as pupil voice, citizenship, personal and social education. In the second part of this book we look at how LMs in primary schools are often charged with this responsibility. It is possible to argue that this participation 'right' is now seen as part of an essential duty, which the educational professionals should encourage as part of their role.

Activity/task 6

As part of the NHS initiative on the 'right to choose' a 12-year-girl was invited by her GP to choose at which hospital she wanted her surgery undertaken. Both she and her grandparent carers felt that she was too young to do this. What sort of provision needs to be put into place to ensure that mature children can undertake this type of task? Whose is the responsibility to provide the support? Do you think schools have a part in this? Do specific educational professionals have a role in it? How do you feel about theoretically having a right to choose your own hospital for surgery?

Children as victims

This view of the child as a 'victim' of circumstance is a common one. It is linked closely with safeguarding and the breakdown of two basic children's rights – provision and protection. It is used to explain delinquency and, although it has led to more support and protection in law, it sees children as vulnerable and passive. However, this can be dangerous; for example, a recent ChildLine advert challenges this through encouraging children to phone them because they have the right not to be abused. Sue Palmer's excellent book *Toxic Childhood* (2006) is written very much in the vein of child as victim, but does provide some good advice to parents. This is incidentally a very readable book, although I think it needs to be balanced with something that expects more of the child, such as Robb and Letts *Creating Motivated Kids* (2003).

The child as a victim can quickly become a stereotype, which 'labels' the child but does not help. The cycle of poverty is often linked with this, explaining unhelpful parenting away as being a product almost of some genetic disorder, rather than questioning whether the long-term labelling of families as victims has encouraged them to become such.

Children as threats

'Stabbed six times by a teenage neighbour' – we are all familiar with an increased number of these sorts of reports and it is easy to see how such views and constructs about young people/children as threats move into the primary school. The two police workers, interviewed for this book, were quite clear that part of their role within primary schools was to identify and support children who already were or were likely to become mixed up with threatening behaviour. The fireman, too, was quite clear that primary children were involved, often as bystanders, in attacks on fire engines called out on real or hoax calls. To some extent this has always happened in a less formalised way – the local bobby might be asked to have a word with a particular child about their behaviour. The formalisation of this through the Safer School Partnerships and its funding in specific agencies highlights the degree to which the age of children as threats to the community has fallen. The three LMs also all identified 'vulnerable' and 'challenging' children who were potential or already 'threats' to the social order in the local community. In nearly every case, they were part of identified 'problem families' who did not 'control' their children.

The key difference between the approach of these six educational professionals and the media is that they the professionals still see these young people as victims and maintain an optimism that a labelled threat need not become a threat and indeed that gang members can be turned round. Nearly all of those interviewed were optimistic about the potential for change, as are many children's charities. For example, the current Barnardo's slogan 'Believe in Children' sums up this optimism.

Children as an investment for the future

The 'Every Child Matters' (ECM) agenda makes this construct of a child very clear in at least three of its stated outcomes. First, the most obvious one is that children should achieve economic well-being. Later legislation made this clearer, with requirements that young people were expected to continue with their formal education until the age of 19 and that this should involve further or higher education, training or employment with training. Another outcome linked with the child as an investment could be seen as that related to making a positive contribution. This included taking part in decision-making, obeying the laws, developing positive relationships and demonstrating enterprising behaviour. The enjoyment and achievement outcome is indirectly related to both the other outcomes and is measured (as we have already seen) almost entirely in terms of test and examination outcomes.

The importance of this philosophy within the ECM agenda should not be under-rated. It permeates all of the inspections carried out which involve children. The Joint Area Reviews (JARs), which are multidisciplinary, add another layer of inspection, with their own protocols. Educational professionals in schools are therefore entrusted to embed the ECM agenda within their practice. A number of support packages – often called tool kits – have been developed for central and local websites to aid this. Experienced educational professionals, who have actually read or even worked through these packages, are sometimes disturbed at the naivety of some of the strategies suggested, and there is certainly room for a much greater discussion than the simple acceptance of yet another government package. Examples are provided on the ECM website.

Table 4.2 identifies some of the strategies that have been directed at seeing the child as being a victim, threat or investment for the future. The third column raises some questions and you can probably think of many more.

It is vital that educational professionals identify and question all of these constructs of children and childhood, because they are used to inform an increasingly centralised approach to schooling, child care and parenting. Those actually working with children know that simplistic strategies do not work, but there can be a good exchange of strategies between practitioners who have trained and often work in different professional silos. It is often lack of opportunity to do this which interferes with proper discussion on the key issues facing those in primary schools. Briefing and information sessions that give information from the top down are frequently weak at grasping the opportunities to hear and learn from the operational workers how practice is working and evaluated; even more rarely is this fed upwards.

TABLE 4.2 Examples of some strategies that underline different child constructs

CONSTRUCT OF CHILD AS:	SCHOOL-BASED STRATEGIES	REFLECTION
Victim	Safeguarding policies – at local and central government level: much of the ICS legislation is linked with this aspect and is increasingly moving into and becoming part of school life, in particular with co-location across agencies. Safeguarding policies – at school: policies and strategies related to bullying, health and safety, discrimination	Who decides what is, or is not, bullying in school? How realistic is it to expect all children to be free from bullying?
Threat	Behaviour management policies. Educational professionals providing counselling and support across a wide range of agencies; these increasingly involve carers	How are these interventions measured? Over what time frame? What sort of support do educational professionals working solely within school get for this work?
Investment	Raising achievement for all children. Citizenship – schemes of work, outside speakers, pupil involvement and voice, enterprise initiatives	How controlled is pupil involvement? What happens when school councils request controversial changes to practice?

The child in need of services

This view presents a construct of the child in need of services. Barron *et al.* (2008) suggested that these include the deprived child, the vulnerable child, the market child and the distributed child.

TABLE 4.3 The child as in need of services

THE CONSTRUCT	POLITICAL/POLICY BACKGROUND	MEANING	STRATEGY USED
Deprived child	1960s – important concept in the Plowden Report	A child whose proper development path is prevented by adverse social circumstances	Ensure appropriate support in school and create educational priority areas with increased funding for schools and for staff working in them
Vulnerable child	1970s – arising out of the Maria Colwell inquiry	Child in need of protection from inside own family as well as outside	Establish ACPCs to coordinate agencies that are responsible for ensuring the safety of children at risk
Market child	1980s and early 1990s	Child whose opportunities were shaped by consumer choices of parents/ carers – for good or ill	Broaden the 'choice' of school for children
Distributed child	'Every Child Matters'	Eligible for integrated service provision to ensure that all terms of the ECM agenda are fulfilled	Build into all services a more holistic approach to child care and protection; in schools this also included curriculum provision
Insufficient child	Across all the decades	The child and their family are seen as deficient because they have to resort to using agencies; the ideal child/family is one who does not need the additional support; this construct of 'insufficient' can act as a barrier to uptake and effectiveness of services	Try and involve greater and more genuine involvement of local communities and families in what happens to them, e.g. support groups for child carers

Adapted from Barron *et al.* (2008).

Table 4.3 shows this as a timetabled development, based on the theory of the child as being an individual in need of services. Having lived through all of these periods as a child, parent and grandparent, I am not convinced that these constructs of 'serviced' children can be separated out so neatly. Indeed, the same child could be each one of these constructs. The integrated construct is probably the most political. Barron *et al.* suggested that the concept of the 'insufficient child', whether voiced openly or not, drives encounters between primary schools and other agencies. This tends to ignore the fact that many of those working at an operational level in health, social care and education have incomes that fall below the poverty line or only slightly above it and are themselves in receipt of specific welfare services.

Unhappy children

On Valentine's Day in 2007, a headline in *The Independent* newspaper read 'Britain's children: unhappy, neglected and poorly educated'. This was based on a Unicef report on childhood in twenty-one of the world's wealthiest nations.

Table 4.4 provides an outline of this, which makes it clear that the UK did poorly in all six categories. Some of this has to be questioned. For example, is it really that our children are the least content in the wealthy world, or is it just that they say they are? Other figures are harder to question as they are evidence based, for example being ranked eighteenth for material well-being and living in households in which the income was less than 50 per cent of the national median. The UK was also in the bottom third for homes with fewer than ten books; perhaps something which those concerned about reading levels in schools should be looking at more closely.

In spring 2009, a revised league table of child well-being in European countries was drawn up; this time the UK came in twenty-fourth place out of twenty-nine countries. The Child Poverty Action Group (CPAG 2009) published a useful booklet on where the UK stands in the European table and which explains from where league data came.

Bob Reitemeier, Chief Executive of the Children's Society, addressing a conference on 'Childhood, Well-being and Primary Education', looked at similar issues that were raised in the society's *The Good Childhood Inquiry*, for which 9500 children and young people had been interviewed, as well as 1500 adults and professionals. He ended the presentation with a series of questions, rather than a conclusive strategy for making childhood better. His questions would be useful for all of us to have some time to discuss under his presentation title of 'What is the Purpose of Education?':

1.   Given the importance of friends to children, what can we do inside and outside schools to better support children's friendships?

2.   What should the respective roles of schools and parents be in children's learning and how might we better support the relationship between them?

3.   How can we improve the learning experience of those that are not doing well in the current system, for example children with low attainment, who regularly truant or have been excluded?

TABLE 4.4 Unicef findings on the well-being of children in 21 countries

COUNTRY	AVERAGE IN ALL DIMENSIONS	DIMENSION 1: POVERTY AND INEQUALITY	DIMENSION 2: HEALTH AND SAFETY	DIMENSION 3: EDUCATION	DIMENSION 4: FAMILY AND FRIENDSHIPS	DIMENSION 5: SEX, DRINK AND DRUGS	DIMENSION 6: HAPPINESS
The Netherlands	4.2	10	2	6	3	3	1
Sweden	5.0	1	1	5	15	1	7
Denmark	7.2	4	4	8	9	6	12
Finland	7.5	3	3	4	17	7	11
Spain	8.0	12	6	15	8	5	2
Switzerland	8.3	5	9	14	4	12	6
Norway	8.7	2	8	11	10	13	8
Italy	10.0	14	5	20	1	10	10
Ireland	10.2	19	19	7	7	4	5
Belgium	10.7	7	16	1	5	19	16
Germany	11.2	13	11	10	13	11	9
Canada	11.8	6	13	2	18	17	15
Greece	11.8	15	18	16	11	8	3
Poland	12.3	21	15	3	14	2	19
Czech Republic	12.5	11	10	9	19	9	17
France	13.0	9	7	18	12	14	18
Portugal	13.7	16	14	21	2	15	14
Austria	13.8	8	20	19	16	16	4
Hungary	14.5	20	17	13	6	18	13
United States	18.0	17	21	12	20	20	21
United Kingdom	18.2	18	12	17	21	21	20

At the same conference Robin Alexander, who headed the Primary Review, outlined findings from their regional witness sessions on children's well-being. They had found widespread concern that many primary-aged children were under excessive pressure from:

1. An overcrowded curriculum in school

2. A high-stakes national testing regime

3. A backwash of teachers' anxiety about league tables

4. Inspection and the public, somewhat punitive, character of school accountability

5. The degrading of children's values and aspirations by consumerism

6. The cult of celebrity

7. The pressure to grow up and adopt the trappings of adolescence too soon

8. The loss of personal freedom due to increased traffic and parental fears about safety, and this has led also to lack of outdoor play provision generally.

As this chapter shows, learning clearly takes place everywhere and when it is formalised in school, attention has to be paid to what are seen as unhealthy trends both outside and inside schools for children's well-being.

Conclusion

In this chapter we have looked at some very traditional philosophical, as well as psychological, theories that have, in different ways, informed how learning – in theory – takes place in school. Certainly, many of these theories have been used to inform policy and practical strategies; for example, behaviourism with its heavy dependence on extrinsic motivation to aid learning.

These theories were linked with views/constructs about what a learning child is. Ironically, it is still possible to show how those very early philosophies of Locke (the blank slate) and Rousseau (the active learner) inform practices today.

5

Identifying and Lifting Hidden Curriculum Barriers for Children

School and education should not be confused; it is only school that can be made easy.

(Anon.)

Chapter overview

- To look at different forms of curriculum within schools, which may influence children's learning

- To identify the hidden curriculum of building space and how this may influence learning

- To identify ways in which these barriers can be challenged by educational professionals

- Jeanne Willis and Tony Ross (2002) have written a lovely children's picture book about some alien school children who are studying the topic of 'Earthlets'. Before their visit to Earth, their teacher, Dr Xargle formally instructs his class of aliens about the appearance and habits of these 'Earthlets' (human babies) before embarking on their trip. This chapter is rather like that. It involves us stepping back and looking at what goes on in school as if we were completely alien to it. It looks at the curriculum first and then at the buildings and organisation of schools. It builds on a largely sociological perspective to education.

Four types of curriculum

The curriculum

Pollard and Tann (1994) and Pollard (2002) distinguished between the official or formal curriculum, the hidden or latent curriculum, the observed curriculum and the curriculum as experienced. These are all part of children's learning experience and can deeply influence the effectiveness of the learning outcomes.

The hidden, observed and experienced learning experiences in the curriculum are harder to identify than the formal curriculum and for this reason they are particularly relevant when looking at ways to raise barriers to learning for particular children.

The official curriculum

When the National Curriculum was first introduced in 1988, it was a statutory instruction for all children and young people to be taught specific and recognised subjects. This has altered considerably since, but our Victorian ancestors would have recognised most of what was set down in the 1988 requirements. They would have questioned the right of all children to 'receive' it, pondering about the wisdom of teaching subjects such as geography and mathematics (rather than arithmetic) to working boys and girls.

The National Curriculum set out the law and, later, published schemes of work (SOW) through government agencies, such as the Qualifications and Curriculum Authority (QCA). These schemes of work set out not only what children should learn, but also when and how they should learn it. As the name suggests, these schemes were non-statutory and schools were not required to follow them. The Department for Education and Employment (DfEE), later the Department for Education and Skills (DfES), and then the Department for Children, Schools and Families (DFCS), have all produced more extended guidelines for both literacy and numeracy for primary schools. The Primary Strategy, for example, replaced the separate National Literacy Strategy and National Numeracy Framework, both of which were produced in the late 1990s. Other guidelines were provided for small group work, which acknowledged and supported the use of educational professionals such as higher level teaching assistants (HLTAs) and teaching assistants (TAs). There have been other more vaguer guidelines to support the 'Every Child Matters' (ECM) agenda, such as those related to 'Excellence and Enjoyment' being an essential part of the curriculum, but being interpreted in very different ways; for example an 'art week' once a year replaced regular sessions or art being embedded in the whole curriculum. The 2009 Rose Review advocated a more holistic approach to the primary curriculum. Only time will tell if this happens.

This 'planned course' of study is also known as the official or formal curriculum. In recent years, central government has made statements (for example in all of the personalised learning documentation) about loosening its hold on what goes on in schools. But the need to demonstrate both nationally and internationally that attainment is rising in English schools means that results will still be published, league tables followed and inspection reports tightly monitored. This means that central government control will remain tight.

There is nothing new about this. Schools that have logbooks dating back to the nineteenth century have some wonderful descriptions of standards and the role of the central government inspector who visited and tested children to see if they had reached the required level. Then, as now, the emphasis was on literacy, in particular writing, reading and numeracy.

The hidden curriculum

This curriculum is 'picked up' rather than learnt. Several chapters of this book have identified aspects of the hidden curriculum, and the findings about children's learning have emphasised the importance of school and classroom ethos in terms of supporting effective learning. Many of the statements made by TAs and LMs confirm their belief in this, without necessarily using the term 'hidden curriculum'.

There are also hidden messages here about the role of the teacher; the role of other adult workers in the classroom and school; the role of the learner, in particular the role of the individual child as a successful learner; attitudes towards learning; and the ways adults expect different groups to behave and contrasts between these and peer expectations. Most primary schools have good personal, social and health education (PSHE) programmes that acknowledge the pervasiveness of the hidden curriculum and its influence on children's progress and attainment.

There has also been a growth in the programmes that look at the rather more controversial idea of teaching for improved emotional intelligence/literacy within schools, as well as moral and spiritual development. The government's Social and Emotional Aspects of Learning (SEAL) programme is just one example. A more scientific slant to this has been provided by developing findings in neuroscience to the school situation. David Sousa's very readable book (2009) on *How the Brain Learns*, with follow-ups for maths, reading and behaviour management, provides an important practical development. Although, at the time of writing, this is not always reflected in other publications or public sector continuing professional development (CPD). All of this is an acknowledgement that programmes are needed to inform the hidden curriculum and ensure that the stated ethos of the school is supported by informed pedagogy, policies and practice.

Activity task 1

What hidden curriculum is permeated through the staffing structure of a school known to you? You might also find it interesting to do this exercise by looking at random at a couple of school prospectuses that you can find online. Gender and ethnicity are relatively easy to identify. Class, age and disability discrimination are much harder to find unless you know the school well.

The most important aspect of the hidden curriculum is that it does need to be identified. A positive ethos for every child does not just happen – it needs to be planned for and created. There may be a specific time for it on the timetable as in a PSHE or SEAL lesson, or indeed the much older daily circle time. It does have to permeate the whole life of a school to be effective. And this has to include all of those who come into the school and those who work with the school as part of the Integrated Children's Service (ICS) agenda. Planning any lesson or activity involves planning for children's personal, spiritual, moral, social and cultural development. At one time, such provision would not have appeared on the formal teaching plan but educational professionals, such as TAs and HLTAs, may be involved with planning for specific groups that are identified as having a particular need.

Those who do come into schools, such as coaches, dramatists, musicians and road safety officers, are obviously required to have gone through the Criminal Records Bureau (CRB) disclosure process, but are much less likely to have informed expertise about planning for small groups, whole class and whole-school presentations and activities. This can influence their effectiveness, as at least one of those interviewed in Part 2 noted.

Box 5.1 provides an example of this in relation to 'passive girls' and helping them in Learning to Learn (L2L). It is important to note that both the class teacher and teaching assistant drew up the plan and evaluated it afterwards.

The government has issued a considerable amount of guidance and commentaries in the past few years on personal, social and health education, and, more recently, has linked many aspects of the hidden curriculum to the concept of citizenship.

The observed curriculum

The observed curriculum is what is actually taking place in the classroom: the lessons and activities you see. This may be different from the intended official curriculum, for a variety of reasons, and one of the skills in lesson, activity and child observation is to note and evaluate the differences and the influence they have on specific children. Good practice involves adapting and changing activities in response to children's different learning needs. The effective practitioner has a sound educational reason for this, and the process indicates the subtle skills involved in good teaching. See Table 5.1 for a timed observation and commentary sheet by a TA.

The experienced curriculum

This is the curriculum as experienced by the children. This is what they take away from the lesson and it is particularly hard to monitor. One of the advantages of working with small groups of children, as many classroom-based educational professionals do, is the opportunity to discuss how they experienced a specific activity, what they felt they had learnt from it and how they had learnt it. This is a very different process from parroting back the learning objectives written on an interactive white board.

Box 5.1 Lesson observation plan prepared by class teacher and teaching assistant to support identified group of: passive girls, Years 1 and 2

ASSESSMENT THAT HAS INFORMED THIS LESSON

Some children have said they were lonely and didn't have a friend.

Qualities of friends and what friends do (incident on playground).

EW and MR not contributing during group or in the classroom (information from class teacher).

Children/teacher/myself feel a longer session would be of more benefit.

Lesson objectives

- Speaking and listening skills
- Confidence
- Awareness of feelings
- To give reasons
- The importance of friendship
- Friendship in an unstructured environment
- Vocabulary – why? friend, forgive, sharing, fun, care, help/look after

Deployment of other adults

Iris – to encourage Molly to interact with the other children and participate in the activities.

Starting points/introduction

Children to talk about something they have brought in from home (letter sent home last week).

Main activities

Strength cards – children to choose a card, give a reason why chose it, then choose a friend who they think could have the same card and give reasons why.

Cards in importance of what they think makes a good friend – can they come up with more?

Children to do hand paintings – this will be on display showing a friendship line that cannot be broken.

CHILDREN'S TARGETS – GIVE STARS IF ACHIEVED	ANY INCLUSION ISSUES?
M – participation with adult support	M – very quiet – Iris to target
E – participation independently	C – very quiet only plays with one child
C – to play/interact with more than one child	
E – to speak with adult prompting	E – very quiet
R – to let someone have a turn. To listen	E – very quiet has a twin in the same class
F – to help other children join in	

Box 5.1 (continued)

CHILDREN'S TARGETS – GIVE STARS IF ACHIEVED	ANY INCLUSION ISSUES?

Resources
Strength cards
Paints, pencils, card
Children's resources from home

Plenary Think of words to write on cards to stick on hand Playtime outside small group demonstrating qualities of friends – stars given for achieving this, i.e. using or demonstrating qualities Iris to hang hands bring children in to see at end of playtime	*AFL* More contribution in group and class Children can name a quality that makes a friend

Self-evaluation of lesson by class teacher and TA

If you were an observer watching your lesson, what are the strong points of the lesson that you would comment on – what went well?

All children contributed towards the lesson – they really enjoyed making the friendship line and all of children talked about and shared the meaning of a friend with each other. Children moved around the table and sat with different people without asking them to do so.

How learning was shared with the children – how effective was this?

Strength cards – children very confident and gave reasons for their choice to ask and answer questions – targets on show. All children listened to each other and were given the choice to ask and answer the questions. Encouragement and praise at all times – essential.

What were the outcomes of the lesson like?

All children achieved their targets – they know the meaning of being a friend and they all care and look out for each other.

What are your reflections on the quality of work produced or learning experienced by children during the lesson?

I feel that all the girls within the group are proud to be a part of this 'special group'; all of them eager to participate and work with each other. Friendship line fantastic.

Even better if . . . ?

I could get to do it all over again and the children could be just as fantastic and motivated.

TABLE 5.1 Timed observation and commentary on an individual child from a TA

TIME	CHILD ACTIVITY
9.00 am	Fooling around in line while waiting to go to class Distracting another boy in front of him by poking him Laughing and had to be told by the teacher
9.20 am	In group situation – guided reading Lounging on a chair and chatting to child next to him – ignoring the TA's input
9.40 am	Sitting quietly on the carpet with the rest of the class Sitting correctly – cross-legged. Playing with his fingers but looking at the teacher
10.00 am	Now in group situation Sitting next to his friend and working independently and quietly
10.20 am	Sitting quietly on the carpet with the rest of the class for plenary Playing with his face and glasses but looking at the teacher Yawning
10.40 am	Playing with small group of children – running around playing a chase game
11.00 am	Sitting on the carpet, playing with the table leg Rubbing his head and face along the table top Distracted by the two observers of the lesson, fidgeting on the carpet
11.20 am	Still sitting on the carpet No longer leaning on the table Fully focused on the teacher, taking in the instructions being given Playing and pulling on his shoes
11.40 am	Flapping his paper round Not sitting on the carpet properly – sitting on his knees and kneeling up above the rest of the group Not watching the teacher and is more concerned with his piece of paper Back to leaning on the table
12.00 pm	General messing around in the dinner queue Running and pushing other children Had to be spoken to by welfare assistant
12.20 pm	In hall having his lunch Rushed through his lunch and went on to boast about 'beating' the rest of his friends Dismissed him from the hall to the playground
12.40 pm	On the playground playing football with his friends Self-organised but then began to argue and shove other team mates away from the goal Welfare assistant had to step in
1.00 pm	Lined up after being prompted by the staff Got changed for PE with a little silliness, drawing neighbouring children's attention to his shorts by stretching them
1.20 pm	Sitting on the carpet, listening to the teacher read the story Looking and making faces at neighbouring child – playing with his tongue, looking 'over' and 'under' his glasses

TABLE 5.1 (continued)

TIME	CHILD ACTIVITY
1.40 pm	Listens to instructions from the teacher, who was supervising changing for PE Little messing in the line – hopping around
2.00 pm	Seemed to be enjoying the session Moving around the room sensibly despite fact that there is great opportunity to 'act silly'
2.20 pm	Sensibly got changed, put his kit away Sat on the carpet, listening to teacher instruction Moves away from other children trying to talk to him
2.40 pm	Fully engaged in the computer Not talking to others near him – occasionally poking his neighbour to look at his screen
3.00 pm	Sitting at the back of the whole class group on the carpet Sitting quietly with his fingers in his mouth Self-distanced himself from his friends
3.20 pm	Waits to be told to get coat Chatting in the line to other children again had to be spoken to by the teacher

What have I learnt about this child? After conducting this observation, I have learnt several things about how this child learns best and how easily this child can be distracted. It became apparent that from the beginning of the day that this child was not in the mood to be in school; he was messing about in the line keen to distract anyone he could. Through my observation it was always with the same child that he was distracted by. As a result I learned that if in this type of mood, moving the child away from the particular group of boys he sits with is one method of ensuring that he is calm and focused. I also observed how giving praise to the child, on a whole-class basis, proved beneficial and acted as a motivator to the child. As a result, he focused on the teacher's input and became keen to volunteer his ideas and opinions to the discussion. I also considered if this child was indeed a kinaesthetic learner. Throughout the PE session, he flourished and was even offering help to other pupils, something I had not observed during in-class activities. During the PE session, he seemed to be a great deal more comfortable in his abilities resulting in a more focused approach on his behalf. Another factor that I also considered was the fact that sitting 'correctly' (cross-legged) may be uncomfortable for him. When he did sit 'correctly' he did so but only for a short period of time. Also playing with his fingers, face and shoes may also be signs of a lack of self-confidence in his ability to conduct the task set by the teacher; as it was during teacher instruction and explanation when he would fiddle with his face, shoes or hands.

The hidden curriculum of the building

This can include the school as a built space, noise, ventilation and heating, lighting, furniture, space, storage and outside space.

Activity/task 2

Note down as many different ways as you can in which you think each of these factors might influence learning in school. Can you think of any aspects that have been missed out?

Rebuilding to transform learning

The secondary school programme Building Schools for the Future (BSF) highlighted the importance of 'buildings for purpose'. The initial vision was 'to provide 21st century facilities in secondary schools across England' and promised transformational education.

Behind the BSF initiative was a considerable and surprising amount of political consensus. The consensus was linked to an awareness that the current school buildings were not appropriate for a twentieth-century population, never mind a twenty-first-century one. Indeed many had not changed substantially for fifty or more years and schools built in the Victorian era can still be seen.

The Primary Capital Programme was not so ambitious, but many of the issues raised about the secondary building stock could just as easily apply to primary schools.

Figure 5.1 models some of the influences on attainment, engagement, affect and attendance. In some areas, children's centres, health, clinics, etc. were already being co-located by primary schools at the time of the launch of the BSF. Primary schools have the clear advantage of having more parents and carers come to their gates/yards and classrooms. Co-location has very clear social and economic advantages and will be looked at later.

The primary school as a built space

As our world becomes increasingly urban, the built spaces take up far more importance in our lives. Children are in their primary schools from 9.00 am to 3.30 pm at a minimum per school day and some are in for far longer with breakfast clubs and extended schools, giving up to a 10-hour school day. The initial BSF programme was very much about buildings that could support transformational learning. Unfortunately, looking at both national and local websites today, some of this initial excitement has been lost in more day-to-day challenges that such a massive building and funding programme brings.

Table 5.2 shows how school buildings have always been seen as important in the learning process over the years.

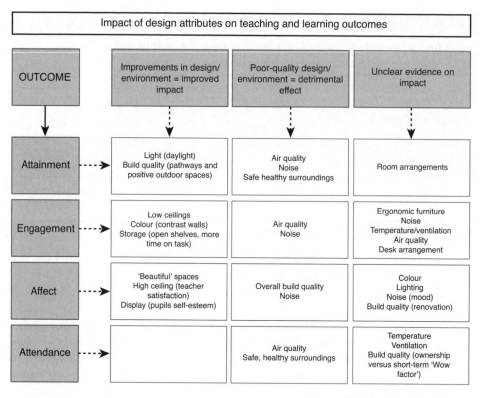

FIGURE 5.1 Impact of design attributes on teaching and learning outcomes. Adapted from Woolner et al. (2007)

TABLE 5.2 Primary building reflecting primary philosophy

DATES	PRIMARY CONCERN	RESULT
Post 1870 Education Act	Space for activity Good toilets Safe environment Pupils taught together in large rooms	Large central space Teacher centre stage Movement of pupil monitors
Start of twentieth century	Access to daylight	Provision of large windows that could open; usually too high for pupils to view the outside world
Haddow Reports 1931	Single-storey buildings Plenty of sunlight Fresh air Cross ventilation (for fifty or more pupils!) Primary curriculum to provide a variety of experience and activity	Longer buildings, rather than higher in areas of high school numbers Quadrangles contained with gardens to provide a view, but not necessarily used by children Continuation of high windows, but greater provision for ventilation and heating

DATES	PRIMARY CONCERN	RESULT
Post Second World War	Space outside the classroom important as part of learning and socialisation across different age groups Create space for pupil to be agent of own learning, rather than transmission coming from the teacher Separate primary and secondary pupils Replace destroyed and damaged schools	Spaces created within schools to support ideal of pupil as agent of learning; although focus continued to be on reading and numeracy
Post Plowden Report 1967	Teachers to become facilitators Vertical grouping Wider range of areas for learning Integrated day	Flexible and adaptable spaces Smaller or non-existent 'whole-class' areas 'Open plan' schools built
Post 1979	Believed no evidence that school buildings made any difference to attainment, so did not need to spend money on them	Changes made internally in schools to recreate larger classroom spaces to ensure whole-class teaching could take place
Post 2007	Newbuilds to take account of: learning methodologies; themed planning; project teaching; learning spaces; administration and support spaces; extended schools; other – sports, play, car parking, external classrooms, climbing walls, shade (from sun), storage Acknowledge changes in primary schooling, e.g. involvement of parents and carers; new technologies; inclusion; energy saving; co-located children's services; green spaces; ability for staff and pupils to modify the environment	?

Table drawn up from Primary Review and report from Hickton Madeley Architects.

Activity/task 3

Imagine you are back in Dr Xargle's world and you are given the task of designing a learning environment for pupils between the ages of 5 and 11 years. Money is no object and you can design your own teaching spaces, specialised teaching space, multipurpose teaching spaces (halls, foyers, etc.), circulation space (such as corridors), administration space and other spaces that are normally found in a school today – playground, dining area, etc. Does your design look very similar to schools/learning centres you see around you or have you managed to have some more original ideas, e.g. multipurpose spaces with folding walls and storage? As Henry Ford most famously said on whether he had consulted the public about the design of the Ford Model T car, 'If I'd asked people what they wanted, they would have asked for a better horse'. It is difficult to think 'out of the box' without having seen and experienced working in a new environment.

It is difficult to 'think out of the box' without having experienced new ideas. The Primary Review makes it clear that all of the evidence collected by their researchers shows that the built environment, both inside and outside the classroom, has continued to be important in order to achieve effective learning and socialisation, while being aware of changing health and safety regulations.

Case study

Hickton Madeley Architects were asked to prepare some exemplar studies for provision of new-build primary schools for a local authority. Their design concept acknowledged that they were hoping to provide 'a launch pad for transformation in primary and children's centre nurturing and education'. Such a launch pad would be child focussed 'rather than teacher or carer focussed' and was intent on 'equipping, facilitating, enabling and empowering a child to become a responsible and active individual to play their unique role in society'. Their report quoted from a report of 700 interviews of primary children, their teachers and their parents. It found that the building designs will need to reflect:

- Independent study

- Peer tutoring

- Team collaborative work in small and mid-sized groups (two to six students)

- One-on-one learning with an adult

- Project-based learning

- Technology-based learning

- Performance- and music-based learning

- Community service learning

- Naturist learning

- Social/emotional learning

- Art-based learning

- Storytelling (floor seating)

- Learning by building – hands-on learning.

You may be able to think of areas that have been missed. I would be concerned about the lack of any specific mention about provision for sport/dance/gymnastics, etc. The performance- and music-based learning is not a wide enough category. There is also no mention of drinking and eating, sitting or lying space, or, indeed, restrooms. The American terminology of 'restroom' implies perhaps what should be provided.

The organisation of classrooms and offices can have both negative and positive effects on pupils and staff, as we all know from our own experience. One of the most positive things I have seen over the past few years is the move away from taking small groups of pupils into very small spaces and the acknowledgement that those educational professionals working with them need a proper, well-lit working space, with room for movement and stimulating and informative displays.

Another positive development has been a move away from established and traditional school retailers, who in the past held a stranglehold over schools. One local two-form primary school called in the retailer John Lewis to advise them on their dining area. This was a 'compromise' area, used for dining and for the provision of breakfast and after-school clubs. John Lewis transformed it from a large hall, with chairs, tables and a serving hatch, to the sort of restaurant you might go to with a family. The central area had a salad bar, which served to break up the kitchen canteen look. There were small tables seating four people and a couple of sofas to sit back on later. Behaviour in the dining area was transformed and the numbers of children taking school meals increased. The transformation has been real, as I have witnessed it. Costs were marginally higher than for a more traditional refit by a school supplier. A similar transformation was later used for the staff room. It replicated the things we enjoy in our spaces outside school, for example a dignified eating space.

Display, toilets, noise, heating, light, furniture and space

Display

Primary schools have been traditionally very much aware of the potential for display on their walls, although there are still very mixed views about it. The current thinking looks at display space where children sit for some time, as an opportunity for visual learning – word banks, number lines, etc. Display in circulation areas in these schools is more likely to consist of celebrations of children's work and whole-school themes.

Some children find too much colour and display distracting and the Zen approach to house decoration is finding its way into some areas of primary schools.

Toilets/restrooms

Toilets and restrooms are key areas in schools and often too little attention is given to them. When I first started primary teaching in the late 1970s children had to ask for toilet paper; there was no soap and often no paper towels. The toilets were cleaned at the end of the day, despite being smelly and dirty by the end of first break. They can also be frightening places; most of us can remember bullying taking place in the toilets in both primary and secondary school. No wonder so many children choose not to use them and rush home at the end of the day. This is unhealthy as well as preventing learning from taking place. The primary review found research evidence to show that poor attendance is still encouraged if pupils seek to go home to use the toilet. Bog Standard is a pressure group that aims to improve school toilets. Their website ran a competition with a complete toilet refit for the winning schools, where pupils had to design their own toilets.

Noise

Everyone working in primary schools knows something about the effect of noise on both themselves and their children. The Primary Review looked at the research literature on noise and found that the majority concentrated on the influence of classroom acoustics on children's learning and attainment. There was far less research on the impact of noise on children's health and behaviour. We all have our own personal tolerance of noise in different areas of our life. When I write, for example, I need almost complete silence, whereas my daughter needs music in the background. The Open Plan Schools of the post-Plowden era were often very noisy (Table 5.2).

Activity/task 4

What sort of noise levels do you find challenging in (a) everyday life and (b) working in a school? What sort of strategies do you use to tackle these? The Primary Review suggested that teachers try: using raised voices (33.3%); using specific attention-gaining strategies (21.6%); stopping teaching (17.6%); and ignoring the situation (3.9%). The review suggests that additional strategies could include class layout, class grouping and using classroom spaces in strategic ways. Interestingly, nothing was mentioned about flooring and furniture, which can make a tremendous difference, e.g. carpets to deaden the noise of furniture and movement.

The literature survey showed that poor classroom acoustics can create a negative learning environment for many pupils, as we would expect, most obviously for those with hearing impairments, learning difficulties or English as an additional language (EAL). Not mentioned are the numerous children who move in and out of hearing difficulties because of things such as glue ear, heavy colds and ear wax problems. Ongoing excessive noise, as might be expected, has a direct effect on test performance as well as annoying and stressing both staff and pupils. The review also makes the point that when teachers are trying to compete with an acoustically difficult environment it may place severe strain on their voices and lead to them needing time off. If we examine where many educational professionals work, they are often subject to particular challenges with noise. When working in corridors, for example, both they and their pupils are distracted not only by noise, but also by movement.

Ventilation and heating

There is limited research in this field, but we will know from our own experience that classrooms that are too hot or too cold affect concentration. I suspect that there are health hazards as well in poorly ventilated classrooms in which the environment easily becomes very humid – and indeed smelly. There is also some evidence that poorly controlled classroom ventilation may lead to raised carbon dioxide levels, which are associated with a reduction in concentration. It is also extremely difficult to maintain the personalised levels of ventilation and heating for individual differences; I have seen many educational professionals advising individual children to take off a jumper when they are clearly overheating themselves.

Lighting

This is one of my favourite themes, as I blame poor school lighting in my secondary school for my need to wear glasses – whether true or not the lighting was certainly poor. The ideal is good natural light, and evidence points to having a view from the classroom that impacts positively on teacher and pupil well-being. Most of us have attended briefings, lectures and continuing professional development (CPD) in rooms and halls that have no windows and, although technically less distracting, many of us find them quite claustrophobic. Lighting has more facets than this; for example, glare can arise from reflective surfaces and make vision difficult. This aspect has become particularly important with the growth in the use of Big Books, overhead projectors and interactive whiteboards. Not only can it be uncomfortable, but it can also make it virtually impossible to see what has been written. Sometimes children are not even aware of how little they can see as a result of poor lighting and/or high glare. The Primary Review also points out that 'low exposure to natural light may negatively interact with individual circadian rhythms and are associated with reduced concentration, disturbed sleep and depressed mental and social activity'. This, in turn, can lead to both pupils and those working with them missing school. The Primary Review also found some research that indicated that women were more perceptive to light than men, and both perform differently under different types of lighting. Very little work, however, has been done with primary children.

Furniture

In schools, most adults have spent time sitting on furniture that is completely unsuitable for us. The same applies to children. How many of us would choose to sit in most school chairs, on which we expect children to spend a large part of their day? Chairs that are uncomfortable, too small, too large and too crowded can be the daily lot of many children. An article on children's behaviour and the design of furniture in an ergonomics journal pointed out the obvious point that children spend a large part of their school days in classrooms and yet little work had been done of the design of school furniture in relation to their behaviour and health. The authors worked with a new type of chair in order to try to reduce back pain. Their findings were mixed, but did point out the need to provide children with a choice of chair to allow for different ways of sitting as well as different sizes of child. The TA's careful observation in Box 5.1 showed the effect that having to sit cross-legged had on the observed children. Much the same applies to our furniture in classrooms and the positioning of it in relation to the interactive whiteboard, encouragement of collaborative learning, etc.

There is much in this area that adult support workers can do to raise barriers to learning. They are often in the same position as the child – subjected to stuffy rooms, high noise levels, inadequate lighting, inappropriate furniture, lighting and reading materials. Often the teacher 'at the front' is not putting up with the same condition; for example, sitting on a carpet for 40 minutes. Ideally, the relationship between educational professionals working in schools should mean that they have the confidence to point out physical difficulties for learning. It is often much easier for them to see than it is for staff who become accustomed to conditions.

Space

Use of space in schools is also interesting. Most primary schools now have welcoming foyers, with a reception area. Part of this is linked with security, but it also means that those coming into the school are welcomed, signed in and accounted for. Increasingly, visitors may even be offered a drink by an assigned visitor-support volunteer. I remember one school that I visited as an Ofsted inspector, in which the headteacher's office could only be reached through two other rooms. The unavailability message was clear – to visitors, staff and pupils.

Activity/task 5

Make a sketch map of a school space where children work. Ideally, this should be a designated teaching and learning space. Measure the size of the room and work out how much space is allocated to each child. Is there room for children to move around without touching each other? Is there storage space so that children can find things easily? Does the space allow for independent and flexible learning? How could the space for learning be improved?

Hidden curriculum of school organisation

The ways in which schools are organised have also hidden messages for all of those working in them. In theory, institutions tend to be organised in ways that best meet their stated objectives, and sociologists have looked at ways in which different institutions have done this. Systems management is just one subdivision of sociology that comes out of this particular bit of Dr Xargle analysis.

Systems

Schools have been categorised as being total institutions in the sense that those inside them are cut off from the outside world, like prisons, residential schools and armies. For some children (James 1968) schools can appear like this when total features include:

1. Competition rather than sharing

2. Superiority rather than equality of consideration

3. Incoherent learning rather than coherent

4. Learning being unpleasant rather than joyful

5. Learning consisting mostly of listening in groups

6. Fragmented knowledge.

This can be seen as a means of cultural exclusivity, when particular groups are excluded because their interests and needs are either unrecognised or identified as being unimportant. This may – and often does – represent their less powerful position in society.

Task/activity 6

How might some children in a primary school feel about the organisation of their lives within the school? How might this influence their learning? What sort of strategies could be used by educational professionals to ease the situation over which the child has such little influence? Even reception and Key Stage 1 classes are set by ability in many schools. What hidden messages would you read if you were organised into the tortoise group for literacy and numeracy from four onwards?

Organising by ability: hidden messages?

At this point in time, we tend to take it for granted that children in most primary schools are streamed for literacy and numeracy. In some schools, these ability groupings cover all areas of the curriculum. It is therefore a challenge when we find out that in other countries, such as France and Spain, it is illegal to do so. This is because it denies some children the right to a full curriculum. The French and Spanish 'results' are not significantly different from those in the UK, so this very different approach to 'personalised learning' is interesting in terms of outcomes as well.

Personalised learning, learning style preferences and differentiation have all-important components in common. They represent a current trend in English education to try to match curriculum content to the learning needs of pupils. This is a complex process in which there are no 'right' answers. Genuine individual plans for each child provide a political and bureaucratic answer, but the operational feasibility of this in most classrooms with the current state of technological software is another matter, unless they are limited to just the SATs subject areas.

Challenging barriers within the curriculum

Hopefully, this chapter has demonstrated how there are many hidden barriers to learning within the curriculum, and these are often more obvious to educational professionals visiting the school than to those working full-time in one primary classroom.

Figure 5.2 provides some of the things that could be usefully challenged as a means of raising actual or potential barriers for learning.

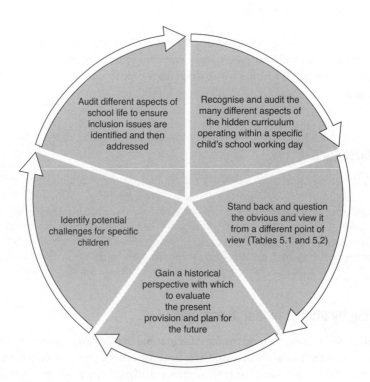

FIGURE 5.2 Challenging barriers to learning in the curriculum

Another issue here is that all those working in schools, including pupils, should be involved in plans to refurbish, rebuild and transform schools. Architects' plans are not easy to read and, as we all know to our cost, they are often weak on practical details. For example, a brand new primary care centre that I attended, which looked wonderful, had a large main waiting area, with doors at either end. The net result was a wind tunnel that cost thousands of pounds to change. So, *question* plans and *ask* for clarification. Professionals, such as architects, auditors, lawyers and, yes, educational workers, should be prepared to demystify their technical jargon. Otherwise we nod through in our ignorance.

Conclusion

In this chapter you have been invited to step back and look at the hidden messages that primary children may be learning from their schools. This may cover curriculum, buildings, display, noise, ventilation and heating, lighting, furniture, space, organisation, systems management and differentiation. Many of these are challenges at a whole-school level, but a considerable number, once identified, do enable change to take place at a micro level. It is this sort of change that can often make a huge difference to children's working days in a school.

6

Change and Challenges for Primary Schools

Change is the process, by which the future invades our lives.

John Seeley Brown

Chapter overview

- Identify some current challenges for primary schools in identifying and breaking down barriers to learning

- Review aspects of the 'revolution in learning', including what is meant by 'transformational learning' and changes in the planning for learning

- Investigate the role of technology

- Look at school support for basic needs

- Explore implications of a developing knowledge base about neuroscience and how the mind works

- Examine strategies to raise barriers to learning through direct teaching of Learning to Learn (L2L) and thinking skills.

Introduction

Educational professionals working in primary schools are an essential part of change and challenge. Figure 6.1 looks at several others, which are requiring a change in how we see our schools. The rapid growth of the Children's Workforce is just part of this.

First, because the future is speculative, we do see through a glass darkly. Second, central government control over children's lives, inside and outside schools has increased, and although it is easy to say we need to prepare children for the uncertain future, it is less easy when we are faced with sudden and frequent central curriculum directives. These changes are as likely to take place with changes of ministers, as well as changes of government. Bartholomew (2006) makes this point very clearly in his book *The Welfare State We're In*.

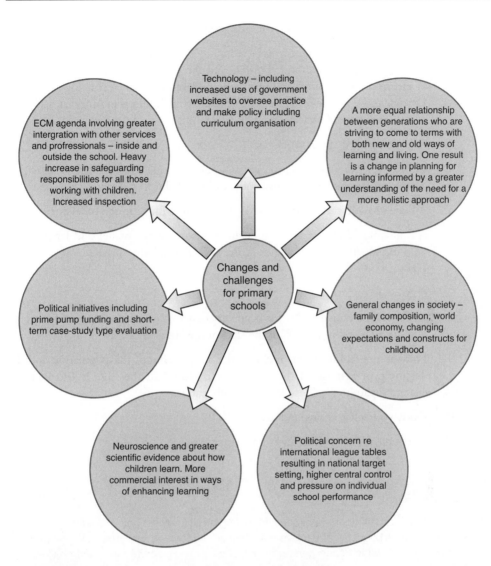

FIGURE 6.1 Some changes and challenges for primary schools

General changes in society

1n 1993, Gordon Dryden and Jeanette Vos published a global bestseller entitled *The Learning Revolution*. It sold millions of copies and has been updated at least six times. The copy that I have at present was revised in 2005, edited for the British market and retitled *The New Learning Revolution* (Dryden and Vos 2005). It is makes an interesting and polemic read, although many statements need to be questioned and you may need to research the subject area further elsewhere. It does provide a good overview to why 'Education is about to change more than it has since the modern school was created by the printed book over 300 years ago' (Drucker 2003). Dryden and Vos suggested identifying this as the birth of a new society, arising as a result of:

1. Having access to instant and free communication

2. Living in a global economy, which includes internet commerce and learning, the breakdown of economic borders and the changing leadership in the fields of electronic innovation and productivity based on high technology; in 2005, Dryden and Vos gave the leadership of the new technology to America, but a few years later they redirected it to India and China

3. The changing shape of work

4. New developments in neuroscience, which, among other things, can provide greater information about how both adults and children learn

5. A huge growth in the service industry, coupled with a growth of leisure

6. A fundamental change in how businesses work with smaller and larger firms working together and a growth in the rise of social enterprise initiatives in the UK

7. A growing underclass

8. Cultural nationalism – this has been very easy to see with the reaction to foreign national workers in the UK at the start of the 2008 recession

9. New demographics – this includes the active aging of the population and the declining percentage of the younger age groups in the UK; it also includes changing patterns in lifestyles and family patterns

10. Do-it-yourself learning and health

11. Cooperative, networked and social enterprise.

Activity/task 1

Which of these challenges are already impacting on primary schools? What do you feel has been missed out? What barriers may they create for learners? This makes a good group activity in which each person or group take one exemplar and then challenge each other to see what barriers and/or opportunities to learning it may provide. Then the task is to look at how it will impact on school provision.

Technology

This is always a dangerous area, as what you write today will almost certainly be wildly out of date in a few months time, or even in 30 minutes' time. One of the most useful, readable and challenging texts that questions the use of technology in today's schools is Nicola Yelland's *Shift to the Future* (Yelland 2006). In this book, Yelland looks at the huge opportunity of rethinking learning in relation to the new technologies. Her basic argument, which is echoed elsewhere, is that, sadly, new technologies are being mapped on to old curriculums, instead of being used to change and expand the many ways in which both adults and children learn. As an anonymous contributor to a blog on the subject wrote 'if you work in schools and are worried that you may be replaced by a computer, then you should be'. The specialist ICT parent volunteer in Part 2 of this book makes much the same point. Figure 6.2 illustrates this rather conservative view to show how the traditional views of learning have been translated into modern use of potentially much more powerful and creative technology.

The failure to transform, or even radically change, the learning medium in many schools, has serious implications for pupils, most of whom are attracted to technology. This is particularly poignant when children have and use web technologies at home and then discover that the uses of such technology in school are very different. Indeed, schools work hard to 'shelter' children from very basic technologies, such as the Internet and mobile devices. Will Richardson (2008), in his book on blogs, wikis and podcasts, outlines this restricted use. He suggests that whereas about 90 per cent of US students connected to the Internet use of Web technologies in their personal learning lives, only a small fraction of classrooms have 'begun to understand fully what these networked learning environments mean'.

The 2009 Rose Review on the overhaul of the primary curriculum goes some way to suggest strategies to do this. The media outcry at the time of its publication indicates that the media at least need to be persuaded that technology has an important and transformational role in the curriculum. 'All Balls and Twitter: How the so-called "Schools" secretary is wrecking our children's education for his political career' (*Daily Mail*, 30 March 2009).

Yelland uses the terms 'new technologies' and 'learning technologies' interchangeably, and includes computers, digital cameras, televisions, MP3 players, mobile telephony, electronic whiteboards, scanners, electronic musical instruments, laser printers, the Internet, Skype and Messenger, iMovie and Moviemaker, Garage Band,

Old media and delivery technologies against the new			
0	Writing	Interactive computers	1970s
1400s	Paper	Local drives and disks	
1600s	Indexes, paragraphs	WIMP interfaces	1980s
1400s	Printing	Internet	
1800s	Photos, sound, film	Multimedia	
1900s	Libraries	Worldwide Web	1990s
1500s	Published books	Laptops	
1800s	Postal services	Email	
1900s	Bibliographies	Search engines	
1940s	Television, phones	Broadband	
1950s	Paperbacks	3G mobiles	2000s
1700s	Pamphlets	Blogs, wikis, podcasts	

FIGURE 6.2 New and old media for knowledge development (adapted from Professor Diane Laurillard, inaugural lecture)

Kid Pix, and the whole suite of software programmes, both commercial (Microsoft Office) and free (Linux). And as I type these words in, I know that you, the reader, will be thinking of many more developments that should have been included. We become fearful of new technologies if we deny their potential importance in our lives and also seek to control for ourselves the knowledge of what is available. The new technologies challenge the traditional idea that conventional education passes knowledge, skills, understandings and concepts on to the next generation. It should provide a more equal relationship between generations, who struggle to come to terms with both old and new ways of learning.

The term 'transformational learning' is often used as an over-riding term that incorporates many of these ideas. It is an aspirational hope that learning can become transformed so that it involves the learner experiencing a 'deep, structural shift' in the way that they think, feel and act. There are a growing number of people, who believe that appropriate technology can do this. Just as the printing press opened doors to reading for all in the past. Anyone who has experienced transformational learning knows exactly what it means, but it is difficult to explain the excitement of shifting your original understanding and beliefs to those who have never experienced it.

Palmer's *Toxic Childhood* (2006) provides the more conventional viewpoint of the 'electronic village' in which many of us live our lives. She focuses in particular on electronic entertainment becoming the 'default activity' in houses and suggests some rules to prevent and shelter children from this – 'no family members automatically switch on the TV or log on to a computer when they enter the family space'. Although I understand her concern, her image of family life is very different from the one I have now, and have had in the past, and is very different from that of most of the children with whom I work in schools.

For educational professionals working in primary schools, however, the contrasting views concerning the uses of technology to promote learning are serious and involve them in developing knowledge, skills and confidence with new technology. Frequently, this has to be done in their own time and usually at their own expense.

Neuroscience and greater scientific evidence about how children learn

In the past fifty years there has been a revolution in the study of the mind and this has brought with it important implications for school learning. It has moved studying how children learn, both inside and outside school, from the realm of speculation to one where evidence can be drawn from different scientific areas.

At the same time this has led to a growth in research that looks at the characteristics and qualities of effective lifelong learners. This, in turn, has led to specific strategy work in primary schools, which has examined how young learners may be given frameworks to learn how to learn. These include De Bono's Thinking Skills programmes, Claxton's Learn2Learn, Fisher's Philosophy for Children, and Learning Inventories such as that produced by ELLI (Effective Lifelong Learning Inventory). Claxton was involved with ELLI as part of a research programme at the University of Bristol.

Many of these programmes are commercial, promoted and disseminated by consultants. The scientific element here is less obvious, but perhaps more useful to those working with children to support their learning in subjects such as language and mathematics.

There is also a formal recognition that learning does not take place in a vacuum. The child is not a blank sheet. Other concepts and strategies have been introduced to raise barriers to learning. These include emotional literacy, brain gym, accelerated learning and mind-friendly learning. They are strongly linked to creating a positive learning environment for more children within school, but still draw more on speculation than scientific evidence. This is fine provided that the strategies are carefully evaluated by the users, including, of course, the children themselves.

The 'Every Child Matters' (ECM) agenda, linked with a strong Integrated Children's Services agenda, means that all of those involved in these multi-agency services have responsibility to respect children's rights and recognise that they themselves have a duty to ensure that they provide children with positive learning experiences. Linked with the neuroscience element this means that what we do in our work with children can make a difference to the physical structure and functional organisation of the brain. The Common Core of Skills and Knowledge for the Children's Workforce requires study on children's and young people's development. So it is important that those who deliver these programmes, directly or indirectly, challenge workers to look at new developments and support learning about some of the quite complex understandings involved. The initial documentation was fairly light on this and the popularity of workbook activities for training does not necessarily help to promote new ideas.

In theory the growth of scientific knowledge about how the brain works has moved the knowledge base for learning substantially from just observation and interpretation, to the ability to collect hard data about the way in which the mind works. It draws from a number of different branches of science: developmental and cognitive psychology; learning and transfer of knowledge; social psychology; neuroscience; and technology. It has also produced, indirectly, strategies to help people to learn how to learn. Two of these are briefly described later in this chapter. They were chosen because they have been used successfully with primary school children.

Neuroscience is potentially one of the most interesting areas for those working with primary-aged children. It is also possibly the most transformational in terms of our understanding about how the brain works and how this impacts on learning. Neuroscientists study the anatomy, physiology, chemistry and molecular biology of the nervous system, with particular interest in how brain activity relates to behaviour and learning. The Teaching and Learning Research Programme has published a very useful and free booklet *Neuroscience and Education* (TLRP 2007). Andrew Curran's *The Little Book of Big Stuff about the Brain* (2008) also provides some very accessible diagrams and information about new findings in neuroscience, as does Blakemore and Frith's *The Learning Brain: Lessons for Education* (2007). Curran has been heavily involved in the SEAL project. As a paediatric neurologist, he has used his very specific expertise to help to inform and publicise this central government project, with its very detailed guidelines and links to scientific knowledge about the brain.

Key findings related to implications of neuroscience on primary education include:

1. The functional organisation of the brain and the mind depends on, and benefits positively from, experience.

2. The brain learns from every experienced event and its development is not merely a biologically driven unfolding process, but also an active process that derives essential information from experience.

3. Research shows that some experiences have the most powerful effects during specific sensitive periods, while others can affect the brain over a much longer time span.

4. Neuroscience supports the value of multisensory approaches to teaching.

You do not of course have to agree with all of these. The implications, however, for those of us working in primary schools are very optimistic. First, let's consider the finding that experience makes a difference to the physical structure and functional organisation of the brain. This means that our young learners cannot be written off at any age because they come from specific catchment areas; speak different languages; have carers who do not fit the norms of the learning organisation; behave inappropriately; are disaffected; are too young or too old to learn, etc.

The change in the physical structure of the brain is easier to measure than the other three areas. It is possible to take one scientific example from *Neuroscience and Education*. It suggests that 'a particular concept in science may depend on neurons being simultaneously active in visual, spatial, memory, deductive and kinaesthetic regions, in both brain hemispheres'. It also makes quite clear that ideas such as left-brain/right-brain learning, or unisensory 'learning styles' (visual, auditory *or* kinaesthetic) are *not* supported by the more recent developments in neuroscience.

David Sousa's practical guides (2004, 2006, 2007, 2009) to classroom management, reading and mathematics are sent out under a general editorial title of how the brain works. He looks at scanning technologies which give us more information about how the brain functions; he explains the terminology and then uses the science to provide evidence-based strategies to improve learning in areas such as reading, mathematics, special needs and improving behaviour management. The technological procedures mentioned are:

- Electroencephalography (EEG)
- Magnetoencephalography (MEG)
- Positron Emission Tomography (PET)
- Functional Magnetic Resonance Imaging (fMRI).

The book makes a very successful attempt to show how scientific findings about the brain can be translated into effective classroom strategies. The American slant to his work does make a quite refreshing change from linking everything with the Primary Strategy.

Brain care: exercise and food

These findings bring into conflict several strategies that are recommended to improve the workings of the brain. These include those involved with educational kinesiology and food supplements.

Educational kinesiology

This is often better known as 'brain gym' – 'An education movement based programme which uses simple movements to integrate the whole brain, senses and body, preparing the person with the physical skills they need to learn effectively' (www.braingym.org). And this is where educational professionals need to sift out what they find useful, i.e. breaking up sessions with movement or using particular sets of exercises to help children to concentrate or to relax or practice fine motor movements. However, the claims that doing particular exercises influences particular parts of the brain, thereby improving performance, need to be treated with caution and certainly children should not be sitting still on the floor or in a chair for long periods of time. So, be wary about claims that specific movements enhance particular parts of the brain to improve:

- Academic skills – reading, writing, spelling and maths
- Memory, concentration and focus
- Physical coordination and balance
- Communication skills and language development
- Self-development and personal stress management
- The achievement of goals, both professional and personal.

Brain Gym was originally developed to help adults and children with learning difficulties, such as dyslexia, dyspraxia and Attention Deficit Hyperactivity Disorder (ADHD). It has now developed into a more generic action programme, claiming to improve everyone's lives.

Over the years I have watched many children (and adults) atrophy when their experienced curriculum was too static. Indeed, in my own learning, I need to move around to wake myself up and refocus. But this is not the same as believing with Paul Dennison, of Brain Gym, that the human brain functions in terms of three dimensions, laterality, focus and centring: 'Successful brain function requires efficient connections across the neural pathways located throughout the brain. Stress inhibits these connections, while Brain Gym movements stimulate a flow of information across the networks' (www.braingym.org).

The exercises suggested in the guidance for Brain Gym participants, and those seen in school, are nearly always related to the laterality dimension of the brain. This is based on the traditional belief that the right side of our brain is programmed for creativity, whereas the left side is programmed for logic. The theory is that exercises that force us to think across this laterality will therefore build up nerve net formations in the brain, across the two sides. A very popular exercise, which you may have seen, is known as cross crawl and involves touching your right knee with your left hand and then changing to left knee and right hand. This is done quite quickly and is very much better to music! There is now much more doubt about this very tight distinction between left and right brain patterns, and certainly a lot of evidence to show plenty of cross laterality.

More information can be found on the UK Brain Gym website, together with a list of accredited trainers. The training sessions that I have attended with an accredited trainer have been very useful and have certainly provided plenty to bring back to the classroom in terms of short, manageable exercises to revitalise learners. The trainer in question, Louise Cook, has produced a DVD called *Moving Minds*. This provides a good introduction, and she and other brain trainers (of varying competence!) can also be found on YouTube. Also on YouTube, you can find a fairly critical interview between Jeremy Paxman and Paul Dennison, the founder of Brain Gym, as well as some good short videos, showing children and adults doing different forms of Brain Gym.

Accelerated Learning in Primary Schools (ALPS) and brain breaks

Alistair Smith (Smith and Call 2000) takes a far more cautious approach to linking exercise with brain care. He calls these types of exercises 'brain breaks' and suggests that they support improvements in learning. They can be broken down into six different types:

1. Laterality exercises – any exercise that involves crossing the mid-line of the body, for example the 'cross crawl' described above.

2. Focus exercises – exercises, such as 'nose 'n' ears', when children put their right hand on their nose and their left hand across the front of their face to hold the right ear lightly. They then swap round, so that the left hand is holding their nose and the right hand is across the front of the face and holding the left ear. Smith suggests that these type of activities require intense focus and this can be transferred to learning once the activity has been done – it is certainly fun.

3. Relaxer exercises – 'ear rolls' – with the finger and thumb massage ears slowly, starting at the top and rolling round to the ear lobes.

4. Learning numbers, letters and words – clasping hands together, with index fingers or thumbs pointing out. Then in front of their faces, moving their hands in the shape of the numbers, letters or words.

5. Handwriting – as above.

6. Chaining material – encouraging children to remember information in sequence by linking it with a series of physical movements, for example miming.

It is clear here that the exercise is combined with some fairly traditional methods of supporting learning, such as tracing letters, words and numbers with fingers.

Primary children, in particular, really seem to enjoy the physical activity that is involved with these movements, and they certainly seem to provide much needed breaks in schools when less physical education is taking place than ever before. It may also be because so many children have so much less exercise outside school. These exercises can be taught and used at home as well.

Food

Sue Palmer (2006), in her book *Toxic Childhood*, has a chapter on food, looking at it in relation to how we are 'poisoning our children'. She covers junk food and the marketing messages for unhealthy foods; high sugar intake generally; food additives; fats and fish oil; snacking and the decline of the family meal. This section of this book examines only those aspects that have been directly linked to brain activity, but Palmer's chapter does raise important issues about primary school children's eating habits. Both *Toxic Childhood* and its sequel (Palmer 2007) are addressed to parents and carers and they contain a series of 'detoxing' strategies. Like *The Learning Revolution*, Palmer's book is a polemic one, but is well referenced and reads easily for a mass audience. It is also a welcome recognition by a primary specialist that schools are not responsible for pupils '24/7'.

We are all well indoctrinated now into the importance of a healthy diet, and even the most hardened chocoholic knows that stuffing yourself full of the top layer of a box of chocolates does not do you much good – even if it does taste lovely! Both the Healthy Schools initiative and the more general health promotion programmes run by local authorities (LAs) and charities have taken this up nationally. Existing research, as identified by the texts recommended in the bibliography, show that good regular dietary habits, such as having breakfast, are the most important nutritional issue influencing educational performance and achievement. How much this is linked to improved brain performance is very much harder to work out. However, this has not stopped several nutritionists putting forward ideas on specific food and supplements. The sections below look at fish oils, caffeine, water and prescribed drugs.

Fish oils

In 2004, the Durham LA undertook a whole-authority trial to examine the effects of fatty acid supplementation on learning in pupils. The idea was to give three million fish oil pills to 2000 children over an 8-month period to see if it improved their performance. This was closely linked to an advertising campaign by the providing company, Equazen, so there were clearly commercial interests involved as well. In the event, despite wide initial publicity, the eventual performance results were disappointing. The commercial company was 'chastised by the Advertising Standards for the Authority for its misleading use of the Durham data' and the LA denied that it had ever intended to produce data on children's performance as a result of taking the pills.

Trials like this are sad in many ways. They appear to provide a wonderful, simplistic solution to improve learning for all pupils, in particular those underachieving because they have particular problems concentrating. Claims were also made for pupils with specific learning difficulties, such as dyslexia, dyspraxia, dyscalculia and ADHD. The Durham trial website had many testimonials from parents, teachers and pupils about the efficiency of the pills and this has helped to spread the word into commercial markets. So supermarkets and food manufacturers stock and advertise supplementary omega-3 on their products. The implication is that we all need it as a supplement to our diets. This is despite the fact that at the moment there are no published scientific studies that show supplements enhance either school performance or more generally cognitive abilities among children.

Ben Goldacre's *Bad Science* (2008) provides some useful background information on this, as well as a more general critique of the qualifications of nutritionists to make claims about specific strategies to improve health/performance based on weak research data.

Caffeine/cola/coffee

Caffeine has long had a reputation for keeping those who take heavy doses awake and alert. Recent research (Palmer 2006; TLRP 2007) showed that children aged 9–10 who habitually consumed the equivalent of two cans of cola a day demonstrated decreased alertness relative to low users of cola. They needed caffeine to raise their alertness and then it was only temporary. This appears to indicate that caffeine does not keep us alert for longer.

Drinking water

In recent years there has been a recognition that children can become very dehydrated in school, and most primary schools now have easy access to water and encourage children to drink it. The drinking of water is sometimes promoted as being good for the brain, so, the more you drink the more effectively you think. There are no clear findings about this and indeed some evidence to show that drinking too much water can be harmful. Most schools do adopt the sensible approach of ensuring that children drink water when they are thirsty. This is often after activities such as PE and when it is particularly hot. This does contrast sharply with what happened 10 or 15 years ago, when the very idea of children having bottles of water easily available in a primary classroom would have been anathema.

Drugs to manage behaviour

ADHD is often treated with a drug called Ritalin, or similar types of drugs, such as Concerta and Equasym. These are used to stimulate the central nervous system and help the learner to become more responsive to feedback from his or her social and physical environment. It is claimed that a drug such as Ritalin has a 70–75 per cent 'success' rate and that it reduces disruptive behaviour and helps to improve relationships with parents, teachers and peers. It is also claimed that it helps the child to concentrate long enough to complete academic work, thus improving achievement. This is generally given alongside a programme to teach the child acceptable behaviour, and he or she is kept on it from 2 to 7 years. Anyone who has seen the difference between a child before and after taking Ritalin can understand why it is seen as some sort of panacea for severe behavioural problems and it is not surprising that there was a 156 per cent rise in the prescription of drugs to treat ADHD between 2001 and 2007 in the UK. But it is extremely controversial. There are negative side-effects, such as sleeping problems and weight loss. It is also claimed that at least nine children have died in the UK from its use and there is currently a push from the medical profession for it to have a 'black box warning' on the package insert for prescription drugs.

The idea of drugging children into compliance is disturbing and there is little evidence about the long-term effects of such treatment. Robb and Letts work with children identified as having ADHD and their book *Creating Kids Who Can Concentrate* (1997) is an excellent read for anyone concerned about finding proven strategies for beating ADHD without drugs. It is a comprehensive guide that shows how lack of concentration has become a medical condition. It then moves into do-it-yourself mode and uses children with whom the authors have worked as case studies to suggest solutions. The final section shows how adults helping such children can help themselves. This includes using relaxation to 'give you a tranquil moment as you work your way through the book'. Medical, nutritional and educational experts have suggested that the disorder is a psychosocial issue that should be treated without drugs, for instance by changing the child's diet or environment.

It is also worth noting that there may be a financial incentive for some parents to register their child as having a special need with ADHD. And there is evidence that it has been used as a mood enhancer for adults, including students who have taken it to enhance examination performance.

Perhaps the simple solution to good brain care is very much simpler and what is really plain common sense – plenty of sleep, exercise and a good diet; sadly, of course, Maslow's basic needs pyramid (see Figure 3.1) puts many children into a category of basic need when this common sense approach is not possible.

Activity/task 2

In the next week, note how many advertisements in the commercial and public sector suggest different ways in which you can improve your brain – by eating, drinking and/or doing a specific activity. Increasingly we are advised what not to do as well as what we should be doing.

Changes in planning for learning for educational professionals

Many educational professionals coming in to school are given a 'teaching' role. Figure 6.3 shows just one way in which activities undertaken by a variety of educational professionals can incorporate some of these new ideas about effective learning into their planning. This particular model is aimed at classrooms and attempts to cover all the many different ways in which those coming into school will be involved in presenting information and/or skills to primary-aged children. Obviously, the ability to plan more tightly for individual or small groups of children will be much easier for a teaching assistant or LM than for a vicar, police/fire personnel or a theatre group who visit the school in a series of one-off sessions. What it does demonstrate is the

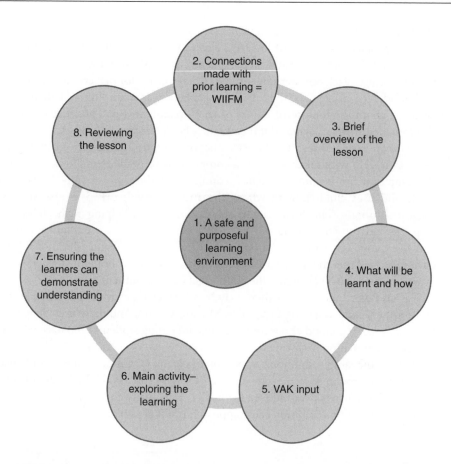

FIGURE 6.3 Model for planning a mind/brain-friendly input

importance of preparation and knowing exactly who will be in the audience, what prior experience they have, etc.

The need to start with a positive learning environment provides a good starting point for negotiation with the school about the conditions under which the presentation is being made. Having the whole of the primary school aged 4/5–11 years, or even 7–11 years, sitting on the floor in a large hall for any length of time is unlikely to make for effective learning. Many children can do this very successfully, but the learning aspect may be minimal. It is worth trying to sit down on a floor yourself for more than 10 minutes to see how it feels. Nor is it useful if staff use the occasion as a non-contact time, as several of those interviewed said they did. In at least one case, this was seen as a slight about the worth of what the visiting staff were doing. If the presentation is important for children then it should be important enough for adults as well, and participation avoids having to deal with crowd control rather than the activities and messages intended.

The figure is fairly self-explanatory and is intended to cover all the different types of formal teaching inputs with which educational professionals may have to deal, some of which may last for a short period of time, whereas others may last for much longer.

School support for attendance and basic needs

The central point of planning for learning, and obviously breaking down barriers for learning, is that those involved need to feel positive about the experience. Feeling positive about school is not necessarily the same as feeling positive about learning, nor does being positive about learning mean that the child feels positive about school. There are also distinctions between what a child might want to learn about at a particular moment in time and what is being offered.

Attendance

A major barrier to learning is attendance and some poor attendance may be linked to the parent and/or child having a negative view of the school. The roles of educational professionals differ considerably. Some educational professionals, for example attendance officers and LMs, often spend time persuading children and their parents/carers to come to school in the first place. They have to create a positive mind set for being at school; although as both the mentors in Chapter 8 and the attendance officer in Chapter 10 stated they were also aware that some of the work with hard core non-attenders had to be done with the stick of prosecution. All the LMs interviewed for this book emphasised the importance of their work on attendance. So too did their head teachers. Non-attendance is a clear barrier to learning.

Poor school attendance can be result of a number of different factors:

1. Fear – this may be of the institution itself, of fellow pupils (older, younger or same age), of adults working in the school with whom they have to interact, of learning situations generally.

2. Rules, routines and regulations which differ from those outside school – the limitation to personal freedom, lack of personal space, requirement to sit for periods of time, ways of eating, toilet facilities, boredom.

3. Language, cultural and/or special needs challenges with which the school is unaware; not successfully dealing or with which it is unable to manage.

4. Long-stay holidays/visits with other members of the family either at home or abroad, or parents who travel frequently taking their children with them.

5. Frequent hospital appointments leading to erratic attendance, which builds up into not wanting to attend.

6. Child in care or child care shared between a number of adults who do not all live close to the school.

7. Difficulty involved in travelling to school – no-one able to travel to school with the child, transport difficulties, bullying/taunting/isolation on journey itself.

8. Financial – lack of clothing, footwear, owed monies (trip, dinner money, voluntary contribution).

9. Chaotic family/outside home lifestyle which results in difficulty keeping up with routines. This may be linked with mental illness, substance misuse, sickness, whole family responsibilities, general inability to cope, damage to property or potential damage if their home is left empty.

10. Bored by school and both parents/carers and children finding more interesting and motivational activities to undertake at home. Many parents who have successfully (and unsuccessfully) opted for home tuition have followed this through.

11. Care responsibilities at home – such as caring for an adult, caring for other children, acting as an interpreter.

12. Condoned absent – families where regular attendance was not part of parents' or carers' own lives and therefore they rated it low in their order of priorities. Condoned absence, particularly at primary level, is a bigger issue than truancy. A couple of those interviewed mentioned the difficulties of working with third and fourth generations of families who had never worked.

13. Involvement in criminal activity – with or without home adult knowledge. This may include illegal working and may be condoned as a means of improving family income.

14. Bereavement – in school this may involve building up strategies to cope, when the situation at home does not enable these to happen. Many schools now recognise that this is a highly specialist area and call in professionals such as Jigsaw4U.

15. Children who have fallen out of the system – they may have been excluded, moved from one area to another, live in homes where the responsible adult has a reason to 'disappear – abusive partner, wanted by the police/criminals/debt collectors.

Activity/task 3

Some of the reasons for non-attendance may seem more justified to you than others. How many of these can be 'solved' solely by a school-based professional such as a LM? How many would require the use of other agencies? Several of those interviewed in the second part of this book are involved in school attendance.

School support for basic needs

Table 6.1 provides some suggestions for ways in which basic needs are addressed. It is worth noting that many of these needs are at different levels. The child abused at home who has safety needs comes into the agency service provision. Another child who is being bullied, or fears bullying in school, may need support in a different way and there will often be very effective whole-school strategies to follow. Educational professionals visiting a number of schools may or may not be aware of whole-school strategies available and the visibility of procedures is key to the success of their visit. Their success is what needs monitoring. Much attention is given to cipher bullying, but it is also true that, for many children, social networks such as Bebo and Facebook, form an important part of their support and social lives together with texting, emails, chats and phone exchanges.

Emotional literacy

Many of the educational professionals whom I interviewed, particularly those working with individuals or small groups in school, talked about how they found the need to work on children's 'self-esteem'. Several of those working with parents/carers said exactly the same. The term has a specific meaning within the field of psychology, but much of this is diluted in schools and equated with the belief a child has in themselves. Children at risk are often seen as having low self-esteem, but in fact this may be limited to how they see themselves in relation to school.

A researcher working on urban regeneration was involved in a children's voice project that looked at how children saw their lives within their community. She gave out digital cameras and asked Year 5 children to take photographs of their neighbourhood. One quite timid girl produced two photographs. One was of herself in the classroom. In the back of this photograph, a child was trying to get out of a window and the classroom looked confused and the photographed child looked withdrawn and silent. The following photograph showed a picture of the child at home, confidently holding her youngest baby sister. Also in the photograph, all smiling, were her other six younger siblings. In this photograph the child looked confident, self-assured and in control. I wonder how many of us would feel so confident – first, holding a baby, and, second, helping to care for so many children.

Corrie (2003) in her very practical book on *Becoming Emotionally Intelligent* found that 98 per cent of the staff with whom she worked, in schools all over the country, felt that the most worthwhile attributes a primary school could give to its pupils were self-esteem, self-worth, self-respect, self-love and self-confidence. The book provides a really good guide to ways in which primary children can develop their emotional intelligence through their internal and external environment; being able to manage their own behaviour; and identifying and dealing with fear, love, grief, motivation, self-identity, self-esteem, spirituality and communication. I have deliberately put this into the active tense for the children because it can seem that much of the work on personal development is being done 'to' children, rather than 'by' and 'with' children.

This approach is closely linked to the SEAL curriculum resources that were developed by the government to help primary schools develop children's social, emotional and behavioural skills. The materials were developed as part of the Primary National Strategy's Behaviour and Attendance pilot. And it is worth questioning why they felt that this programme was relevant for all primary pupils, rather than a targeted minority. Certainly, this contrasts significantly with European schools in countries

TABLE 6.1 School support for basic needs (Maslow)

BASIC NEED (FROM MASLOW'S HIERARCHY OF BASIC NEEDS)	SCHOOL SUPPORT – SHORT TERM (OFFERED TO ALL PUPILS, BUT OFTEN SPECIFICALLY TARGETED FOR IDENTIFIED PUPILS AND PERSONALISED PROVISION MADE)	LONG TERM
Physiological needs – survival needs: hunger, thirst, shelter	Extended school provision, e.g. breakfast club, water, milk, fruit. Individual/small group support to identify and report extent of neglect, physical, emotional and sexual abuse	Child Protection Plan, Common Assessment Form, involvement of other ICS agencies and workers, e.g. social care/family workers, health/mental health workers, housing, asylum advocates, police, charities
Safety needs – security, freedom from danger	As above if external need. If safety needs are linked solely to school-based issues, e.g. bullying, then school policy intervention with recommended strategies and parental involvement	As above if external need. Internal risk assessments for specific children
Belonging and love needs	Understanding of school as a community; encouragement for positive relationships	Nurture clubs and other non-age-related groups to which children can belong; a broad curriculum that acknowledges and values all the individuals who make up the school community
Self-esteem needs (competence, approval, recognition). Cognitive needs (knowing, understanding and exploring). Aesthetic needs (symmetry, order, beauty). Self-actualisation needs (self-fulfilment, realisation of personal potential)	Formal policy statements with audited strategies and tracking procedures. All-inclusive provision and monitoring to identify those who need more personalised provision	Provision under SEAL and more general curriculum provision

such as France and Spain, where such interference in their pupils' lives would be seen as taking away from the primary responsibility of schools to educate.

The SEAL guidance covers what the government sees as the underpinning qualities and skills that help us to manage life and learning effectively. The magic five social and emotional aspects of learning are identified as self-awareness, managing feelings, motivation, empathy and social skills. The resources are seen as having a whole-school approach and increasingly being directed towards planning for six whole-school 'themes' taught through assemblies and themed work. The materials are variable in quality and their comprehensiveness requires a fairly dedicated member of staff to inform the rest of the school-based staff what the message is and how it should be delivered. Ideally, it should be linked explicitly to the appropriate inputs from other educational professionals who come in and work with primary children or when primary children are involved in outside learning activities. Many schools have welcomed these materials and made sensitive decisions about how they should be used. A couple of those interviewed said that they found the materials overwhelming and, although using some of the more colourful paper resources, felt that they already had a good Personal, Social and Health Education (PSHE) curriculum in place.

Learning to learn

Developing thinking skills

Another way in which primary schools are breaking barriers to learning is looking at ways in which children can develop their own learning strategies. Many schools, for example, have looked at the idea of introducing a framework of thinking skills, which, when done successfully, have involved pupils in changing their views of themselves as being poor learners. They also provide a strong and memorable framework for tackling challenges both at school and at home.

Edward de Bono's Thinking Hats (2000) has been a popular set of thinking tools for primary schools and has been used very successfully in many schools. His six thinking hats each serve a slightly different purpose:

1. *White Hat* – signifies the gathering of information, data, facts and figures
2. *Red Hat* – represents intuition, hunches, feelings and emotions
3. *Black Hat* – covers thinking linked with assessment and checking
4. *Yellow Hat* – looks at the benefits and advantages of what is proposed
5. *Green Hat* – represents creativity, action, proposals and suggestions
6. *Blue Hat* – supports thinking that gives an overview and control of thinking process itself.

The 'thinking hats' idea has taken off well in primary schools because the hats can be made visible and 'funny'. I have seen all sorts of hats in use – woolly ones, character ones, paper ones and imaginary ones. In some primary class rooms you can see them

117

on display on the wall and they stand as a reminder of different ways of thinking. This is particularly useful for discussing PSHE issues.

And why 'hats'? Because you can physically put them on and take them off, i.e. you can think in one way and then in another. Something happens, my gut reaction is the 'red hat' thinking, then I spend some time with some 'white hat' thinking, etc. They are useful for role play, drama and talking heads activities.

Guy Claxton's work with primary children on learning to learn has also been very successful in helping both the adults and children in re-assessing themselves as learners. Claxton's work on building learning power (2005) is very much about the importance of identifying what makes an effective learner and how this can be developed.

Like many other action-based researchers, Claxton and his co-workers audited what learners needed for Learning to Learn (L2L) and then developed strategies to help them achieve these characteristics. This is all part of a programme about Building up Learning Power for lifelong learning.

For L2L, the effective learner should have:

1. Resilience
2. Resourcefulness
3. Reflectiveness
4. Reciprocity.

Claxton calls these the '4Rs' of learning power, and makes it quite clear that in order to develop learning power, educational professionals need to work on all of these four aspects of learners' learning. *Principles of Primary Education* (Hughes 2008) describes this in greater detail.

Effective Lifelong Learning Inventory (ELLI)

Claxton was also involved with the creation of a self-report questionnaire that was designed to find out how learners perceive themselves in relation to the key dimensions of learning power. The aim of the inventory is to encourage a greater degree of learner centred strategies. This seems to ignore the fact that our school curriculum has so much statutory content but school-based educational professionals do have room to manoeuvre. The increased inspection regime for Integrated Children's Services has also meant that educational professionals who act as providers of services to school have their own targets to achieve and work in circumstances in which learner-centred learning may be a challenge. The ELLI profile measures seven dimensions of learning power, which seem to have little compatibility with Claxton's other work on learning power:

1. Changing and learning
2. Meaning making
3. Curiosity
4. Creativity

5. Learning relationships

6. Resilience

7. Strategic awareness.

The personal, learning and thinking skills (PLTS) framework for secondary pupils, introduced nationally in 2009, is also likely to have some impact on primary pupils and those who work with them. Its aim is to develop independent enquirers, effective participants, team workers and reflective learners and to raise attainment, and the guidance could certainly be easily transferred into primary schools.

Summary

In this chapter we have just touched upon some of the changes and challenges that face primary pupils and educational professionals. We have also touched on some of the strategies for supporting a positive learning environment, in the hope that this can be seen as a starting point for children to get the most out of an education system that is increasingly taking up more of their lives.

Introduction to Part 2

If you don't listen then I may as well be,
Underwater, in the midst of the sea
Without my voice I might float away
While my trail of bubbles make their way
Up to the top of your great big boat
And burst on the surface or merely float
Without my voice, I might float away
But I have plenty of words to say

(Jordan, Year 6)

In this second section we listen to and record the voices and stories of some of the educational professionals who work full- or part-time in classrooms (Chapter 7, teaching assistants), and inside and outside primary classrooms (Chapter 8, mentors). Chapter 9 provides an example of how one primary school organises and runs its own pastoral support team. Chapter 10 includes the views of six educational professionals who are employed either directly or, in the cases of Jennifer and Stasia, indirectly by the local authority (LA) to support learning in school. Chapter 11 then provides a LA case study of multi-agency working for schools. Chapters 12 and 13 look at the work and views of workers who are in public services, such as the police and fire services, and then charity, private consultants and volunteer workers.

The distinctions between the groups are not always quite as clear as this appears, but the section provides a good snapshot of the sort of educational professionals that may be found in primary schools.

The interviews were held in a number of different local authorities and schools. They were informal and covered five basic questions.

- How did you get to be where you are (i.e. your journey to this point in your career?)
- What is your role? What are you doing to help primary pupils in their learning?
- What are you most proud of?

- What areas do you see for development in your school/organisation/personal development?
- What barriers for learning do you find in your role? And how are they being overcome?

It is worth noting here that nearly all of those interviewed said that their formal role description bore very little relationship to what they actually did! A feeling that I am sure many readers will find familiar.

Obviously a book like this cannot hope to cover all of the many aspects of the school that are focused on the Integrated Children's Services programme and it does not aim to do so. It looks simply at how those at the operational level in schools see themselves, their role within their school/organisation, the ways in which they help and support children and areas that they think could be developed. Their stories may be – and often are – different from the formal policy version from government websites, including the case studies often provided. But one of the things that comes over most strongly is the passion that many of these educational professionals feel about their work and their power to change children's lives. It was humbling and I am really grateful to those who gave up their time to be interviewed. I need also to apologise if I have misunderstood or misinterpreted what I was told. All names have been changed and names of specific LAs have been taken out.

7

Teaching Assistants

My life is a fairy story, I come in every day and never know what to expect, new challenges, different challenges. Every day is different.

(TA, during interview for this chapter)

Chapter overview

- Exploring the changing role of teaching assistants

- Listening to the voices of teaching assistants who work daily with primary-aged children

- Identifying some key issues arising out of their work and strategies being used to overcome them.

Introduction

In exploring the current role of teaching assistants (TAs), it is useful to look at their dramatic growth as key personnel in schools. All of the headteachers whom I interviewed identified TAs and LMs as the key personnel who had changed the way in which classrooms operated. Two of them used the term 'breaking down barriers to learning' and all were enthusiastic about the difference it had made to their school and children's learning and behaviour.

Five TAs were interviewed for the book. This includes one Higher Level Teaching Assistant (HLTA) and one who is now a designated Senior Learning Support Officer. Initially, the plan had been to interview two TAs, but it quickly became obvious that although their titles were the same, their roles were significantly different. It also was clear that they shared particular experiences that helped to support their relationships and 'credibility' with the children and parents with whom they worked.

The Training and Development Agency (TDA) role definition of a TA

TAs usually work alongside teachers in the classroom, helping pupils with their learning on an individual or group basis. Some specialise in areas such as literacy, numeracy, English as an additional language, and the creative arts, as well as special education needs.

Day-to-day tasks could include:

- Getting the classroom ready for lessons
- Listening to children read, reading to them, or telling them stories
- Helping children who need extra support to complete tasks
- Supervising art and craft activities and displaying work
- Looking after children who are upset or have had accidents
- Playing educational games with children and encouraging younger children to learn through play
- Helping with outings and sports events
- Carrying out routine administrative tasks.

TAs are not required to lead lessons but may supervise a class should its assigned teacher be temporarily unavailable. Only HLTAs may be expected to take classes as part of their routine duties.

The TDA currently see TAs as forming a team of learning support staff, which also includes HLTAs, nursery nurses, sports technicians and assistants, and cover supervisors – the last two are more likely to be found in secondary schools.

The history of TAs in the primary schools

When I first starting teaching in a primary school in the late 1970s, the only classroom support in the school was a National Nursery Examination Board (NNEB)-trained nursery nurse who worked across two reception classes. Since then there has been a massive increase in the numbers of primary school support staff. The number of TAs in English schools rose from just 60,000 in 1997 to more than 153,000 today. There were several reasons for this, which include:

- An increase of children with special educational needs within mainstream schools
- Ofsted expectations that all pupils should be learning
- A general increase in the numbers of children identified with special educational needs
- A growth in government control over small group work in the primary curriculum.

These four factors brought more 'bodies' into classrooms, but it was really the introduction of specific literacy and numeracy strategies that transformed special needs and classroom assistants into 'teaching assistants'.

The process of training up assistants started in the mid-1990s, with specialist courses carrying accreditation for Special Teaching Assistants and easier local access to National Vocational Qualifications (NVQs). The introduction of a Foundation Degree, targeted at staff such as TAs, showed a major commitment to improving and accrediting the knowledge and skills of support workers who were working directly with children in classrooms. Newly appointed TAs are expected to have the basic qualifications of a GCSE in maths and English and to commit to undertake NVQs.

In addition the career development for teaching assistants was taken over in 2006 by the TDA. Details of the Career Development Framework for Support Staff can also be found on the TDA website.

It is still, however, very much left to chance what is available for TAs in any one local authority, and, of course, the ability and desire of schools to release support staff for training. You will find big differences between schools on the qualifications of TAs, despite the fact that Workforce Remodelling has technically rewarded those who undertake higher qualifications, including that of assessment for the HLTA.

The following five interviews, like all of those in this book, were carried out informally at the TA's place of work.

Marie: Senior Learning Support Officer

Marie's title has developed from TA to Senior Learning Support Officer and she now manages all seventeen TAs in the two-form entry primary school. When she left school herself she became an office worker and later stopped work when her children were young. When her oldest son was at school, he was very badly behaved and she was asked to come in to see him in the classroom and explore ways in which he could be helped to concentrate and learn. His behaviour did improve, but, as she said, he never became very academic. She was then taken on by the school as a 'dinner lady' and found herself continuing to work in classrooms as a volunteer because she had enjoyed it so much when working with her son. The class teacher noticed that she was really good with the growing number of children who had English as an additional language (EAL) and she was appointed full-time to the school as a TA and part of an ever developing EAL team.

Marie describes it as a fairy story because she was so keen to be with the children, passionate about the job, and woke up each morning wanting to get up to face the challenge of working with children with EAL.

The school has supported her professional development both in time and in funding and she has been on many courses over the past 8 years. These have been generic courses for support workers and teachers as well as those specifically for those working with EAL children. These have included courses that looked at specific features of work; for example, working with the families and children of asylum seekers, courses for children with speech and language difficulties, courses for working with children identified with autistic spectrum disorders (ASDs), Attention Deficit Hyperactivity Disorder (ADHD), special educational needs (SENs) and children with EAL who also have special educational needs (EALSEN). Marie now does many course inputs herself, both within the school with teachers and support workers, but also in other local authorities and with Initial Teacher Training (ITT) students. Figure 7.1 shows some of the different aspects of Marie's role.

Both the LA and the school have a policy of full inclusion that includes all EAL children. There were twenty-four different languages represented at the time of

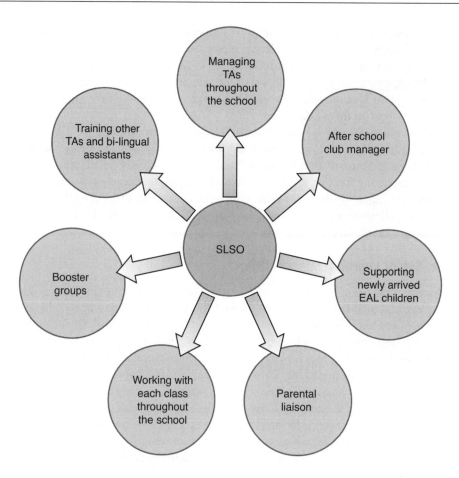

FIGURE 7.1 Marie's current role as a senior learning support officer

the interview and the school had well over 50 per cent of its population with EAL. Children and their families are arriving – and leaving – all the time from Slovenia, China, the Far East, Poland, Somalia, Bengal, the Czech Republic, Slovakia, Burma and Kurdistan. Many are asylum seekers. Marie had a full teaching timetable and at the time of the interview had a case-load of twenty newly arrived children. The fully inclusive provision involves Marie in providing small group or one-to-one sessions. It also includes a 'pre-teach' time. This takes about half an hour before a specific lesson, and she and the class teacher prepare what will be useful for the child to understand in order to become part of the session, for example key words.

When children first arrive in the school, there is a set programme for welcome and induction. This includes looking at their previous educational experiences because not all the children have been to school before and so the very routine of going to school is unknown. There is provision of a welcome booklet in their own language. They are also welcomed in their own language (if possible) and given a tour round the school. Children are also assessed on language using a five-sheet initial picture assessment that the EAL coordinator and Marie have designed together.

This assessment is redone every half term. There are also assessments in their home language and if appropriate the Foundation Stage Profile administered. Marie has also developed a EAL 'survival pack' for these new arrivals with slightly different versions for Key Stage 1, Lower Key Stage 2 and Upper Key Stage 2. Materials from the Qualifications and Curriculum Authority *A Language in Common* (QCA 2000) are also used.

The EAL team consists of a part-time teacher, two language support assistants, one teaching assistant, a nursery nurse and all of the staff. The language assistants are bought in from the local authority. The team review their work formally every term and meet regularly. The school work hard to provide positive messages and a supportive ethos with good role models. They also work on ensuring that EAL children are provided with opportunities to activate their prior knowledge and hear from other more fluent speakers of the language they will be expected to use. Good peer language models are particularly important, which is why EAL children are seated not with children with special needs, but with those pupils who can model the language for them and give them time to process and mentally rehearse their own speech. Then their own contributions can be scaffolded with graphic organisers and talk frames.

Marie also runs a coffee afternoon on a Friday as a means of supporting the local community. This is proving very popular. Interestingly, but not surprisingly, I noted that this was run when Marie was timetabled for her own Planning, Preparation, Assessment (PPA) time.

Most proud of

- 'Watching the progression when the child starts to use their language skills. It is a real thrill because it is a team effort and seeing the child smile when there is real communication taking place.'

- 'On a personal level I've come from being unemployed eight and a half years ago to what I have now and hoping to become a HLTA and eventually a teacher.'

Barriers to learning

- The lack of talking buddies for some children: for example, a single Burmese child did not share a language with any other child, so was currently not getting the opportunity to work collaboratively with other children in his own language. Children are very supportive to each other's learning and this buddying up approach has been very successful.

- In some schools, making sure that EAL children are not put on the SEN table because this does not provide a good language model.

- Attendance – at this school there were two LMs to keep this up.

- Community cohesion – our coffee afternoons are supporting this.

- Emotional health, particularly with asylum seekers, many of whom have had traumatic experiences and you get glimpses of this sometimes through the children's own pictures. The small group work also enables them to feel safe and that they can open up.

Sally

Sally trained as a nursery nurse 20 years ago when she was 16 and had first worked as a live-in nanny. Prior to that, she had worked voluntarily in a children's club, run by Save the Children Fund, and for council play schemes. She then came to work in her current school nursery as an NNEB-trained nursery nurse, then in Key Stage 1 with a special needs support remit supporting individual children who had statements of special educational needs. When the role of the NNEB nursery nurse was discontinued, her role was identified through the Children's Workforce Reform as a TA. Her NNEB qualification was recorded as equivalent to a Level 3, which she felt devalued it and was linked to saving money. Box 7.1 shows that Sally is probably correct in this, as she is successfully performance-managed against a Level 4. The table shows an extract from a nationally recognised scheme that Sally's school uses.

Sally had found the special needs responsibility challenging so she enrolled in, and subsequently completed, a Foundation Degree course in Special Needs. This had made no difference to the level to which she was assessed and paid; indeed, for the first 2 years of the degree she had had to pay her own fees and make alternative child-care arrangements. For the first year of the course the previous headteacher had insisted that she made up the afternoon when she attended the university. This seemed unfair as others on the course were having fees paid for them by their school and, in some cases, were given laptop computers through SureStart funding. The budget in her school had been tight and the salary structure was changed so that she was paid for 46 weeks, rather than 52.

Role

Sally had no specific role description, and Figure 7.2 outlines her current activities. SHARE is part of 'ContinYou' a national community learning organisation – it aims to 'offer opportunities to people who have gained least from formal education and training'. As part of the school programme, weekly workshops are run for parents, in a specially adapted parents' room. They use the national SHARE materials to plan home-learning activities for parents to work through with their children. The materials cover from Foundation Stage to Key Stage 3. Parents put together a portfolio, based on their SHARE diary, which is accredited through the Regional Open College. It is a very flexible programme, which Sally felt worked well in different contexts.

There was a distinct difference between the level of personal development supported by Sally's school and that which Marie had enjoyed. Sally loved her job, but felt deskilled when asked to do activities for which teachers had had training and she did not – for example, the latest Primary Strategy phonics training run by the LA. She discussed the difficulties of getting extra training for her special needs work and the recognition of its importance in moving children with special needs on. As an example, she described when she had been able to go on a special course for the visually impaired and had used the recommended strategies to support the child involved and had seen great progress. Sadly, the following year she then had to observe him with an untrained parent and saw him regressing as he was babied, picked up and removed from assemblies. Basically he was being 'cared for' but without aspirations for his education, and was being encouraged to be dependent on adults.

Box 7.1 Extract from 'Recognised and Rewarding Staff Performance'

COMPLETED BY: Sally Wood

STANDARD SET – 4   Teaching and learning: monitoring and assessment
The skills required to contribute to the monitoring and assessment of learning

In order to demonstrate the National Occupations Standards, teaching assistants should:	Evaluation response	Sources of supporting evidence
4a	Be able to observe and record pupil performance as specified by the teacher	✓	Initial profiles, team planning, observation of work by deputy headteacher
4b	Monitor pupils' responses to learning tasks and modify approaches as agreed with the teacher	✓	Recorded observations – written and recorded on computer, identify matching needs and modify weekly planning
4c	Monitor pupils' participation, provide relevant information to the teacher about pupils' learning achievements and provide support to pupils as specified by the teacher	✓	Discuss with teacher after each lesson co-signing assessment sheets, providing support as appropriate. Lesson/activity evaluations, monitoring records
4d	Contribute to maintaining pupil records as specified by the teacher	✓	Records designed by me, after attending LA course, agreed with teacher; observations by deputy headteacher
4e	Be able to support teachers in evaluating pupils' progress through a range of assessment activities	✓	Records drawn up as a year team, agreed with school assessment officer
4f	Monitor pupils' responses to learning tasks and modify accordingly	✓	Observations, profiles, PDA input
4g	Monitor pupils' participation and progress, provide feedback to teachers and give constructive support to pupils as they learn	✓	Observations by deputy headteacher, recorded assessments with c/t and co-signed by me, pupil and parent responses
4h	Contribute to maintaining and analysing records of pupils progress	✓	Completed records on all pupils throughout the year. Specialist records on SEN and EAL groups. Ofsted outstanding report on work!

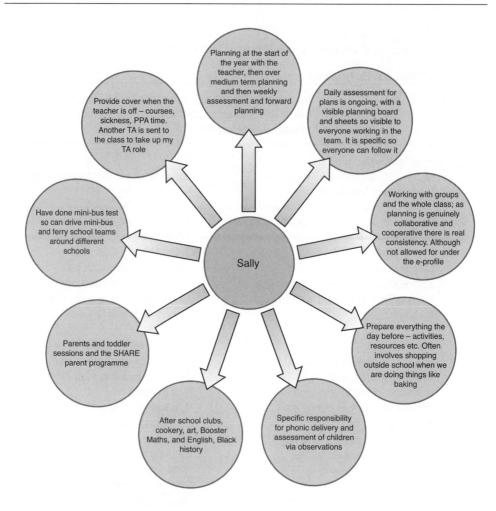

FIGURE 7.2 Sally's responsibilities

Most proud of

- Introducing the letters and sounds phonics programme and seeing the improvement for the children with whom she worked. It was particularly rewarding when children read aloud and she could see how proud they were of themselves

- When working with one child with special needs over a year as a learning support assistant (LSA): the child started to reach his goals, concentrate, and extend the boundaries and targets set for him. Working one-to-one with the child meant that it was often possible to work closely with his parents and show them how to give support. As an example, she described when she had taken child S to be measured for splints and then for her follow-up visits. Her own mother had not been able to take her because of lack of child care and transport.

Areas for development

- In the speech unit, it was common to see the same programme being used for all children, whatever their speech and language needs.

- The limited opportunity for personalisation; for example, Jon needed to work in a quiet room, because he had limited spatial awareness, but there were no facilities for this.

- The lack of equipment – in particular books. This resulted in the TA supplying a lot of materials herself, using her own money and of course borrowing resources from her own child!

- The general lack of training for TAs was seen as an issue – no phonics training was just one example, but there was minimal support for delivering a variety of programmes. TAs were expected to work through and learn by trial and error. Often, with special needs it involved a therapist coming in, just once, to show the TA how to deliver the programme and then leave her to get on with it. There was no later check to see that it was being done correctly, that it was useful for the child and whether the child needed to move on.

- In the current climate, there were issues with having such intimate contact with incontinent children and the general expectation from some teachers that it is the TA who will clear up all the time, even if the TA is working elsewhere.

- There were no real networks for integration of appropriate services; for example, Sally had found out, by chance, about a programme for 'Splash and Sing' and enrolled the child herself and took him to the swimming pool each week.

Figure 7.3 shows some of the barriers to learning, as provided by Sally.

Sabba

Sabba came to the UK in 1972, when she was 7 years old. She and her family were refugees, which had the advantage that she now can speak several languages, including Urdu, Punjabi, Swahili, Turkish, Hindi and Kutchin. Kutchin, she explained, was the language of her ancestors. There were several Kutchin speakers in the school.

Initially, Sabba worked with the LA Ethnic Minorities Achievement Service (EMAS) as an EAL worker supporting two Turkish siblings. The remit of the service was quite wide, and involved not only supporting language to overcome barriers to learning and achievement, but also supporting pupils across the curriculum, including emotional, social and cultural needs. It was this agency that assessed and advised new pupils on their admission to schools and provided loans and teaching resources to help reflect the LA's population diversity.

She did this for 5 years with different languages, at different levels. This included running a parents and toddlers group. At this stage it was largely Asian, but that had changed over the years. Another change had come when money from the service was transferred into schools and this resulted in a drop in the numbers of workers employed.

FIGURE 7.3 Some barriers to learning from Sally

Some of the work from the EMAS service was taken over by another LA service called Starting Points, which was based in an old school. It took all new EAL admissions into the school, focusing on the children of asylum seekers, refugees and anyone else who did not speak English. Initially, the service provided for children aged 4 to 16, but now covers 3- to 18-year-olds. Starting Points was really aimed at children who had never attended school before, so that not only were there language challenges but also socialisation into school attendance. It also advised parents. The Starting Points school worked through a curriculum of literacy, numeracy and life skills. It aimed to move children into mainstream schools within 6 weeks, although some children were there as long as two terms. All of the school's EAL pupils now go to Starting Points prior to coming into this school.

At about this time, Sabba started in this current school as a 'dinner lady' and later was appointed as a TA as the number of EAL children in the school rose.

Role

Sabba's role (see Figure 7.4) is considered to be at Level 3.

Most proud of

- Everything – all of it. She had always been welcomed in the school, colour does make a difference, and she had found that this welcome was not always there when she had visited other schools. It was wonderful to work in such a supportive school, which was not precious about doing things in a particular way. There was a relatively new leadership team and the headteacher and deputy enabled staff to try things out. It was the current headteacher who had changed the organisation of the support staff a couple of years ago. There is now a TA in every class in the school. All of the adults worked well in a team and this provided good role models for the children.

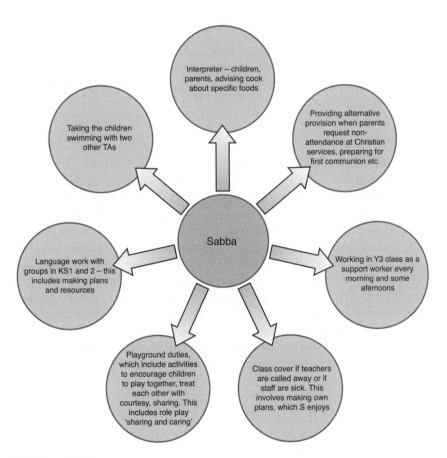

FIGURE 7.4 Sabba's role

- She really enjoyed running the after-school homework club. When she had realised the children were hungry, she and the other TAs made provision for them to have fruit. They had also drawn up rules with the children for being in the club. It covered just Key Stage 2 and was in two organisational groups, which they had found worked best. Years 4 and 6 worked together, as did Years 3 and 5. The children came in with homework from the class and this provided a booster for those children who would not or could not do homework at home. It helped them to feel good about coming to school. The class teachers provided TAs with a list of homework from each class, usually numeracy and literacy.

- Helping and supporting parents. This involved having a regular timetabled session each week, for which Sabba was timetabled to be available for interpretation and support. This was also the case for parents' evenings.

Areas for development

- More EAL courses for herself and other staff.

Barriers to learning

- Sabba felt that these was quite easy to identify: the children's behaviour, their ability to listen and their own speaking, pronunciation and ability to communicate. She felt that these barriers were issues that affected not only EAL children, but all of the children generally.

Amy

Amy left school with some GCSEs and went into the retail industry as a shop assistant, later becoming a cashier. Then she had a daughter who did not sleep and so she could not later return to the same sort of work after having her. This resulted in doing various part-time jobs such as cleaning. Once her daughter started at this school about 12 years ago, Amy became a volunteer mum in the school to help children with their reading. She was then employed part-time to cover the various initiatives being introduced in the literacy strategy and later with the mathematics framework. These involved a lot of small group work and provided training for the support worker who worked with the groups. They included ALS (Additional Literacy Strategy), AFL (Assessment for Literacy) and ELS (Early Literacy Support). Then when the numeracy strategy moved into small group work with TA support the TA's at the school were trained and covered this too. At about the same time, Amy started to provide support for a girl with severe emotional and behavioural problems and transferred to full-time employment.

Role

See Figure 7.5 for an overview of Amy's current role.

Most proud of

- One-to-one behavioural support with child J, who had tremendous difficulties at one time but is now much more settled, although it has taken a long time and is not always all right.

- When working with small groups on reading support and seeing a child who has had the extra support suddenly realise that they can make words from the sounds and can read these words. Also when younger children realise that the squiggles on a page make sense.

- When a child, who has not spoken very much to either adults or other children, confides and we can take some action on it to help him/her.

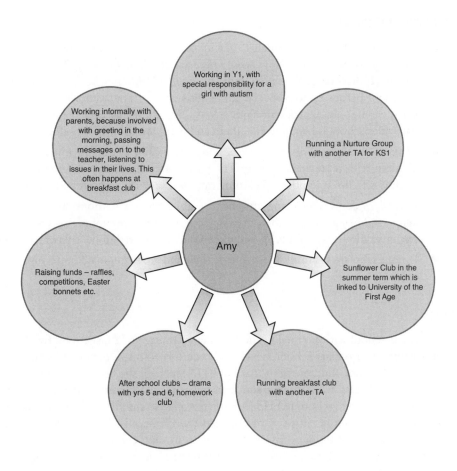

FIGURE 7.5 Amy's role

- When ex-pupils come back to have a chat and show how much they had enjoyed their time in our school.

- Role play and drama when supporting learning, such as London's Burning – Samuel Pepys.

- The outcomes of the investment, by current headteacher, in play materials. She has an understanding of what is needed and this has greatly improved the classroom environment. The school now has some really child-friendly rooms, such as the Rainbow Room, in which this interview took place.

Areas for development

- More courses so can keep up to date with general changes in education as well as the things that are more specific to TAs.

Barriers to learning

- *EAL*. The school has a much larger intake at all ages, at all times of the year, and they cover far more languages. There are children speaking Polish, Turkish, Arabic, Indian (sic), Somalian and Sudanese. Children who have never been to school before go to a special admissions centre. The authority then tries to get them into an appropriate faith school, but often this isn't possible and this particular school is happy to take them and make special provision for them.

- *Manners and respect*. This involves speaking and dealing with both adults and other children with respect and dignity. The pleases and thanks are important, as is the readiness to listen to others. Learning cannot take place without basic respect.

- *Parental support*. A growing number of children are without much parental support. They are left to their own devices as parents do not seeing this as their responsibility. It is as if it is up to the school to do the traditional role of parenting.

- Parents who always think their child is right and are manipulated into supporting them.

Diana

Diana left school with no qualifications. Later, at the age of 20, she took five GCSEs at her former secondary school, which had been turned into a further education (FE) college. When her children went to school 11 years ago, she became a parent helper. This started because the teacher sent letters home to ask parents if they would be willing to come into school to help with the reading. So she started with one morning per week and then it became five mornings per week, because at that time there was a policy in the school about every child reading to an adult every day.

She really enjoyed doing this and quickly became involved in doing Link courses at school, which were run by the local FE college, and were designed to teach parents how to help their children with their school work. The school was very supportive and when the courses finished in 2001, there were jobs advertised for TAs. She became a TA for 2 years, starting on five mornings per week. This expanded, as the literacy and numeracy hours involved TAs every morning, and she became full-time.

It was at this stage, that Diana wanted to become more involved and she enrolled at a Higher Education institution for a Foundation Degree. This was being held locally and went on for 3 years. It was very hard work, because she was working full-time in school and had a family with two children. Towards the end of it, she was able to do the HLTA module, so she came out with the Foundation Degree and the HLTA qualification. She had found the Foundation Course to be very repetitive; there were changing staff and often they did not seem sure of what they were doing. However, she felt that it did give her knowledge and skills about planning, assessment, subject knowledge, teaching skills and confidence. The course had been funded by SureStart, and the funding also covered books and a laptop computer for her studies. Her fees were paid by the school.

When Diana finished, she got one of the six places available for a 2-year course to bring her qualifications up Qualified Teacher Status (QTS). She started the course, but it lasted only a few months because the course was a new one and there was often no tutor, so the students would arrive and nobody would be there. Then, when tutors were there, they did not seem to know what they were doing and they heard comments such as 'wish I'd known what we were doing this week'. It was very disappointing because she expected that she would have really enjoyed it.

At the same time as she qualified as a HLTA, PPA time was being introduced into school. This resulted in teachers getting non-contact time for one morning or afternoon per week. The school advertised for people who had HLTA training or evidence of further study to fill these gaps and Diana got one of these HLTA posts. Initially, the job involved just two sessions of PPA time per week, so she was paid the TA rate for the rest of the time. Now, the HLTA element is full-time, which means getting paid for 32.5 hours per week over 46 weeks per year.

Now, Diana feels that the HLTA post really suits better than being a teacher because of the wide coverage of classes, so she can move on and avoid being frustrated about the behaviour of any individual children. This makes the work easier than being in the same class all the time. She feels she is very lucky: 'I love coming in, I'm not on a tread mill doing numeracy and literacy all the time and so get the best of both worlds. What I get to do every day is great.'

Role

Very loose term – more as a level descriptor for Level 4. This was a role that Diana had been able to create for herself.

Most proud of

- At a personal level gaining the Foundation Degree because it was such hard work.
- In terms of her role in the school:
    - Being able to work creatively with the children. Through covering the PPA time, I am able to take over the planning, assessment and resourcing as part of a block and organise. It generally covers areas like DT, Art and RE, often the areas the teacher do not want to do, because it is high resourcing, making a mess, higher noise levels and more creative. I've built up a bank of resources

– they fill my spare room. We've just made a Sikh temple in the Y6 class and I've got things like antlers and yoghurt pots in my care. When we plan we match as much as possible with literacy and numeracy objectives and work through those in a more creative context. It is not always possible, but it does reflect the Excellent and Enjoyment remit.

- Being trusted by the teachers and feeling very confident now in the classrooms.

- Working in classrooms through the school from nursery to Year 6. This provides a really good overview of the curriculum, which is fairly unique because teachers don't get this experience. It also means you get to know children well, and can see and support their development. It helps understanding about learning for example, seeing a child struggle with something in Years 3 and 4, and then being able to succeed in Year 5. 'Any child, any concept at the right level': it helps to see how the spiral curriculum makes sense.

- Having the opportunity to work with the same children on topic areas, for example I was in a Year 4 class this morning and we covered religious education and design technology.

- Being a parent and having the experience in school means that I've got good knowledge of the school, its curriculum, parents and children. Coming from the area helps as teachers seem to be more middle class and don't really understand what it is like to be poor, or what children have to put up with at home if a parent is a drug user or alcoholic, whereas I do.

Areas for development

- Would like to be more included; for example in assessment meetings. Covering for PPA time can mean you just get left to get on with it and do not get the opportunity to see others teach. We do not get paid for staff meetings and they aren't always relevant. We are very much on our own island.

- I'd like a more defined role – what you are doing can get dropped and you never know what to expect. I enjoy having a flexible and loose role, which has developed over the years, but would like it to be more defined.

- Student teachers – one HE institution asked us in because they wanted to provide students with more of an idea about what we did. Students can resent us because we are generally older and more experienced.

- HLTAs here are more qualified than the HLTA qualification, yet are still classed as 'support staff' but actually we are not with teachers. I teach all the time with covering for PPA and indeed have PPA time myself. Other HLTAs have combined roles. This role is a new one and pay has improved, but it still changes in conditions and status.

- Higher expectations of HLTAs – I am a HLTA mentor and some of those being assessed should not be on the course. HLTAs are doing less elsewhere.

- Nature of HLTA qualification – doesn't reflect the nature of the job.

Barriers to learning

For details, see Figure 7.6.

Summary

Table 7.1 provides an interview summary, with some of the key points that came out from the interviews with the TAs. They are of course very personal views, but, over the past 3 years, I have worked with several hundred students on an Educational Professional course, during which they have been asked to interview TAs as part of their module programme. Many of my findings from these interviews have been replicated in theirs, in particular the huge time commitment from TAs. The bibliography includes some reports on TAs, but even the 2008 one fails to identify the huge amount of goodwill and commitment involved, which results in them spending so much volunteer time at work and skilling themselves up outside work. It also partly explains the improvement in this element of the workforce since previous surveys (Ofsted 2008).

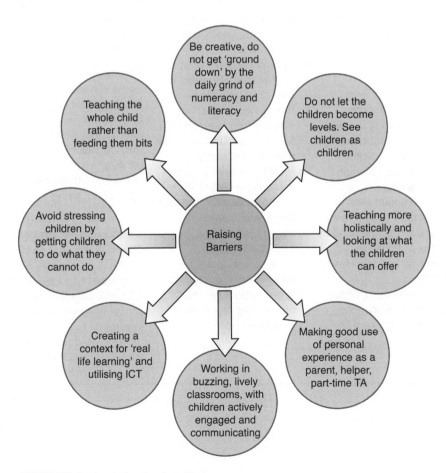

FIGURE 7.6 Barriers to learning from Diana

TABLE 7.1 Summary of interview findings

ALL INTERVIEWED	SOME OF THOSE INTERVIEWED	DIFFERENCES
• All those interviewed were very optimistic and positive about their work. • Perhaps related to this was their ability to provide many individual examples of children who had made real progress – academic and/or behavioural – because they had worked over a period of time either one to one or in a small group; relationships were seen as a key factor in this success and had been built up over time. • The willingness to spend a large amount of extra time and often extra personal expense to support children. • Pride in their school as a good place for both children and adults to work and its ability to be making a difference to children's lives, often in challenging circumstances. • Many had undertaken a large number of courses, both chosen by the school and many chosen by themselves and sometimes self-funded. • All those interviewed had additional qualifications from when they were first appointed.	• All except the trained nursery nurse had had non-conventional career paths and none had any A Level or HE qualification prior to becoming a TA. • Three of the five had started as parent volunteers in their children's school and discovered something they really enjoyed; clearly, staff already employed at the schools had evaluated their performance as volunteers – later when an appropriate post arose, then they were in a strong position to apply for it. • Several lived in the local community, with their own children attending the school in which they worked; two mentioned in the course of the interview that they felt that this meant that both parents and children felt more comfortable with them and they were trusted. • Mixed funding was available for post-holders, with a number on temporary posts, e.g. in one school four out of the eight TAs were in temporary posts.	*Financial support for HE:* The HLTA had received good support and encouragement from school, which, she felt, valued the fact that she was moving on; the former NNEB, undertaking a different Foundation Degree at the same time, did not receive any funding or support until there was a change of headteacher. Variable CPD support available for TAs in different local authorities; central government directives for TA training, i.e. as in the literacy strategy initiatives, were particularly useful in ensuring that TAs were trained. *Salaries:* Some sensitivity regarding the levels and rates of pay. One of those interviewed said directly that she would not tell me how much she earned, although I had no intention of asking. Others were quite open about being a Level 3 or Level 4. *Variations in the rates of pay:* The HLTA only got paid at a Level 4 during school-term time but it reverted to a Level 3 payment during school holidays; it would be interesting to see how the unions would react if teachers went on to retainer pay during the school holidays

Table 7.2 provides a summary of the barriers to learning that have been identified and some of the strategies that are being used to overcome these.

It is interesting to note that some of the features identified here by TAs were also identified by Ofsted in their 2008 summary report on the deployment, training and development of the wider school workforce.

This report identified that:

1. There were weaknesses in the training and development of the wider workforce. Too much 'continued to rely on the extent to which individual members of staff identified and requested professional development themselves'. Evidence from the TAs shows that there are important inconsistencies among schools in terms of support given for this – in terms of both funding and time.

2. The diverse backgrounds and life experiences enabled them to engage well with disaffected pupils and often managed to establish regular contact with parents and carers to help improve attendance and 'to enjoy learning more'.

TABLE 7.2 Barriers and strategies identified

IDENTIFIED BARRIERS FROM TAS	SPECIFIC STRATEGIES
Poor attendance	Employment of learning mentors with remit to improve attendance; all TAs who identified poor attendance as an issue that created barriers to learning in their schools said mentors had improved attendance Improved quality of teaching and support – so children want to come to school

ENGLISH AS AN ADDITIONAL LANGUAGE (EAL)

IDENTIFIED BARRIERS FROM TAS	SPECIFIC STRATEGIES
Children who do not have 'talking buddies' because there is no-one in the school with their language	Currently there is no strategy in this TA's school to manage this, but for another TA in another authority it was not an issue because all EAL children coming into the authority who have not been to school before attend a special admissions centre and are then directed towards an appropriate school One-to-one 'pre-teaching' sessions prior to specific class inputs
Seating EAL children with SEN children does not provide a good language model and inhibits development of good language skills	Ensuring that EAL children are seated with groups who have really good language skills and identify those who do really have SEN as well as EAL needs TA trained up to do this and ongoing training within in the school
Emotional health – particularly with asylum seekers, many of whom have had traumatic experiences	Small group work by trained worker (all schools with EAL said this); examining, but not questioning, children's pictures if they are showing particular signs; trained counselling (one school); small group work generally helps children to feel safe and to open up to adults
Increased admissions, all over the year, covering far more languages	LA with specific centre to take children who have not been to school before – has specialist personnel to deal with initial issues arising

TABLE 7.2 (continued)

PARENTING

Lack of *parental support* – parents unable, or unwilling, to give children the support they need in order to succeed in the school environment; this included low expectations and aspirations, poor communication, social and developmental skills, little play experience, fear and lack of respect for authority, general poor behaviour	Working towards more community cohesion, informal strategies and opportunities to meet before and after school, coffee mornings, provision of on-site café run by volunteer Home visits carried out before children come to school to provide insight into home circumstances; this enables those who visit to have an idea of what child's prior experience is and how they can build on it Strong parent mentor programme (in one school). Modelling behaviour and language expected – saying 'please' and 'thank you', listening to others, using clear pronunciation
Large families, teenaged pregnancies resulting in very young parents with a number of small children. Having difficulty coping	External support from SureStart, teenage pregnancy programmes
Parents always assuming their child is right	Improved relationships over a period of time, helped by being able to use personal experience as a parent and helper
Stressed children	Teaching the 'whole' to children, rather than feeding them bits of knowledge, helped by a general move towards more holistic planning Being creative, creating a context for 'real life learning' and utilising ICT Creating a buzzing lively classroom, with children actively engaged and communicating Not letting the children become levels – see children as children; provide challenge but not stress
Poor training of support staff	
Too little time in college, and the time doing the job is heavily dependent on quality and competence of those in school – the TA who said this had undergone NNEB training 18 years ago and felt this had been a much better qualification; this was balanced by an HLTA who felt that her university-based Foundation Degree had been poorly organised, although she had learnt from it	Strategies require good training institutions and schools working together in partnership. The whole purpose of the core training for anyone working with children does effectively recognise the need to improve the quality and consistency of training and professional development. There were huge inconsistencies between TAs in terms of school support for training
Proper time allocation for meetings, CPD, resources for courses, laptops	Currently an expectation that most TAs will attend briefings, in-service training, etc. that are relevant for them, whether or not they are paid for it

8

Mentors

The parish priest was talking to our children about our relationship with God: 'If you could live with anyone who would you live with?'. The usual responses came out such as footballers, pop stars and celebrities generally. What also came from this very simple question were some important insights into children's lives. One child said he would like to live with 'people who don't argue' and another wished for 'someone who can change me'. The message we try to give to parents is to get the support now, before the child – and themselves – become lost in the system.

(Angela, LM)

Chapter overview

- Review the development of mentors in primary schools

- Examine the different ways in which mentors undertake their role to break down barriers to learning

- Evaluate their role in terms of the 'Every Child Matters' (ECM) and Integrated Children's Services agendas.

Introduction

This chapter will look at the work of five different sorts of primary mentor. Only two of those interviewed were working in the full-time mentoring post: one was a learning mentor (LM) (the only mentor who was a man) and the other a parent mentor. In addition, there were three part-time mentors: two LMs [one of whom also worked as a Higher Level Teaching Assistant (HLTA), the other as a Teaching Assistant (TA)] and one behaviour mentor.

Background to primary learning mentoring

Ten years ago it would have been rare to find any sort of mentors in the English education system. In this chapter, we look briefly at their introduction and growth in primary schools, examine the initial training given, and explore their current role, both inside and outside school. I hope to show how this particular initiative has produced a very distinctive new professional in primary schools, who is a key educational professional within the Integrated Children's Services agenda.

Background

Initially, LMs formed one strand of the Department for Education and Skills (DfES) Excellence in Cities (EiC) programme. This was introduced in 1999 to tackle 'specific problems facing children in our cities. Through a combination of initiatives, it (EiC) aims to raise the aspirations and achievements of pupils and to tackle disaffection, social exclusion, truancy and indiscipline and improve parents' confidence in cities' (Hughes 2005). Initially, the EiC programme focused on secondary schools but the following year it expanded into primary schools.

There was plenty of hard data from Ofsted inspections to show that a much greater proportion of schools in the EiC areas were seen as in need of special measures. Levels of attainment as monitored through GCSE and Key Stage 2 Standard Assessment Tasks/Tests (SATs) results were lower than in other schools.

Later, it was taken up by individual schools, who saw a useful initiative and were prepared to pay for a full- or part-time LM out of their budget. A National Training Programme for mentors was established in 2001 and materials for this programme were updated and revised each year until 2003 (Liverpool Excellence Partnership 2003). The initial training programme provided mentors with a formal qualification if they went ahead with the proposed accreditation.

The Children's Workforce Development Council provides an overall description of the work of LMs, pointing out that there are a number of issues that may get in the way of learning and this was part of the role of LMs. These can include family problems, bereavement, bullying, low self-confidence and poor study skills.

At one time, much of this would have been seen as part of the teacher's role. Certainly, when I was a primary governor on the appointments panel for two LMs in the very first phase, we had very little idea of how their role would translate into reality or, indeed, what we were looking for.

Initial training

The initial establishment of LMs had high priority and primary headteachers in the EiCs involved were seconded to manage the programme. Their task was to ensure that the essential primary and local expertise was available in the recruitment, training and management of the LMs.

By January 2001, there was a national 5-day training programme in place. This had been designed to ensure that all primary LMs had the skills needed to carry out their duties. It covered four accredited modules:

1. *The primary school as a learning organisation* – its structure, literacy and numeracy strategies, managing inclusion.

2. *The role of the LM* – enhancing personal and professional effectiveness; child protection; statutory frameworks for health and safety and workplace regulations; the 'extended' role of the LM; managing transition; and the role of external Providers.

3. *The nature of children's learning* – learning hand-in-hand with development; working with diversity in learning; educational support services; enhancing children's motivation and monitoring; and assessing children's learning.

4. *Supporting children and their families* – basic helping skills; working with children on their behaviour; addressing emotional growth; fostering personal, social and emotional development through circle time; developing home–school liaison

All mentors were expected to take part in this training course, which was delivered locally, initially by the National Training Team. The training was updated in September 2003, when the pattern of LMs had become more established and other priorities had come into focus. These included underachieving gifted and talented pupils and strategies to support boys' learning.

Today, the TDA oversees the training of support workers, such as LMs; ironically, this has made it much more dependent on LAs and individual schools. Some LAs set up lead mentors to do the training, but certainly two of the mentors I interviewed felt that they were not getting the sort of developmental training they needed. This included changes in the law, safeguarding of children and other developments within the Integration Children's Services Agenda. The CWDC Induction Standards Training Programme at Levels 3/4 replaced the EiC materials and included two role-specific modules for LMs. These were to support the National Occupational Standards (NOS) for Learning, Development and Support Services (LDSS).

Andy: full-time LM

This interview took place in Andy's office, which was a small, comfortable room, big enough to fit in a couple of easy chairs, storage space for games and files, and space for displaying posters such as the School Food Trust 'Eat Better to Do Better' and the NSPCC and ChildLine numbers. Several children 'dropped in' to see Andy during the course of the afternoon and this provided a very useful demonstration of the easy, but professional, relationship that the mentor had established.

Andy's background

Like many of the TAs interviewed for the previous chapter, Andy had underperformed himself when he was at school; had then left at 17 and worked for 6 years in an insurance office. He then went into teacher training, and got as far as his final year when he decided it just was not for him. Fortunately, he was able to continue the degree but without the qualified teacher status (QTS) qualification.

When he finished university he was out of work and, as he was living several hundred miles from home, he was dependent on what he could earn to support himself while lodging with friends. It was at this stage that he first applied for a LM's job. He did not get it but a friend who did had another job with a children's charity and suggested he tried for that. He did so and became an environmental education officer for 3 years. He found the QTS skills useful and liked working with the children more creatively than he had been able to as a student teacher. He then applied for, and got, his present job.

What Andy does

Box 8.1 shows his job description as of October 2006. Of course a role description and personal attributes only go a small part of the way to describe a very complex post. Andy discussed some of the things that he does on a regular basis, which included:

1. Starting the day at 8.00 am while running a breakfast club with the parent mentor and a volunteer parent. This costs 50 pence per child and cereal, toast and fruit juice are provided. Games are organised either inside or outside. Then Andy goes on to the school yard, 10 minutes before school starts, and uses this time to chat informally to pupils and parents. He regards this as crucial in building up his relationship with parents and the breakfast club ensures that children get an opportunity to eat and drink something before they come into school.

2. Between 9.00 and 9.15 am he stays in the playground to encourage punctuality for those children who arrive slightly late. After 9.10 am the children have to go to front door of school.

3. Each day he scans attendance of the children who are known to have poor attendance records. Some teachers send him lists of absent targeted children, which makes the process faster. He then contacts the home as the first response. The national average for attendance is 95 per cent, but Andy's school only reaches 92 per cent, and so Andy's attendance role is crucial. The school has a policy on attendance and punctuality, and, at the time of the interview, it had identified 13 children as persistent absentees (PAs). Currently, the workload is such that the school receives additional funding to support this first-response work. The figures also include nursery children, of whom 32 have a below-85 per cent attendance rate. The issues here are more complex because there is no statutory requirement to attend, but the school recognises that attendance habits are formed early and non-attendance tends to follow these children from non-statutory placement into statutory requirements.

4. Initially, when Andy started, he was timetabled to carry out individual work in classrooms with specific children. Experience showed that this timetable was difficult to fix because of variation in his work. It has also been rendered unnecessary because of the growth of TAs and parent volunteers in the school. Andy also felt that it sometimes made his role as an advocate for children difficult, because there was a conflict between advocacy and teaching more formally in the classroom. Certainly, the initial idea of the role of an LM was to build up a professional, but different, type of relationship with children who were having real difficulties with formal learning within schools. The more formal one-to-one and small group work is undertaken in Andy's office. Teachers identify children to work with the mentor or who need mentor support, sometimes

Box 8.1 Role description for a learning mentor

Metropolitan Borough of Aspiring School

POST TITLE   LEARNING MENTOR

GRADE   LEVEL 2

RESPONSIBLE TO   HEADTEACHER

MAIN PURPOSE
Working within an agreed system of supervision, to develop and provide a
complementary service to teachers and support staff in school, addressing the
needs of the children who need help to overcome barriers to learning both inside and
outside the school, in order to achieve their full potential

MAIN DUTIES
- Support for pupils
- To promote the speedy and effective transfer of pupils through the various phases
  from pre-school settings to secondary, including within the school
- Develop a 1:1 mentoring relationship with pupils needing particular support to
  achieve the goals defined in their individual action plans
- Act as a role model for all pupils, setting high expectations
- Develop and promote inclusive practices and acceptances of all pupils
- Encourage pupils to interact and work cooperatively with others and engage in
  activities
- Promote self-esteem and independence, developing and employing a range
  of strategies to recognise and reward achievement within established school
  procedure
- Provide feedback to pupils in relation to progress and achievement
- Support for the teacher
- Working with the teacher and support staff, taking the lead in the comprehensive
  assessment of children selected by the headteacher or his/her nominated
  representative, to identify those who need extra help to overcome barriers to
  learning inside and outside school
- Identify those children who would benefit most from a learning mentor and
  working with others take the lead to draw up an action plan for each pupil who
  needs particular support
- Support the development and work within a clear framework for pupil discipline,
  anticipate and manage pupil behaviour constructively, promoting self-control and
  independence, in line with established school policy
- Maintain regular contact with families/carers of children in need of extra support,
  keeping them informed of the child's needs and progress and to secure positive
  family support and involvement
- To work closely with the class teacher and SENCO to ensure that the needs of
  the gifted and talented children and those with special educational needs are met
- Support for the curriculum

Box 8.1 (continued)

- To have knowledge and appreciation of the range of activities, courses, opportunities, agencies and services that could be drawn upon to provide extra support for pupils.
- Support for the school
- Comply with all school policies and in particular the procedures relation to child protection, health, safety and security, confidentiality and data protection, and report all concerns to the appropriate person
- Be aware of and support difference and ensure all pupils have equal access to opportunities to learn, develop and feel valued, respecting their social, cultural, linguistic, religious and ethnic background
- Contribute to the school ethos, aims and development/improvement plan
- Facilitate the sharing of relevant information between local agencies and schools and be the joint point of contact for accessing a range of community and specialist support services, for example Social Services, Education Welfare Service
- Report on the implementation of all action plans to the line manager and the EiC Partnership
- Attend and participate in network meetings sharing best practice to support others
- Undertake personal development through training and other learning activities, including performance management as required
- To comply with all the Council's Standing Orders and financial regulations

Note: This is not a comprehensive list of all of the tasks that may be required of the postholder. It is illustrative of the general nature and level of responsibility of the work to be undertaken, commensurate with the grade.

parents ask, and sometimes requests come from the headteacher, for example when reports are needed for parents and the local authority (LA) in relation to looked-after children (LAC).

5. After school, Andy runs and organises sports, which he finds helps to set targets for attendance and behaviour. Sports are used very much as a carrot to encourage children to work towards their targets. Andy covers the yard both before and after school, and the welfare staff and the headteacher cover at lunch-times. Welfare staff have been specially trained for this and the playground is sectioned into different sorts of play areas. These strategies have cut down on much of the difficulty when children went back to classes and largely avoids teachers having to settle children's playground disputes when they should be learning.

6. Andy arranges external speakers and visits for specific classes, for example with the fire and police services, conferences such as 'Your Choice', and invitation to speakers to cover several issues related to the ECM agenda, such as healthy eating and cycle safety.

7. Andy set up the school's council, which at the moment is for children in Key Stage 2. It meets every fortnight and has moved from having two representatives from each class to one from each class. In this two-form entry school, this gives it

eight members. Recently they have discussed the LA travel plan, which involved conducting surveys for comments from the pupils and the local community. In another recent survey on the school, they used the findings to help to fund a new gate into the yard. On a healthy schools initiative, the school's council drew up a letter that was sent to parents about the contents of lunch boxes. This is an issue, even in a school in which at least three-quarters of the pupils are entitled to a free school meal, because many children bring very unhealthy lunch boxes into school. The school's council have also discussed the equipment that is needed for the playground. Sometimes children themselves bring up issues such as the death (from cancer) of a neighbour and a request to raise funds for cancer research.

8. Meetings:

   (a) Andy attends many meetings that take place outside school and link directly with the Integrated Children's Agenda. These meetings cover transition into secondary school, so that vulnerable children are identified well before they leave. He meets with the relevant professionals in the secondary sector, including the LMs, and ensures that the children have met them before they leave primary school.

   (b) He meets with Social Services to discuss, both formally and informally, the children who are involved with Child Protection Plans that replaced the Child Protection register and there is an educational social worker who regularly visits or is called into the school – most recently, when a mother had to be sectioned and the children taken into care. In an earlier interview with Andy's headteacher, the headteacher told me that Andy now covered for him on all of the day-to-day issues and regular meetings with other agencies. He felt that this was happening much more efficiently than it had been in the past because Andy knew the children and has had time to make good formal and informal links with individuals working in the many agencies that are involved with the school.

   (c) Once a term there is a formal meeting in the school between the Special Education Co-ordinator (SENCO), headteacher and mentor. This is used to discuss children who are being seen by other agencies (for speech therapy; problems due to sensory impairment; specialist teachers for learning, access and inclusion; educational social work; and educational psychology). They use this as an opportunity to look at new referrals. He also has regular breakfast briefings with the SENCO to look at report cards, target sheets and individual plans. Box 8.2 provides an example of a relatively informal target sheet for a child who is displaying challenging behaviour on the school playground.

   (d) Although, this looks rather unimportant, football and sports meetings with the LA and other schools are important, because the children themselves value this. Many schools in this area have the same agenda, and see these as ways of breaking barriers to learning because they provide disaffected children with something to do, which motivates them and makes them more positive towards institutions such as schools.

Box 8.2 Informal target sheet for playground

NAME:

CLASS TEACHER:

This week I am trying especially hard to:

1.

2.

DAY	MORNING BREAK	LUNCH-TIME	END OF THE DAY
MONDAY			
TUESDAY			
WEDNESDAY			
THURSDAY			
FRIDAY			

Please ask your teacher to put a tick in the boxes for each of your targets met.

HOW MANY TICKS WILL YOU GET?

Most proud of

■ Providing an outlet for children, outside the classroom. He is there as someone to talk to and feels that his work is valued by both the children and staff. This was evidenced by the number of children who came to see him while I was there. It must have saved many children having a much more formal interview with the headteacher and gave both the child and teacher a time to reconsider and re-establish a working relationship within a small classroom. He feels that it does give both teachers and TAs another person with whom to discuss strategies to help vulnerable and often disaffected pupils.

■ Many sole parents welcome the opportunity to talk to someone about how their child is getting on at school. As an LM, Andy meets many on the school yard, building up relationships over a period of time. This also provides many opportunities to discuss events that are taking place outside the school which may influence what goes on inside it because children are involved, either actively or passively. For example, recently the uncle of several children was knifed and one of the gang of youths who was found responsible had a sibling in Year 6. Another parent, who is a taxi driver, had picked up a fare and the next minute found guns through the window of his cab. He had not told his daughter, but was concerned that she might hear from other children.

Areas for development

- Andy feels that his own career is not developing. This is not helped by the fact that there is no clear career path for mentoring.

- The LA training is run by two lead mentors and is good at supporting newly appointed mentors but does not, or cannot, respond to needs; for example, LMs have asked for training about restraint procedures but have been told that this is not possible.

- Poor attendance of a small minority of pupils distorts the school's attendance records, which are important indicators of school performance. The other work that Andy does makes this attendance aspect difficult to follow up; so, although he is able to measure it and follow up with phone calls, but he would like time to make more visits and work with parents and carers. He gave as an example that day's absence rate of 25 children in a two-form entry school – six of these are on the school mental health concern list.

Barriers to learning

Andy sees these barriers to learning as being very broad. They include the nature of the school learning itself; the school and home environment, which may not be helpful to learning for some children; local and home circumstances; medical needs, both physical and mental; and the cultural norms in the area. That morning, he had discussed with a boy's father about his son being very aggressive and the father had explained how he had encouraged his son to hit back if he was in trouble, because otherwise he would not be able to survive in this neighbourhood.

Angela

Angela works 60 per cent of her time as an LM and 40 per cent as an HLTA. She started going into school a volunteer when her children were little. She had worked in insurance prior to having her children, having left school at 16. When working for the insurance company she had taken courses and learnt how to touch type and use a computer. So, initially, she had gone in to school to help with the computer and then ran a computer course for parents. As she became more interested in working in the school she had attended a special teaching assistant (STA) course for teaching assistants, for which the school sponsored her, and then she began working at the school as a lunch-time assistant. After she finished the STA course, she got a paid for a year as a TA, but then there was no money in the budget to continue paying her. She did continue to work as a volunteer and was eventually persuaded to become a mentor by the headteacher, but had expressed concerns because she lived in the community and felt it might be too intense.

Role

Angela realised quite quickly that the closeness to the community was an advantage because when children spoke about different gangs and peer pressure that they were under she knew who they were talking about.

There are several different elements to her role:

1. Attendance – there is a first-day response and she works closely with the education welfare officer (EWO). Good attendance is rewarded with trips out half-termly for those with 100 per cent attendance. Initially, these trips were funded by the school and then 'regeneration' money was used. The school is currently looking at just targeting poor attenders for small half-termly trips and then having a really big trip for the 100 per cent attenders. There are difficulties as parents come and ask if child can go on the visit, because although the child's attendance was not 100 per cent he really was just ill. The mentor does visit the house if it is known that the child is usually a regular attender, but she has to make judgements about making the visit in a potentially dangerous area.

    The school provides early-morning alarm calls, supplies alarm clocks, if needed, and has developed individual target certificates. It has hard data to show that attendance has improved. Angela is not sure, though, how much this has been due to the school itself improving under the new school leadership and how much to the fact that the procedures on attendance have sharpened. The attendance rates have gone from 88.5 per cent in 2000 to 92 per cent in 2004, and last year were 95.3 per cent. So the school is now above the national average.

2. Angela also works as an HLTA with Year 6, spending time in the mornings on numeracy and literacy. Unlike Andy, who found it difficult to combine the formal teaching role with the mentoring role, Angela has found the in-class work useful because she can see the children in the classroom and tries to identify what barriers to learning may be appearing and which strategies to use to overcome these. As an HLTA she covers other classes and does not see any conflict between the HLTA and LM roles. She is able to act as a role model and often takes out small groups.

    She runs the breakfast club, with the help of the headteacher and a TA, and it is attended by between 40 and 50 children. Only those having food pay. However, as well as food, activities such as football, computers, games and reading are offered. Angela feels that these provides a useful social opportunity for the children at the start of their day.

4. After school, she runs three evening clubs for an hour each. These are varied, and have included a performing arts club at the school's main feeder secondary school, a gardening/growing club, enterprise, first aid and computing. On another evening during the week she works with children to produce the school newsletter, and on the remaining evening she waits to see what crops up. They have found that the children prefer clubs that cover wider life skills work, rather than that of the curriculum. This makes them keener to attend and it is useful to be able to share good practice with the feeder secondary school.

5.   Angela also does lunch duty outside every day and the school has developed a policy of having a game of the week, which helps to build up games skills. The school also has zone park leaders. These are pupils who lead games and are in Years 4 to 6. The school also has a 'Friendly 15' group who act as mediators and buddies for other children – again, these children come from Years 4 to 6. The 'Friendly 15' are appointed and trained by the LA Pupil Advocacy Team, and they cover mediation and buddy support through both Key Stages 1 and 2. Initially, those interested in becoming one of the 'Friendly 15' are trained to apply for the job. They are told how to find someone to give them a reference, fill in an application form and then have an interview. Angela sees this as being particularly important as they come from an area of high unemployment and may never see this happening at home.

6.   In the afternoons, Angela runs and organises other activities, including:

   (a) *The school council/Pupils' Voice*. This involves two children from each class and they have to be elected. They set their own rules, sit in for job interviews – both pupils and staff – and have strict rules for attendance; for example if a child misses three meetings then they are dismissed. The school council feeds in to governors' meetings, has a weekly spot in assembly and sets its own ECM targets. For example, 'economic well-being' involved improving the school bank, and now 50 per cent of the pupils are savers; 'staying safe' involved taking part in a neighbourhood forum with police, the leader of the council and local councillors. Linked with the school council is the school parliament, and three of the school's council members attend the LA school parliament. There are 150 children altogether, and this has resulted in children producing statements such as 'want to be PM'. Speaking and listening here has changed ideas about their power and resulted in school-based initiatives, such as the tree house and drinking fountain in the playground. Children have also made a visit to the Houses of Parliament and stayed overnight in London.

   (b) *University initiative on widening participation into higher education (HE)*. This included their 'Professor Fluffy' project and follow-up work.

   (c) *Being the 'link person' with other agencies*. This includes the EWO; the school nurse; behaviour and education support teams (BESTs); Child and Adolescent Mental Health Services (CAMHS); the Youth Inclusion Project; the Pupil Support Centre; the secondary schools; local wardens; the Nugent Care Society; and pensioners' groups.

   (d) *Having responsibility for special events*. These include live radio, fun days, young citizens, sailing, tennis, and PGL holidays.

   (e) *Running 'golden time' or 'rewards time' on Friday afternoons*. As with the running of the breakfast club, this involves the headteacher, a TA and the LM.

   (f) *Weekly meetings* – with lunch-time supervisors.

   (g) *Attending reward visits*. Recently, Angela took children to the main City library, where they were allowed to go behind the scenes and look at some of the very rare books that the library holds. The children were really fascinated, as well as being made to feel special because they had been allowed to do something that most people never get the opportunity to do. Other rewards visits have been to the theatre, museum and football club. The funding of a visits bus by the City made it easier for several years for schools such as Angela's to go out on more visits and actually introduce the children to their own city. Recently, a group of children have been involved with the Philharmonic Hall – as well as going to concerts, pupils had the opportunity to try playing musical instruments, such as the double bass, violin and guitar. This led to doing work with Classic FM and Hymns of Praise.

(h) *Mentor intervention on a one-to-one basis and also small group work, during afternoons.* Angela also works on circle time over the whole school with pupils from Key Stages 1 and 2. Basically, she reacts to what the school needs; for example, at the moment she is supporting parents in their appeal for a pupil's placement at a specific secondary school.

Most proud of

1. School council/*Pupils' Voice*, because she can see confidence growing as children are getting to think for themselves and have a forum in which to express ideas. It provides a challenge for those pupils who want challenge.

2. Challenge also comes from extracurricular activities, which can provide wide and opportunities for learning, for example the Big Write Project.

3. Running a reading project, during which a grandmother came in to the school to tell Angela that she had bought her grandchild four reading books rather than a game for the PlayStation.

4. Teachers answering questions in a particular way that allows children to answer them.

5. The school, as it has developed a lot since her own children were pupils there, and it has been greatly helped by the arrival of headteacher (now in post for 3 years) who allowed things to happen. This has enabled the school to become an 'I Can' school, giving children experiences, aspirations and improved expectations: it is their school, and the pupils know this, and they are well informed about what is going on: 'It has been wonderful to watch a cultural change of willingness to say yes.' Angela is convinced that this has been responsible for the highest academic standards in the school's history in terms of Key Stages 1 and 2 SATS.

Areas for development

Needs to be more independence among pupils who still need a lot of reassurance.

Barriers for learning

Home life – lack of support and/or interest. Parents, who love their children but do not parent. What happens at home comes through to school, for example when the parish priest was talking about our relationship with God: 'If you could live with anyone who would you live with?' The expected responses came, with children suggesting they would like to live with footballers, pop stars and celebrities, generally. But also there were more profound statements, such as from the child who said 'live with people who don't argue' and another who wanted 'someone who can change me'.

Audrey: working 2 days per week as a LM

Audrey trained as a graphic designer and had a degree in graphic design. After finishing this she worked in the industry. During this time, as well as getting older, she had her family and found that the design job was no longer satisfactory, so she went to work as a volunteer with a LA-based charity known as ITS (Intermediate Treatment Scheme), which provided a range of services for vulnerable children, young people and families. During this time, she became a mentor to a girl who came to the school and then began to work as a volunteer with her in the school. This made her realise that she wanted to do more, so she undertook a basic counselling skills course with Compass, a regional counselling organisation, and went into work voluntarily in schools.

After realising how much she enjoyed it, she started to look for jobs. The first job was as a part-time classroom assistant working on the Additional Literacy Strategy (ALS). Then the LA came up with a post for a creative mentor to work in primary schools, funded through the Excellence in Cities programme. Her current school was one to which she been assigned and in which she had built up relationships with both pupils and staff. The money stopped, however, when funds were moved into the extended schools programme. At this stage, the headteacher at Audrey's school approached her about being a mentor in the school. The work as a creative mentor had involved vulnerable children and focusing on them, so the two roles were more similar than they might have seemed. The National Learning Mentor Training Programme was in place, so Audrey undertook this and found it really useful.

Role

Audrey has been enabled to identify priorities and created active and passive files. She sees her post as filling some of the gaps where parenting slips. The role has changed, as the school has changed and as a result of a strong pastoral team within the school.

- Initially, it had involved a lot of firefighting with older angry boys. Seven years later the position has changed. The school is much calmer, and it is possible to put more input further down the school.
- Now there is less frequent work on anger management and it can be done in groups. The pattern was to help children identify anger; where it is felt in the body and how it makes the individuals involved feel.
- The school has run, and continues to run, its own very successful pastoral programme, Second Steps. This is similar to SEAL, but the Second Steps programme is well embedded and has been independently evaluated by a local university team. The last two Ofsted reports have recognised the school as outstanding across the board, making statements such as 'pupil personal

development, including their spiritual, moral, social and cultural development is outstanding'.

- Audrey uses Silver Seals for small group work with children in both Key Stages 1 and 2. At the moment the focus is on self-esteem and work with needy boys with no father figure. The programme has five themes, for which points are awarded when children show the behaviour wanted – caring, co-operating, concentrating, challenging and celebrating.

The school is also focusing on the 'Saying No to Bullying' campaign; how it is 'Good to be Me' and New Beginnings.

- One of the ways in which support needed is identified is a *worry box*. Children can put their worries into this and they know they will be dealt with on a one-to-one basis. Some examples of what goes into the worry box include quite light ones such as 'Nan going on an aeroplane', but there has been a move towards deeper concerns. 'Nobody pays attention to me' and 'I am worried because . . . is nasty to me'. There are some straight child protection ones, for example the 9-year-old girl who was watching drug deals at home and was worried that someone might shoot her parents. Clearly, the school had to involve other agencies with this, but this is not always easy.
- Audrey uses the box to look at both general and specific concerns and the need to react. A more general example, was when twenty Year 6 children put in twenty slips mentioning the same child bullying. This was brought to the attention of the headteacher, who dealt with it. Many of the children had come in with a friend when submitting the slips, so that they felt protected about what they had written. Mental health issues are quite frequently mentioned, such as feeling sad all the time. Teachers also make referrals about particular children 'looking glum and sad'.
- Audrey's work involves quite a number of mental health issues. A few years ago she worked one-to-one with a very angry and sad child who was encouraged to do a home–school diary. Initially, this had been a referral from the child's home. It seemed to have been worked through two years previously, but had now started up again. As the child had become older, he had been spending time with older boys in the community and was trying to establish himself as a 'top dog' in the primary school.
- She also gives strategic talks about how to cope with challenges and talking through issues with other children. A small incident outside the classroom can upset the whole ethos of the classroom; for example, a group of Year 4 girls were not getting on well with each other and this was disrupting the whole class. As an LM, she worked with them and the matter was resolved.
- Part of her work involves generic things, such as lunch-time issues and working with both staff and pupils. The lunch-time issue involved changing the way in which the dinners service was organised. Initially, there had been one sitting and children were rushing meals. Now the school runs two sittings: one for the dinners and one for the packed lunches; there is a seating plan linked with chosen

lunch-time partners and four older children from Years 5 and 6 are at each table to act as support for the younger children and ensure better behaviour. There are also lunch-time rewards, with congratulations slips to make it clear what behaviour was rewarded, for example 'You waited patiently'; the slips mount up for the child to exchange for cinema tickets.

■ Other areas covered by Audrey are house teams with suggestion boxes, training and developing of pupil mediators, school council, and play work.

Most proud of

■ Developing good relationships with children over a long period of time. They know they can come and talk. Trust has to be built up over time. It's a real privilege and 'keeps you on your toes'.

■ 'I'm rich working in this wonderful school.'

Areas for development

■ Courses, in order to keep up to date, in particular mental health awareness courses.

■ The opportunity to network with other mentors and learn more from each other.

■ School council – making it more of a whole-school approach.

■ Increased work on the Eco-cycling initiative, because this is self-empowering for children, as well as highlighting the wider issues of recycling.

Barriers for learning

1. 'Many children are just not ready to learn.' The school provides a structured world, in which they can function and achieve and where it is safe for them; this often contrasts with their world outside school.

2. Lack of motivation and aspiration. 'Having a baby' is often seen as the most aspirational aim that many girls have, even at primary school level. This is fuelled by what they see outside school.

3. Linked with this is the need to getting parents on board in order to raise aspirations. It can seem an uphill task for the school because emotional health and literacy is all embracing.

Anita: part-time behaviour mentor

Anita described how she had initially got into working in school, because she had found herself very isolated when she left home and got married. After she had her first child she began helping out at playschool and by the time her son was aged 3 she had 'got sucked into it'. Now she has five children. When she had originally left school, her mother had said to do the NNEB course, which she hated, and gave up after a term.

Later she decided to do an Access Course into social work. As part of that course she had worked on a national charity project that involved working with children. She already had some experience of play therapy and this gave her more. She also learnt some quite useful 'negative' leadership skills! This voluntary post led to a job as a relief cover at a play centre. She spent 9 months at the play centre, which was held in the school hall. She started to bring in other mothers and eventually they ran it. The project involved the whole family, so she was working with mums in groups as well as working in the crèche. There were also holiday clubs and after-school clubs. Initially, this was just within one LA, but then it moved into many others.

At this stage, Anita was not doing much in this, her children's school, except for the occasional school trip. She was then asked if she would be interested in a job in this school as a classroom assistant. Initially, this involved working with children with learning difficulties on a one-to-one basis. She really loved the school because of its culture of 'can do' and 'are allowed to do' and being able to suggest things which are taken up.

The school work was part-time at this stage and Anita continued to do volunteer work for the LA Family Groups, as well as working as a group and play leader. This involved a lot of sessional work and then this headteacher offered more paid hours as a TA, which she took up. Later she was appointed to cover TA responsibilities and be a 'Behaviour' member and a member of the school pastoral team.

Role

- She felt was her role was not entirely clear and varied with the needs of the school. It has changed over time because school needs have changed and also the personnel who are giving support have also changed.

- It involves working one-to-one inside and outside classes and working with parents to look at behavioural and learning strategies.

- Attendance is a crucial issue and at 9.10 am each day Anita works through the registers. Then a first-response phone call is made. In practice, not all children are covered and the school has different procedures, depending on the record of child absence. There are a number of regular non-attenders for whom procedures vary. A new non-attender gets the first-response call. If the first-response calls fail, a letter is written; if there is still no improvement the EWO, school nurse and the mentor meet. The class teacher is aware and involved in all meetings and correspondence. Anita attends a formal meeting every half-term with the EWO, at which the focus is on those children with below 90 per cent attendance. At the start of the school year there is an increased percentage because of the number of children taken on cheaper term-time holidays.

- Linked with attendance is punctuality and the school has a number of strategies to deal with this. These include 'spot on time wall': this is a bookmark with a spot, then a prize.

- Funding for Anita's post came initially from the Behavioural Improvement Project (BIP), but she felt that primary schools did not get the same level of support as the secondary schools. After 3 years, this money disappeared altogether and money from the extended schools budget was used to pay her.

- She does a lot of informal work, as well as more formalised one-to-one and small group work. Informal counselling takes place on the way to school, while walking in to school and in corridors. She makes a point of speaking to particular children every day. It gives them some concrete proof that someone cares and acknowledges them each day.

- They have found that young carers may need a little time between school and going home and Anita plans for this.

- She covers Planning, Preparation, Assessment (PPA) time with some classes, usually teaching RE, and SEAL, which the school has adopted as its Pastoral Programme.

- She has found that often when a child is having learning difficulties they behave badly, to mask the learning difficulties. It is possible to have a good relationship with the child concerned, but this does not, by itself, stop the poor behaviour. For example a child in Year 6 with learning difficulties was helped by working through some simple handwriting and comprehension exercises. This helped him to get back into the habit of concentrating and trying to do the tasks set. It was a very slow process, but the behaviour improved. Teachers can miss these learning blocks in a very busy classroom, so the barriers to learning are not always with the child.

- Referrals come to Anita by staff referrals, the LM, direct referrals from outside the school, the deputy and children who refer themselves.

Most proud of

- Pleased when something works with a child and brings them through to a better place. This can be very intensive and often involves a very different sort of relationship with the child from that which the teacher has.

- Having the respect of other children. These relationships are different and delicate and often needed to help a vulnerable child get the support required from other children.

Areas for development

- Anita has done nurture group training and would like to set up a nurture group within the school. The training involved doing a 5000-word essay, for which she was awarded 64 per cent and she has now earned thirty credits towards a degree.

- Social Services. The relationship is not always easy; for example, recently a child came into school with drugs. Initially, the child just said that they had something they should not have. It was good that the child felt comfortable enough at school to say something to someone. The behaviour mentor looked in the child's coat pocket and found a white powder. Social Services were called, but did not come in or want to act. The police pointed out that the child's pocket should not have been searched and were concerned about this. Both pointed out that there was no evidence that the drugs came from home and the child could have got them on their way to school.

- Dyslexia and behaviour management training. Eventually, Anita would like to go down the special needs route and is applying for a foundation degree.

Barriers to learning

- Lack of support and encouragement from home. This covers both motivating children and having some sort of positive expectations about what they want out of the education system.
- When Anita had her own children she said she did not know much about children, but loved watching them develop. She does not see this happening today and some parents just do not value their children.
- Children and parents with low or non-existent expectations.
- Attendance problems.

Evie: full-time parent mentor

When Evie left school she trained as a hairdresser and had two children, one of whom was very poorly. This was a turning point in her life, as one of the products of having a sick child is that you have to fight for them all the time. This resulted in her getting involved with support groups for parents with sick children. As a result of this work, she was asked by her children's primary school to run a support group for parents as a volunteer. This led to her being trained, with the school's support, as a nursery nurse at the local further education (FE) college. She was also doing voluntary work for Home-Start and supporting a LM in another primary school.

After gaining the NNEB she felt she was in position to take on a paid job and initially worked for a private agency as a family support worker, based in another primary school. The provision was poor and it made the job impossible to do properly, so she resigned.

Role

Box 8.3 provides Evie's role description. Evie herself identifies fourteen different aspects to her role, which include:

1. Organising courses for parents through the local authority Family Learning Team (FLT). She draws up a list of is what available and then asks parents what they want. When the numbers seeking a course reach seven she begins to rally support to get the numbers up to ten, which will make it viable. It costs £10 to register and then £40 to register if the person is employed, with a sliding scale for those who are not. Box 8.4 shows the availability of courses held in her two-form entry primary school.

2. She also works along side the LA well-being team, which runs activities such as 'boxercise', healthy cookery, keep fit, and drug awareness. Recently, these have been made available to staff after school. The local Aim Higher team comes in to support parents who might want to go into HE or FE.

Box 8.3 Role description for a parent mentor based in a primary school

MAIN PURPOSE

Working within an agreed system of supervision, to provide support to families and the wider community to help them to overcome barriers to learning; achieve their full educational potential; be healthy and make a positive contribution to their school and local community

MAIN DUTIES

- Support for parents/carers and the wider community
- Develop trusting and supporting relationships with families and the wider community
- Provide support and encouragement to families and the wider community to enable them to engage in activities, access support and interact positively and cooperatively within the school community
- Act as a role model for parents and carers and the wider community, setting high expectations
- Promote self-esteem, confidence and independence amongst families and the wider community, developing and employing a range of strategies to recognise and celebrate achievement within established school procedures
- Develop and promote inclusive practices and acceptance of all members of the community
- Develop, facilitate and deliver programmes and activities that help parents/carers and the wider community contribute to the delivery of 'Every Child Matters' outcomes for children at the school, including targeted programmes and activities to engage and support individuals who are under-represented or who have a high degree of need
- Support for the school
- Support the development and maintenance of positive and trusting relationships between the school, parents/carers and the wider community
- To work closely with members of the school staff, Extended Schools Co-ordinators and with a range of statutory and voluntary sector agencies to develop and support the delivery of the core offer within schools.
- Contribute to the identification of families who would benefit from additional support and to planning and development of appropriate support packages
- Attend and participate in meetings and network formally and informally, sharing best practice, engaging in cooperative working where appropriate
- Comply with all school policies and in particular the procedures relating to child protection, health, safety and security, confidentiality and data protection; report all concerns to the appropriate person
- Be aware of and support difference and ensure all pupils have equal access to opportunities to learn, develop and feel valued, respecting their social, cultural, linguistic, religious and ethnic background
- Contribute to the school ethos, aims and development/improvement plan
- Undertake all associated paperwork and related administration for the role
- Collation of quantitative monitoring data regarding both identified outputs and outcomes and reporting the information to the line manager

Box 8.4 Exemplar of courses available at school in which parent mentor works

- Have you ever thought about trying a new skill? Here at . . . . School we are able to provide you with opportunities to take part in courses and activities that we hope will of interest to you.
- Below you will find a list of some of the courses available to us through various providers. If you are interested in any of the courses please put a tick in the appropriate box/boxes and return this form to your child's class teacher or to Evie Williams (Parent Mentor). This information can then be used to help us planning courses in the future.

COURSE TITLE		COURSE TITLE	
Yoga		Flower arranging	
Salsa		Calligraphy	
Belly dancing		Parenting skills	
Alternative therapies		Classroom Assistant Level 1	
Counselling skills		Classroom Assistant Level 2	
Aromatherapy		Volunteering in school	
Stress management		Learning with young Children	
Assertiveness and confidence building		Helping in school	
Introduction to PSYCHOLOGY		Job seeking skills	
Positive behaviour management		Sign language	
Healthy eating/cooking		Acrylic nails/beauty Therapy	
Maths		Cake decorating	
English		Growing pains (How do I answer those awkward questions about growing up, drugs, alcohol, etc.)	
Spanish		Food hygiene	
Computers for beginners		SHARE	
Computers CLAIT		Healthy share	
Computers ECDL		Family literacy	
First aid		Parent and Child Spanish (NEW)	
Craft		Active dads	
Card making			

Child's name:

Class:

Parent's/carer's name:

Contact number:

Note: You don't need to have a child in the school to access these courses so please share this information with your friends and relatives.

3. The Family Learning Team also run courses over the whole local authority on health, SHARE (see Chapter 7), family literacy, family cookery, family learning through active play, active dance, Reading is Fundamental (in conjunction with the Literacy Trust), Early Years family cookery (for a maximum of six people). Some courses are now being held at a recently opened children's centre.

4. Evie is heavily involved in supporting parents to become involved in both their own and their children's education. She sees this as key to raising barriers to children's learning. She holds meetings once a month for the Parents, Teachers, Friends Association (PTFA). These meetings are more frequent if there is a project on, such as discos, fayres, grotto, fancy dress, etc., which usually attracts more parents.

5. She supervises volunteers. This includes ensuring that all of the volunteers have gone through the Criminal Records Bureau (CRB) disclosure process. She advises the volunteers on school-based courses and has drawn up a volunteers policy, which has been approved by the governing body.

6. She supplies leaflets for specific events, such as the Foundation Stage Open Morning, and gives leaflets out over the whole area. These cover not only what the school provides, but also learning opportunities for adults in the immediate neighbourhood provided by the local FE college and other groups such as Learning in Neighbourhood Centres (LINC).

7. There is a parents' room, which displays a number of posters advertising adult education, healthy shopping, emotional health well-being, healthy cooking, making shadow puppets, and children's work and photos, showing volunteers in action with each other and children. It also gives visiting parents a base, where they can chat, have cups of tea and exchange information. It makes the school a comfortable place.

8. She encourage parents to go on courses, but also to volunteer in classrooms. This has resulted in some of them getting posts as TAs in other schools and, in a few cases, in her school.

9. She helps run the breakfast club every morning, where she works with the LM from 8.15 am to 8.50 am, supplying the breakfast and supervising play activities.

10. There is a parent and toddler group, once per week, and this is where the SHARE programme is undertaken. They are also working hard to involve fathers in the Active Dads programme, which is becoming more popular in many of the schools.

Most proud

- Parents who move on from volunteering and courses to FE, HE and/or paid employment.
- Being responsive to the needs of both adults and children, so additional classes can take place and help given.
- Parental advice in confidence.

- Parents valuing education more because they are involved themselves; children seeing their parents learning and parents more likely to ask questions about their children's education.

Areas for development

- Home visits with nursery staff. Letters about the availability of courses and volunteer opportunities are sent home and given on the yard, but Evie does not feel that this is enough.
- Parents' room. This started as a large room but following school amalgamation the parents ended up with a smaller room.

Barriers to learning

Parents who were let down by the system and who cannot see that their children doing any better.

Findings

Table 8.1 provides an overview of some of the findings coming out of these interviews.

Mentoring, 'Every Child Matters' and Integrated Children's Services

1. The original remit of the primary mentors has changed from its original conception in 2000. They have largely taken on the operational side of the school's responsibilities in relation to the ECM agenda. The primary headteacher takes on the overall and strategic responsibility, but mentors build up the networks and links between different agencies. The first schools to get mentors were those in the challenging inner cities. The schools were charged to break down barriers for learning, which were recognised as being complex and relating to things outside the school as well as within. In order to do this effectively, local agencies needed to work together more closely and there were good practice examples all round the country.

2. Since 2000, schools have been given a leading role in relation to the integration of children's services. This is neatly summed up in the current initiative for schools on 'community cohesion'. If we see the primary school as the centre of the local community then it is not surprising that so many of the agency links are now concentrating on schools. The link agent in school is often the mentor. Figure 8.1 illustrates this relationship between the mentor and other agencies. It draws on a combination of the information supplied by the mentors in this chapter.

3. Figure 8.1 only represents a one-way traffic and this is misleading. The ECM agenda and the more recent Children's Plans require the agencies themselves to undertake specific responsibilities in relation to children. They are given

TABLE 8.1 Overview of general findings

ALL INTERVIEWED	SOME INTERVIEWED	KEY FEATURES
• All interviewed were very positive and optimistic about their work in school and, like the TAs, were able to give many individual examples of how barriers to learning had been broken down; they were also able to illustrate whole-school strategies that had been adopted to break down barriers.	• Work took most of the mentors out of school and involved them meeting and liaising with other agencies and schools.	• Several of the aspects of the work would in the past have been done by the class teacher – for example, the pastoral care programme and citizenship. This may be linked with the changing expectations on primary class teachers, who are expected to concentrate on 'the basics'.
• Extremely positive about the organisation and management structures of the school: 'I'm rich working in this wonderful school'; this was despite – or perhaps because – of the fact that they all worked in 'challenging schools' in terms of economic deprivation.	• Responsibility for teaching the formalised pastoral programme – SEAL/Second Steps.	• Interviews with agency workers in social services, police and fire services, health and attendance confirmed the Learning Mentors role as the vital link between the primary school and other aspects of the integrated children's services agenda.
• Very varied work, requiring great flexibility and adaptability.	• Using teaching time/club time/breakfast clubs, etc. to promote government curriculum initiatives such as citizenship, enterprise and healthy eating.	• Greater awareness in schools about the need to look at the whole child and plan for this if barriers to learning for some children are to be broken down. There was agreement that schools had to be aware of children's circumstances and mediate if appropriate.
• Modest – often difficult to get them to acknowledge that they were responsible for many successful initiatives within the school.	• Heavily involved with agencies in direct response to the Integrated Children's Services agenda. This is probably a reflection of the specific school catchment area.	• Some concern about the ability of social services to respond in the way the schools expected. This may be a result of the misconceptions between services, but may also be linked with the heavy pressure individual operational care workers are under to ensure formal procedures are followed for safeguarding. This in turn may be linked to the very public and humiliating retribution which hits strategic managers when safeguarding fails. The Baby P case resulted in the Director of Integrated Services being forced to resign.
• Significant amount of regular and ongoing volunteer work in the school.	• Two out of the five interviewed had degrees at the time of appointment; all mentioned very specialist professional development courses that they had attended.	
• Good understandings of different streams of funding – including that for their own posts. This was also linked to trying to identify specific funding for school-based initiatives.	• Directly line-managed by the headteacher.	
• Unconventional career paths with rich life experiences on which to draw in their work with both parents and children.	• Some said they had been underachievers at school themselves, and this may fuel the desire to want to make a difference to a child who might be like themselves.	

targets and know that they will be inspected against these targets. This means that agencies themselves have a vested interest in primary school involvement. So, for each arrow going out from the mentor, another should be fed back in, showing requests from agencies for schools, via the mentor, to do something for the agency. Interviews later in the book show this as individuals talk about the importance of their link with the school mentor. There is a concern that this could result in some agencies 'delegating' responsibilities to the schools for which the agency itself has, or should have, the specific professional expertise. Depending on local relationships, the mentors may get these calls to action directly, or they may be fed through from headteachers' briefings.

4.   School councils also provide a useful way of listening to children's voices. One of the mentors mentioned the school council taking a survey on traffic for the local authority. This of course can be greatly empowering, but it can also be a paper exercise and I expect most readers have been involved with closed-question consultations, when the response is so closely controlled that the result is a foregone conclusion. This is as transparent to children as it is to us, and simply teaches apathy, rather than empowerment.

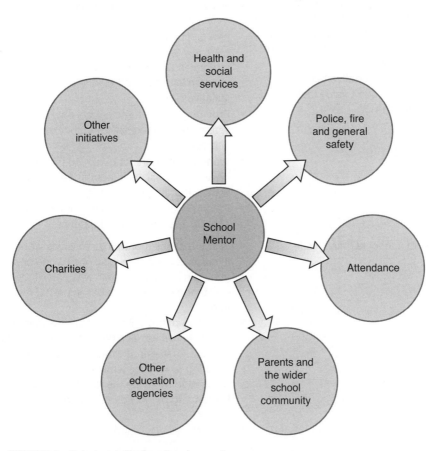

FIGURE 8.1   Role description for a learning mentor

As with the interviews with the TAs, the most surprising and optimistic finding for me was both the enthusiasm the mentors had in their work and their faith in the schools in which they worked, to break down barriers to learning and make a difference to children's lives. Table 8.2 provides a summary of the barriers to learning mentioned by mentors and the strategies.

TABLE 8.2 Barriers and strategies identified by mentors

BARRIERS IDENTIFIED	STRATEGIES IDENTIFIED
Home environment and cultural norms. Interestingly, the focus here was far more supportive towards parents than those in the previous chapter, and this may be linked with mentors having very much more involvement with parents. Quotes included: • 'parents who were let down by the system, who cannot see that their children will do any better'; • 'parents who love their children but do not/unable to parent'; • the most negative being 'parents don't value their children'	• Mentors were doing a lot of work in this area. • The parent mentor's work involved a large number of strategies, supported by her LA, which tackled this directly. • All mentors involved with building up informal relationships with parents/carers as on the yard before and after school, walking to school with parents, knowing parents by name. • Raising aspirations of parents/carers so they can raisen aspirations for their children; recognition that emotional health and literacy were key features in this and working on strategies through PSE initiatives with the children as well as other whole school initiatives. • Providing a structured school environment, where children feel safe and they can function and achieve. • Working with parents/carers so that they can have some positive expectations of what they want out of the education system. • Parents'/carers' room so they have a place in school, and activities around this.
Nature of school learning itself	• In some cases mentors themselves working in classrooms with pupils, one to one or small group; in some cases this was part of their mentoring role, in some cases part of the TA role. • Provision of pre-school, lunch-time and after-school activities; also residential and day trips to broaden views of what learning involved. • Creating reward systems, e.g. sports, which can be used to motivate the reluctant learner. • Building up of individual relationships.

TABLE 8.2 (continued)

BARRIERS IDENTIFIED	STRATEGIES IDENTIFIED
Attendance	• Apart from the parent mentor, all mentors interviewed had this as one of their main roles – to monitor, respond and liaise with other agencies; all operated a first-response system and had a recognised system of rewards for improved attendance. • One mentor raised queries about the need to challenge the current national response to registering whole school attendance, which tended to overemphasise the few families with deeply embedded issues regarding attendance.
More independence among pupils	• Establishment of 'Pupils' voice', including school councils, LA parliaments. • Empowering initiatives, such as 'eco-cycling', fundraising. • Mentoring and acting as buddies. • PSHE initiatives – some mentors involved with working on this programme directly.
Medical needs, including mental health	• Establishment of nurture groups and general training needed on mental health issues.
Raising aspirations	• Looking more closely at aspirations that are just limited to 'having a baby'; discussing children's out-of-school experience. • Involvement in widening participation initiatives. • Broadening horizons – visits.
Conflicting views with other agencies regarding safeguarding, including neglect	• This seems to be in its early stages as the learning mentors gather informal evidence about the operational – as opposed to the strategic – process, e.g. searching procedures, readiness of social services to intervene or be able to intervene.

9

'An Exceptional Pastoral Care Team': A Case Study

The exceptional pastoral care team, in providing a 'team around the child,' ensures every pupil and their family receive support immediately it is needed.

This is an outstanding school which successfully lives out its belief that 'everyone matters'.

(Ofsted report 2009)

Chapter overview

- This is a short case study to describe a fairly unusual pastoral care team that was set up in a primary school in an area of high social disadvantage

- It is directly linked to trying to break down barriers to learning, through its multiskilled team approach to identifying barriers and working through strategies to lift them

- It tries to avoid the sanitised format of so many case studies that find their way on to government websites and in good practice guidelines

- Hopefully, this case study reflects the reality of why Ofsted describes this team as outstanding and digs a little deeper to explain a number of factors as to why it is so successful.

The team

The school is a faith school, very open to those of us who visit without faith, but deeply committed to its mission 'that the Governors and Staff in partnership with parents aim to help each child realise its full Spiritual, Moral, Academic and Social Potential in a happy caring Catholic Community in which every member feels valued'.

The Pastoral Support Group meets monthly, in a small room that is set aside for such purposes, and comprises the school's learning mentor (LM), the higher level teaching assistant (HLTA), a family support worker, a counsellor, an educational psychologist, the school nurse and the deputy headteacher.

Table 9.1 identifies the different employing agencies involved. This marks readiness to consider flexibility in employment practices from the headteacher and the governing body, and also the headteachers and governing bodies of the other schools involved. Anyone who has ever sat on a school governing body knows that such arrangements are often not easy to make or maintain; they need to be worked at and part of this case study is to demonstrate that such working formats enable schools to look 'outside the box'. This is crucial to the success of pastoral support groups, who have fully trained counsellors and family workers. Large secondary schools can, and often do, employ counsellors, but most primary schools could not sustain these on full-time payment.

Box 9.1 provides a disguised version of the agenda of the pastoral team meeting that I attended. It is hoped that this will give a flavour of the discussion, although it cannot provide the in-depth expertise used to discuss strategies to support children and families.

Many years ago I was a social worker and have therefore great sympathy with Social Services. This meeting drew my attention to how family issues had changed over the years. Drugs, which had been a relatively minor issue when I was involved in family social work, were now a major issue for primary schools in terms of both children's knowledge and involvement in substance misuse. The previous chapter identified that police experience, as relayed to mentors, was that primary children were being used to buy and sell drugs. The legality of alcohol misuse is clearly an issue with those who look at domestic violence, but the concerns with mentors and this pastoral team for primary children related to classified substances, drug raids etc. These issues must be influencing how whole communities of children prioritise their lives. I have no doubt that both what the mentors reported in the previous chapter and what was raised at this meeting were just tips of an iceberg regarding the influence of substance misuse within communities.

And for primary children, what does it mean? A detailed deconstruction of a literacy text may be completely lost on a child who has been up all night listening to issues that are well beyond their control. It is often difficult for professionals to accept that children can love and want to protect parents who seem to break every single rule

TABLE 9.1 Employing agencies that are involved in the school pastoral support group

DIRECTLY BY THE SCHOOL	IN PARTNERSHIP WITH TWO OTHER PRIMARY SCHOOLS	IN PARTNERSHIP WITH ONE OTHER PRIMARY SCHOOL AND PART FUNDED BY A FAITH CHARITY	EMPLOYED BY THE PCT
Deputy headteacher (full-time) Learning mentor (part-time) Behaviour mentor (part-time)	Family school worker, covering three schools on 0.6 time	Counsellor	Educational psychologist School nurse

Box 9.1 Exemplar agenda for pastoral support monthly meeting

Minutes of meeting: date

Present

Learning mentor (LM)
Behaviour mentor (BM)
Educational psychologist (EP)
Family social worker (FSW)
Counsellor (C)
Deputy head (DH)
School nurse (SN)

Apologies

SN, and ?

Issues arising

Review of minutes from previous meeting

- AB – Awaiting date for a TAC meeting.
- BC settled in nursery – no major concerns. FSW to run parenting meetings and involve BC's mother, in May, at this school. His older brother (Year 4) – to work with LM, and TAs using SEAL. Ask Sr. T to get involved.
- CD – Child who has attended three primary schools already and has been identified as autistic.

Year R:

- EF – Awaiting speech and language report and review (vocal cords issue).
- GH – Contact advisor for hearing impaired, discuss with parent, still awaiting speech and language report, other report needed for enhanced provision.
- IJ – CAF completed. Needs parenting support.
- KL – LM working with, as sibling in neonatal intensive care unit.

Year 1:

- DH to monitor,
- MN – Concerns remain – EP to assess. ST has seen family and NNEB should be involved. DH and C have met with mother. Noted that noise and change in routine can trigger poor behaviour. To look for any other triggers. Issues because student teacher will be put into this class that will create changes in class routine.
- OP – DH to monitor and identify whether speech therapy required.
- QR – Class teacher to continue to monitor and use DLT form to identify whether ADHD. *(Discussion at meeting itself because this child had a Dad who was a Dad to several other children in the school. He picked up some of these, i.e. of current partner, but left others behind.)*

Box 9.1 (continued)

- ST – All to monitor because social services have been involved in the past and although a closed case now, the class teacher has identified issues of concern and would like parents to be involved. Child speaks about mice in the house.
- UV – Learning support from LA requested an issue here because the LA will only assess and advise and the pastoral team is unhappy about this rather hidden change in practice. At one time more support would have been given.

Year 4:

- WX – Mum has asked the GP to make referral to psychiatrist as concerned over her behaviour. (There are two children in the family who are well known to the team. The mother is currently involved in a lesbian relationship, which is known among the children in school. She is also suffering from depression and the team discusses whether family therapy might be useful as one of the children also seems to be depressed.)
- YZ – The head has spoken with the mother, who seems more involved in YZ's schooling than in the past. Strategies to put in place re. classroom support.
- New concerns for child in Year 4 – BM and class teacher providing support. The class teacher to be part of the group with the counsellor and family support worker to speak with the parents about the fears the child seems to be having about death.
- Explore possibility of support for parents of A, B, C, D, E, F to identify their needs. Possibility of a parenting group, prior to the one planned for May and group therapy. (*Discussion at meeting re. links with the women's centre and generally raising parent self-esteem, so they believed that they had power to change events in their own and their children's lives.*)
- EP identified courses for team to look at re. mental health.

Other issues arising

- Year 5 child – Identified drugs in the house, Catholic agency became involved and referred to social services as agency interpreted as child protection issue. The house was untidy and there was evidence of several siblings with neglect. Led to general discussion re. under staffing of social services and difficulty in out of hours support.
- Year 6 child asking to go into care.

that professionals hold. One of the most impressive aspects of this particular meeting was the awareness of positive aspects of different family structures, and the inside knowledge of the community within which these families operated.

Interviews with members of the Pastoral Support Group

I interviewed two members of this group: the family support worker and the counsellor.

Box 9.2 Family support worker: job description

Job Description

Family Support Worker

This covers three primary partnership schools: St A's & B & C Community Primary Schools, which serve the community of D. We aim together to work with children and their families to help build a stronger, more supportive community.

LOCATION: Primarily at St A's but working through each of the partnership schools

JOB TITLE: Family Support Worker 0.6 part-time

STRUCTURE: St A's Headteacher
⠀⠀⠀⠀⠀⠀⠀⠀⠀⠀B's and C's headteachers
⠀⠀⠀⠀⠀⠀⠀⠀⠀⠀Individual schools' pastoral support teams
⠀⠀⠀⠀⠀⠀⠀⠀⠀⠀Family support worker

ACCOUNTABLE FOR: None

ACCOUNTABLE TO: St A's headteacher

GENERAL PURPOSE OF THE POST

The Family Support Worker works as part of a dedicated team, delivering together or working alone with the family a package of supportive interventions which encourage good parenting, goal setting, meeting of necessary appointments, improving school attendance, celebrating achievements and marking milestones. As part of the team, this will include attendance at and participation in Child Concern meetings, being actively engaged with the Common Assessment Framework and working on agreed goals within Initial Assessments provide by the referrer.

COMMUNICATION

The worker must:

- Report to the line management for regular supervision as per partnership schools agreement
- Report regularly on work undertaken and discuss all planned work with the line manager as per partnership schools agreement to ensure that it meets with their requirements.
- Ensure that all child protection concerns are reported in accordance with the policies and procedure of the schools
- Communicate regularly with other members of staff about issues relating to his/ her work where it affects the schools as a whole and the work of others within it.
- Raise awareness of the schools' work with other agencies and develop and maintain supportive networks for such work with local statutory and third sector agencies and groups as required.
- Contribute to the development of each Partnership School through attendance at staff meetings, etc., as necessary.

Box 9.2 (continued)

RELATIONSHIPS

Develop close working relationships with:
- Partnership Schools' team staff and volunteers
- Staff and volunteers in X Local Authority
- Children and families involved in partnership schools
- Key stakeholders in X
- All other staff and volunteers
- Other agencies working with the same family as part of the Child Concern Model or similar intervention

KEY TASKS

The Family Support Worker will:

- Attend team meetings and contribute positively to action plans for referred families
- Work on allocated pieces of work as agreed and report on these using data management systems (paper and electronic)
- Visit families in their homes and attend necessary appointments in fulfilment of agreed action plan
- Contribute to assessments and action plans as per the Common Assessment Framework
- Attend meetings concerning the referred family as required (e.g. Child Concern Meetings, Case Conferences, Teams around the Child/Family, etc.)
- Ensure participation of children and young people and their parent(s)/carer(s), wherever appropriate
- Provide a safe and ensure a safe and supportive environment for families to engage with the project
- Promote personal development and growth of family members
- Refer families on to other voluntary or statutory services as appropriate
- Undertake general administrative tasks related to the post including using Microsoft Office
- Prepare monitoring and other reports as required
- Undertake training as necessary to ensure competence to fulfil these responsibilities
- Ensure that the project is characterised by anti-oppressive and antidiscriminatory practice for all those involved
- Ensure that service users have access to an effective means of expressing grievances and complaints
- Keep all records in accordance with statutory and internal requirements and best practice
- Ensure that the project is delivered in line with the policies and procedures of the schools
- Meet and uphold the objects and ethos of the schools

Box 9.2 (continued)

ADDITIONAL DUTIES

It is the nature of the work of the Partnership Schools that tasks and responsibilities are in many circumstances, unpredictable and varied. All staff are, therefore, expected to work in a flexible way when the occasion arises, when tasks not specifically covered in their job description have to be undertaken. These additional duties will normally be to cover unforeseen circumstances or changes in work and they will normally be compatible with the regular type of work. If the additional responsibility or task becomes a regular or frequent part of the member of staff's job, it will be included in the job description in consultation with the member of staff.

CONFIDENTIALITY

All employees adhere to the confidentiality of the Partnership Schools.

BASIC PRINCIPLES

The postholder is expected to be familiar with and have regard to the Basic Principles of the Partnership Schools and work within that framework. He/she must be prepared to operate within faith and community organisations, without prejudice to all who would use our services or work with the organisations at any level.

CONDITIONS OF SERVICE

The Conditions of Service are broadly in line with those set out by the National Joint Council for Local Government Services.

PROBATIONARY PERIOD

The Partnership Schools have a probationary period of 3 months.

Lisa: family support worker

See Box 9.2 for details of Lisa's job description. This is probably one of those job descriptions that make you look twice at the responsibility involved. And, also, it says a great deal about the ability of the three headteachers involved, in that they were able to find such a skilled, committed and confident individual to take on the post.

Lisa's story

Lisa had a conventional start to her career. She trained as a teacher and then worked in a high school, teaching cookery and needlework for five years. During this time she had three children, and started to work part-time with adults with special needs, as well as in a young offenders' institute. Her work at the institute involved pre-release courses, practical craft, food and food hygiene. She then moved into residential education, full-time, and spent ten years doing this. It became more difficult as the target group behaviours became more extreme. During this time, she found that she was enjoying the pastoral care side much more than the food technology and science and was seconded to a high school, in another area, to set up provision for students with educational difficulties. This was funded by the Home Office, as it was hoped it would cut down on crime in the area. Although she was seconded to one school, the secondment covered three high schools and this later became part of an Excellence in Cities Cluster. She took on the post on for three years under the funding of the Behaviour Improvement Project (BIP). When this funding finished, she applied for this post.

Lisa's role

See Box 9.2 for details. Initially, she had to spend a lot of time networking to build up links between different agencies. This was helped by the fact that she lived relatively locally and had worked in local schools.

She took over responsibility for the common assessment framework (CAF) for all three of the schools and this has become an important part of the role, for which there has been no training. She was helped by fact that in the past she had developed a multi-agency assessment and referral form (MAARF), which was a means of getting a case opened by Social Services. She had also done quite a bit of work on child protection, so was therefore very familiar with the procedures.

Lisa explained that this particular LA had appointed two CAF co-ordinators. They held all the CAFs and now delivered training on the CAF as part of the LA safeguarding procedures.

She also worked with other agencies such as Action Rights for Children (ARCH) who work with alcohol misuse, adult learning groups, and branches of different children's charities. The key message of all of these organisations is that it is always OK to ask for help.

Lisa also works with the growing number of children's centres and liaises with the support workers there. Locally, there are also a number of other groups with whom she liaises:

1. The Child Development Centre
2. A RISO group (Children at Risk of Offending)
3. Family Intervention Project (FIP), which provides an outreach support service
4. Community Safety Team
5. Police, police community support officers
6. Connexions, the government agency that provides careers, counselling and advice service for those between 13 and 19 years
7. Children and Young People's Area Network (CYPAN): most of the funding comes from CYPAN, along with some from one of the primary schools
8. The local Premier League football team
9. Church organisations
10. 'Mind, Exercise, Nutrition . . . Do it!' (MEND), which is lottery funded
11. The local community centre and the women's centre, and there is also a local relationship centre.

At the moment Lisa has a case-load of nineteen families at this school.

Most proud of

1. Learning to have the tenacity and patience to keep with children, even when it looked very difficult.

2. And, perhaps the most important thing of all, to be able to see success when able to break a cycle of events.

Areas for development

■   Lisa would like time to look at, and learn more about, group therapy and practice. This would also include working on parenting courses, initially as an observer and then helping to deliver them. She has identified a specific course that lasts for 6 weeks and involves 2 hours of work per week.

■   Looking at a summer school programme for families that struggle during this time.

■   Involvement in cookery classes, because they involve both one-to-one working and also getting children to work together.

Barriers to learning

■   Children coming into school who have not slept and have not been fed. Many of these children have come from homes where there is known substance misuse and sometimes children disclose this without realising it. They come from this background into school, where they are expected to learn, sit down calmly to tackle their maths and talk to order. School does often provide the one settled calm environment in their lives and Lisa feels that her school is really good at providing the additional support that so many of them need.

■   The need for children's homes to have an environment that is conducive to learning – even something as simple as having books for the children to read and taking the children out for visits. Obviously, this can be very difficult for parents, especially a single parent who is living in a small housing space with six children under the age of 11 years.

Lisa also reminded me of the Star Fish theory. The Star Fish story is a simple one. A boy stands on a beach and around him are hundreds of stranded star fish. He is picking one up at a time and throwing it back into the sea. A man comes to talk to him and asks him what he is doing. The boy explains that the star fish are stranded and he is throwing them back into the water so that they will not die. The man laughs and says that the boy cannot hope to throw them all back. The boy looks at the man carefully, bends down, picks up another star fish and throws it back into the sea. Then he says to the man, 'Well I did make a difference to that one.'

Perhaps this theory is the one that really drives those TAs and LMs whom I interviewed in Chapters 7 and 8. It is a belief, or philosophy, that we may not be able to make a difference to every single child, but we can make a difference to some. This may be why many chose to stay at operational levels within services, rather than move on to beaches where there are no star fish to save.

Mary: school counsellor

Mary started working life as a paediatric nurse then became a religious sister. She had then started to go into primary schools to work voluntarily and had chosen challenging schools like this one. As a result of this experience she had noted the difficulties involved in the transition between primary and secondary schools and later became a chaplain in a secondary school. This provided the opportunity to go into feeder primary schools and work with Year 6 children. This enabled her to get to know them all, so that when they went to the secondary school, she would be there for them. Through this she had met the deputy head at this particular primary school and began working more closely with her.

The school decided to pilot a particular personal, social and health education (PSHE) programme and this was undertaken by the deputy, the counsellor and someone from one of the partnership HE institutions that were involved in the evaluation. She trained as a counsellor and as this increased her workload it meant that she had to give up being a nurse. The PSHE programme was very going well, and she went to Canada to learn how to train teachers in the programme.

This primary school then became part of an extended schools initiative, which involved the Catholic Children's Society. Mary then applied for, and got, the post as a school counsellor and has held this post since 2003. The extended schools' service in this school came very much from the grass roots, as parents had become much more involved through the PSHE programme. It developed well before the government's guidelines about core offers of care from 8.00 am to 6.00 pm.

Mary's formal role was to provide counselling for parents and children, so it resulted in seeing a mixture of adults and children. Many of the adults had come to this school as pupils themselves and so they had a strong connection. Mary also sees those who may not have children at the school, but have nephews and nieces. She has close links with the school nurse, who comes in nearly every week. The local health centre is opposite the school and this enables good links with the health visitor.

Mary works as a person-centred counsellor, using techniques developed by Carl Rogers. This is long term, enabling children to self-refer, and they do this. It is seen as a normal thing in this school and there is no stigma attached. Like the LM in the school, her relationship with the children is on first-name terms.

Mary worked in two primary schools at the time of the interview. This involved at least one day per week for each school and approximately 20 hours per week. The total number of hours is subject to funding, which comes from the Children's and Young People's Plan (CYPP). The third primary school in this particular group has its own counsellor who is funded as part of the extended schools programme. This school used its funding for a mobile extension unit, which gave space for a breakfast club and parents' drop-in centre with some café facilities. Mary's current case-load at the school involves four children and three adults (the adults are not the parents of the children).

Most proud of

- Working as part of a wonderful team, in which there is support and trust. Mary feels valued, considered and enabled. It then becomes possible to feel pride in the work done, comfortable in the way in which it is organised and confident that it is making a difference to the children and adults involved. The school is a real community and faith school. When events happen, whether they are happy or sad, the school community is involved.

- Looked-after children (LAC). For a term and a half, Mary has worked with a child who had showed very difficult and challenging behaviour. She came into the school twice per week and helped the child to make the transition to another school. This school made a massive commitment to this individual child.

- Mary is really proud of the way in which this pastoral team works. The fact that it is well attended by many very busy people and it is truly multidisciplined. This includes going on courses; for example, three members of the team attended a course on autism, while others attended, and fed back on, a course on setting up a nurture group.

- Mary also recognises and values the fact that her own expertise is used.

Development

- The role is changing and developing; the pastoral support group has realised that parenting groups were not a first step, because some parents needed more small group therapy support before they were ready to join a parenting group. This has to be part of a dialogue in to building up self-esteem and self-worth, so that these very vulnerable parents can feel part of a parenting group, rather than threatened.

Barriers to learning

- Separation and loss experienced in children's lives
- Lack of safety
- Need to be loved.

Mary feels very strongly that the person-centred therapy, which she trained in, offers unconditional, positive regard to these children, as well as the need to delight. It provides a strong framework for helping children and parents in the often chaotic world in which they live.

Possible reasons for the success of the pastoral support team

1. Ofsted also identified inspirational leadership within the school, and an exceptionally caring and dedicated staff with outstanding achievement. It is certainly a leadership that has been dedicated to working through many potential difficulties to create an exceptionally well-skilled pastoral team. Partnerships and funding have been used creatively.

2. The team is a genuine team, in which those employed by other agencies are made to feel part of the life of the school.

3. Employment of a school-based counsellor and family support worker. Schools are the point of contact for many families and having such services within the school means that access is much easier.

4. The willingness of all those involved to put in so much time, enthusiasm and skill. As was clear in the meeting I attended, this was aided by the 'can do' culture of the school.

5. And, I add this with some personal reservation as a person without faith, I did feel that the faith ethos in this school was a truly uniting feature of the success of the team.

10

Attendance, Health and Study Support

Opening up the community for children.

(Study Support Officer)

Chapter overview

- Review the work of some of the local authority (LA) support services in relation to school attendance, promoting children's health and generally raising barriers for children's learning.

Introduction

One of the key features of the work of learning mentors was to work to monitor children's attendance at school. Non-attendance, for whatever reason, is a major barrier to learning. In Table 2.1 we saw the worst-case scenario of a poor attender. It showed the typical prison offender profile as someone who has missed school and/ or had been expelled from school, along with the huge numbers of prisoners with low literacy and numeracy levels. This chapter looks at Richard's work as a school attendance case worker, as an example of how one LA tackles the problem of truancy. Other LAs will have different methods of doing this, but truancy is given high priority in all schools at which attendance falls below the national average.

The 'Every Child Matters' (ECM) agenda quite rightly gave health a high priority, and we all know from our own experience that lack of good health can be a major barrier to learning. This chapter also looks at the work of a school nurse and also that of a LA manager of the Healthy Schools Project. Closely linked to health is activity, and the way in which one local authority is managing the National Schools Sport Partnership is described. Attendance, health and participatory sport all open up new worlds for children. Annie's work as a Study Support Community is also about opening up the community for children, and using different streams of money to help raise barriers to learning among the most vulnerable primary children. Jennifer is involved more specifically in the extended schools support and is far more critical of the provision provided through a private company commissioned by the LA.

Richard: school attendance case worker

The job of monitoring school attendance is nothing new; by the 1900s, schools employed people to walk the streets looking for children who should be in school. Victorian school logbooks record children being taken out of school for child care, planting potatoes and harvesting. So Richard follows a long history of workers who are committed to getting the unwilling into school.

Like many others interviewed, Richard's career was also an unconventional one. He started as a drayman and then worked on building sites. He then did a degree and started to work in a school as a teaching assistant (TA) with a child with cerebral palsy. From this he moved into training to be a secondary teacher, but, although he passed the course, he decided it was not for him. He said that he did not believe that he could help the children to learn. During that time, he did meet some wonderful teachers, who could get respect and did not bully the children into submission, but he did not feel that they were supported by the secondary system. While on his final teaching practice, Richard met an education welfare officer (EWO) who really enjoyed his job, and it was at this time that he applied for and succeeded in getting his current post.

Box 10.1 sets out the formal description of Richard's principal duties and responsibilities. As a case worker, Richard is given a case-load, based on the attendance rate of schools he covers. Currently, he covers two secondary schools and eight primary schools. In his LA there is a strict procedure that must be followed when a child's attendance falls below a specific level:

Box 10.1 Principal duties and responsibilities of a school attendance case worker

- To liaise with School Attendance Improvement Officers (SAIOs), to maintain a caseload and work programme identified in conjunction with schools
- To liaise with the SAIO in the preparation of case notes, files and in the collation and presentation of information and reports for a variety of purposes
- To develop good relationships between home and school, and undertake home visits
- To contribute to effective interagency work
- To participate in a regular cycle of supervision and in-service training
- To demonstrate a commitment to anti-oppressive practice
- To uphold equal opportunities in employment, in advice and in-service delivery
- To comply with all the requirements of Health & Safety legislation and Council Policy, taking appropriate action where necessary
- To comply with all the Council's Standing Orders and financial regulations
- To carry out duties requested by the Director of Education and Lifelong Learning commensurate with the grading of the post.

- *Stage 1: When absences start to occur.* The school will contact the parents by phone or letter.
- *Stage 2: When absences continue.* School will support the child and monitor their progress. The parents may be invited in for a meeting.
- *Stage 3: When the situation does not improve.* The school will inform the School Attendance Service and an officer will visit the parents and make an assessment. The headteacher or deputy will also contact the parents. Richard pointed out that, in practice, this was usually the learning mentor, and the School Attendance Service meets weekly with the learning mentors.
- *Stage 4: When stages 1–3 have not brought about an improvement.* At this stage any further absences will not be authorised by school. The school attendance case worker will work with the parent for 6 weeks and support them in improving the child's attendance. This could include home visits, meetings, phone calls, referrals, etc.
- *Stage 5: When no improvement occurs despite all of the above.* The case will be transferred to the school attendance improvement officer for possible prosecution. This could mean a fine or imprisonment resulting in a criminal record for the parent.

Richard's job is to go out to the family concerned and communicate issues, which include the legal commitment for their children to attend school. This also involves making sure that parents are aware that their children are off school. This aspect of his work involves looking in detail at the barriers to the child's attendance and is reviewed every 6 weeks (half termly).

It all has to be evidenced carefully, and a balance is struck between providing support and the law, which can be a dilemma. The case worker's evidence is checked thoroughly and the senior attendance officer (SAO) uses it to prepare a file for prosecution. This does actually happen, although more in secondary than in primary schools, and incidences are increasing. Richard has found horrifying circumstances when working with some young parents and the associated difficulties with children.

Richard is also part of a team responsible for delivering Safeguarding and Awareness training to everyone in the LA. He also carries responsibility for licensing and performance work in schools.

Most proud of

See Figure 10.1 for an overview of what Richard feels most proud of in his current post.

Areas for development

- Increasingly, key managers, who are not involved at the operational level, are creating strategies that cannot work in practice.
- There are not enough resources. Six months ago, the pay for case workers was effectively cut by only paying them for working term times. This actually meant a cutback in the team's ability to be able to do the family case work because this

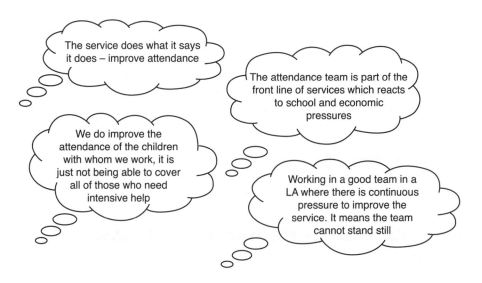

FIGURE 10.1 What Richard is most proud of

was often done during school holidays. Sadly for Richard, because he had said from the start that he had really loved the job, the effective pay cut meant that he applied for other jobs and was moving in the next month to a post in the same field but paying £11,000 more. His political stance on this was that people in this team were simply seen as the tools, whereas the investment seemed to be in structures and systems analysis.

Barriers to learning

1. Richard identified the nature of schooling itself as a barrier for learning for some children and felt that its language, activities, resource choice and use were middle class. The standard assessment tasks/tests (SATs) had also narrowed the curriculum. This meant that children living in households with lower income had a higher level of deprivation because the schooling system did not reflect their lives. He knew that the hard data available confirmed that the higher the household income the more likely it was that the children could gain more out of the education system, despite the fact that the education system should be open and accessible to all. Several of the comments made by children and recorded in the introduction are closely linked to mismatch between rules, routines and regulations in their world outside school and that within it. Richard felt there were real contradictions in the system but remained hopeful that he and others could make a difference to children's lives.

2. Large numbers in classes made it harder for one teacher to make a difference to 25–30 pupils, with so many vastly different learning needs.

3. Parents do not have time to do many of the things a parent needs to do or the government seems to expect them to do. There is still a cycle of deprivation, not aided by single parents being encouraged to go into low-paid work.

4. He also felt that an attitude of resilience to life challenges provided by religion had gone and had not been replaced by anything.

Richard was, indeed, one of the very few whom I interviewed who took a political stance to identifying barriers to learning. He described many of the same barriers that LMs and TAs had done, but put them within a political and historical context. He used very much the same language and research evidence that is used in Part 1 of this book. It was also interesting that finding someone to interview from an attendance team was ironically one of the hardest interviews to arrange as I was moved up from one managerial level to another. There was a level of anxiety about taking responsibility for such an interview, which surprised me.

Stasia: public health nurse/specialist community public health nurse

The ECM website on school nursing has not been updated since 2007, which is quite surprising considering that its first statement under the heading of school nurses is how well placed school nurses were to deliver many of the ECM outcomes for children in *The ECM: Change for Children Programme*; the *National Service Framework for Children*; *Young People and Maternity Services*; and the public health paper *Choosing Health*.

There is a best practice guidance on the website *Schooling Nursing – The Practice Development Resource Pack*, directed at the Specialist Community Public Health Nurse. This indicates a change in title for some of those trained nurses who in the past would have been called *school nurses*. This pack is very much about updating the 2001 guidance for school nurses in relation to the ECM agenda. On one page it covers the role of the school nurse and then looks quite briefly at a child-centred public health approach, how to 'deliver' on health priorities, an audit tool and a development plan. This looked as if, and Stasia implied that, the investment was in structure and systems analysis rather than in human resources, despite the hope in the guidance that Primary Care Trusts (PCTs) would employ more school nurses. There are some short case studies provided in guidance, which give some useful examples of what is possible when PCTs are committed to investing money in the service.

Stasia had undertaken general nurse training 20 years ago and then worked in accident and emergency for 12 years. While doing this, she was seconded to do a diploma in children's nursing, which lasted a year and gave her experience of working in children's wards. It was after this that she became a school nurse and undertook specialised practitioner training in school nursing. Public health was an important part of this specialist training. To follow the specialist practitioner courses, nurses were required to have at least diploma-level qualifications and the practitioner is at degree or postgraduate level.

Figure 10.2 shows the way in which this particular PCT organises its staff. Most school nurses are responsible for a number of primary and secondary schools and work in a team. The LA and the PCT cover exactly the same population in this area

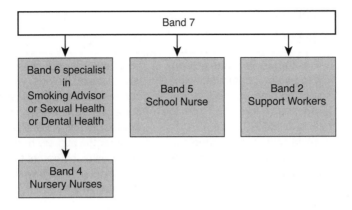

FIGURE 10.2 The organisation of Stasia's school nursing team – the higher the band, the higher the qualifications of the post-holder

and there are four teams. Each one has a nursery nurse, whose key role is health promotion within the school.

The role of support workers (Band 2) is an interesting one and demonstrates the strategic decision to invest in support workers, rather than trained nurses, in order to cover the screening requirements. This involves measuring height, weight and vision, at particular points in a child's school life. They are not nurses, and are just trained for this screening. If there are problems, they feed back to the school nurse. All of the training for these support workers is in-house and it is possible for them to gain an NVQ. In this particular PCT, support workers are placed on Band 2; in other PCTs they might be in Band 3. Nursery nurses are on Band 4 and school nurses on Band 5. This is an interesting contrast to the nursery nurse in Chapter 7, who worked in schools as a TA and was paid on Band 3. The specialist practitioner is on Band 6 and the role carries a specific focus that is shared across the different teams: in Stasia's case this is sexual and dental health. She also carries the child protection/safeguarding role and essentially this has become the bulk of her work. This team is managed by a team manager at Band 7, who will be a nurse, and, again, much of their work is also around safeguarding – attending Social Services meetings concerning children and families who are a cause for concern and/or are on the risk register. The Band 6 school nurse has responsibility for looked-after children (LAC) and writes their reports and does their annual assessment. Table 10.1 shows the regular input by the school nursing team.

Stasia feels that the strengths of current provision are:

- Good relationships with 'learning mentors who seem to know everything about the cause for concern families'.
- The teaching sessions, particularly around puberty, when the children are really interested and ask good questions. Parents are reassured and it provides an

TABLE 10.1 School health team input into primary schools

AGE OF CHILD	SERVICE	COMMENTS
Reception	1. Health questionnaire given out to parents, combined with screening programme 2. Separate information from the health visitor 3. Child screened in school for height, weight, body mass index (BMI) and vision by support workers; *audio screening is separate*	75% return for questionnaire and issues raised include: weight concern and bed-wetting; the school nurse will make the decision about whether to call in parents and decide whether the nursery nurse or school nurse visits the home; the health visitor will provide any safeguarding information
Year 2	Screening for vision	–
Year 5	Dental health promotion team deliver sessions	This team is not part of the school health team and is linked directly to the PCT dental service; schools are asked to contact them separately
Year 6	Screening for height, weight and BMI	–

The healthy schools programme is now based on training schools to deliver the programme, but several schools still contact the school nurse for the sexual health input. When schools do this, it will probably be the nursery nurse who does the input. She will also often be involved in a parents' meeting, prior to speaking to the children. It is hoped that by training up individual teachers or learning mentors in primary schools to take responsibility for the healthy school programme will embed health issues within the curriculum. The team believe that added-on inputs do not embed the issues.

opportunity to refer some of the issues raised by parents (which may not be on sexual health) on to others.

- When it is possible to make a regular time to be in the school, so that parents, children and staff know when you are there. It becomes more informal and Stasia felt it made her part of the school. Unfortunately, she could no longer do this on a regular basis because of the time taken up with the safeguarding procedures and paperwork.

- Parents often seem happier to contact the school nurse than education or social care professionals, as the school nurse is regarded less suspiciously.

Areas for development

- General partnership between health services and education in her authority are good. Relationships with individual schools tend to be more ad hoc and the time allowance can be limited and more task-related than it was 5 years ago.

- Health visitors have responsibility for the under-5s and their records are based with the GP practice. This can make liaison frustrating, but hopefully IT may be able to provide this information to the school.

Barriers to learning

- Children who should wear glasses who don't take them to school. This is often children from vulnerable families and Stasia felt it would make sense to have two pairs of glasses, one for home and one for school. Interestingly, several of the children mentioned in Part 1 identified with this.

- High dental problems in the area. Over 60 per cent of the under-5s have dental decay and poor dental health continues into primary school. It is taken very lightly by parents/carers, many of whom have had false teeth from a very early age. Poor dental health often means that children take time off school because they are in pain or just do not feel well.

- Stasia knows that problems with health are preventing learning, and identification of these is heavily dependent on teachers. Children cannot be helped unless their needs are identified.

This interview was one of the greatest surprises to me, because I had assumed that trained school nurses were regular visitors in school. From this interview, I learnt that unless school nurses had a regular time to go into a school, many children and their parents might never meet one. The safeguarding element of the ECM agenda has essentially taken trained nurses away from the schools. The delegation of the healthy schools programme, to a single trained person in school, has had a similar effect.

Stasia acknowledged that health needs may be preventing learning and that it was down to teachers to recognise health issues within their classes. This worried me – from my own experience I know that teacher training has only a small input on issues such as healthy schools. As a fairly experienced primary specialist and parent, I am certainly not confident that I would be able to identify all health issues evidenced by children in classes I know, in particular mental health issues. The QTS Standards focus on professional attributes, professional knowledge and understanding and professional skills. There is very little here about health.

The under-5s have, in most areas, a well-skilled health link worker, who is provided through the health visiting service and is provided for both children and parents/carers in the under-5s preschool settings. It is worrying that those over 5 years are so heavily dependent on their schools and parents for the identification of health needs.

One of the features of the case study in the previous chapter was that the school had a school nurse in their pastoral support team and the nurse was certainly present in the school at least once a month. This was in a different LA and indicates the difference between investment in the number of trained school nurses.

Naseem: healthy schools manager

Naseem had been a secondary teacher for 20 years and, although she started with teaching design/technology, she found herself gradually doing more pastoral work. Eventually, she was responsible for, and teaching all, PSHE throughout the school. She felt she was lucky to work in this particular LA, which placed a big emphasis on health, as in 1995 this was unusual. Partly as a result of this, she took a part-time secondment, which was funded by the local Community Trust (later to become a

PCT). It initially involved a 2-days-a-week secondment, and later 3 days per week, on the National Healthy School programme. This eventually became a full-time post, but funding was mixed and she was employed by her LA in both the Education and Health departments. This position has been made easier with the establishment of one Directorate under the remit of Integrated Children's Services.

Her current role is to manage the Healthy Schools Programme and this involves being on a number of key health-related committees, which include the Drugs Action Team; the SEAL steering group; PSHE coordination; the teenage pregnancy team; the Partnership Board for Healthy Schools; and the School Health Service. The most recent initiative from central government has been a population monitoring exercise looking at obesity levels, with screenings at reception and Year 6. This had involved Naseem in becoming more involved with the relatively recently appointed School Sports Coordinator.

As manager for the healthy schools programme she also participates in other central government initiatives to ensure that both primary and secondary schools are involved. These include:

1. *Safer Schools programme*, for which police officers are based in secondary schools and spend some time working in their feeder primary schools.

2. *Family learning programmes*, which involve working with both pupils and parents.

3. *Fitbods*, which is a national programme with short-term funding. It is aimed to increase physical activity levels amongst children through provision of supervised activities. In this particular LA there was a financial commitment to the programme. In other LAs the schools themselves have to buy in. This results in them having to generate their own funding.

As this LA has been involved with the healthy schools programme for over 15 years, it has been well evaluated in terms of its input on schools, both by the schools themselves and by independent university-led research teams.

Most proud of

-   Setting up programmes from nothing.
-   Setting up and maintaining a really good network of professionals, based in school, to run the Healthy Schools Programme.
-   The universal coverage of the programme over so many years.
-   The ability of the central support team to supply good curriculum guidelines, which have been updated regularly to comply with new guidelines and disseminate good practice.
-   Being able to ensure that the LA and schools have the necessary policy frameworks that are required by law, for example those covering PSHE, sex and relationship education, drug education, responding to drug incidents, food in schools policy, and anti-bullying.

■ To work in an LA that was one of the first to ban vending machines in secondary schools, which were selling unhealthy drinks and snacks as a means of raising funding; introducing water in all of the LA's schools; ensuring that schools sold only healthy foods; encouraging the establishment of breakfast and after-school clubs, well before the extended schools core offer.

Areas for development

■ The amount of short-term funding becomes an issue if the vital workers are on temporary contracts; for example, a temporary post was made for someone to work with families involved with domestic abuse. This was really supportive for families and meant that the school nurse team had someone to whom they could refer an abused woman/man. The post failed to win longer-term funding and the service previously offered was withdrawn. There is also a funding issue in sustaining initiatives when small teams are all on short-term contracts.

Barriers to learning

Children in schools have barriers to learning through a number of different health issues. These include emotional health and well-being, anti-bullying and their home environment. The healthy schools programme has an important role to play in identifying health determinants and changing them. Training for teachers and LMs is often short on the skilled health input because the skilled people are not available. There is also not a great awareness at strategic level about the importance of primary schools.

Andy, the first LM interviewed, mentioned sport as an important incentive to his reluctant learners. He added that he himself was not particularly sporty and part of his current post had involved understanding and becoming involved in a sports culture, which had never particularly mattered to him. Several other people I interviewed also mentioned sports, so the next interview looks at how some LA are seeking to enhance sports provision, both as part of their healthy schools programme, but also because of the recognition that children's interest in sports can improve their behaviour and attitude to what happens in school.

Wendy: PE and school support manager

Wendy's post is one held within the healthy schools team and she is currently on secondment from a primary school. Her career, like those of many of the other educational professionals, has not been a conventional one. She was in the police force for 13 years before going on an Access course to become a primary teacher. She had always been interested in PE and built up her primary expertise by going on courses and researching into it.

She came into the post by accident. The previous occupant had been seriously ill and a number of headteachers in both the primary and secondary sector were concerned that the 3 months' funding still running on the post would disappear. Wendy's own headteacher approached her and asked if she was interested in a 3-month secondment. She worked this, then another 3 months, and now she is in her third year in post. The line management has been varied – initially it was part of quality assurance, then Universal Services and now Extended Schools. The funding and post were not secure and her seconding school were now looking for her to make a definite decision about whether or not she was coming back to the school.

Role

The post is strategic and the nature of the job has evolved. There was no job description, and the post had proved to be a mixture of delivery and facilitating. The facilitating involved, and continues to involve, auditing what is going on as well as identifying and being responsive to need.

The post arose out of the need to work closely with Schools Sports Partnership, which is a national scheme across the whole country, and also the sport trusts. It currently involves every secondary school releasing a PE specialist to support primary school PE 2 days per week. There are also other funding streams, such as the Big Lottery. There are national aims and targets with which LAs must comply. The funding also enables two schools sports coordinators (SSCOs) to manage the partnerships. They had come from the two specialist sports academies.

Each primary school has a link – Primary Link Teacher (PLT) – and, once appointed, these can access 12 days of supply cover, which is funded by the Youth Schools Trust. They link directly with the secondary specialists and with the SSCOs.

Some of the responsibilities of this post are outlined in Figure 10.3.

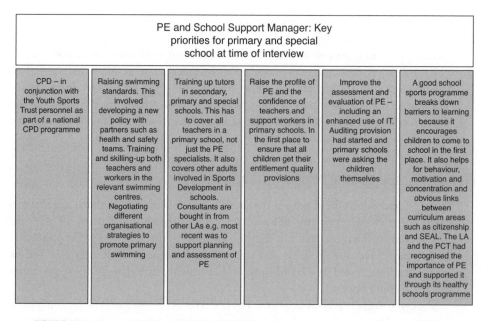

PE and School Support Manager: Key priorities for primary and special school at time of interview					
CPD – in conjunction with the Youth Sports Trust personnel as part of a national CPD programme	Raising swimming standards. This involved developing a new policy with partners such as health and safety teams. Training and skilling-up both teachers and workers in the relevant swimming centres. Negotiating different organisational strategies to promote primary swimming	Training up tutors in secondary, primary and special schools. This has to cover all teachers in a primary school, not just the PE specialists. It also covers other adults involved in Sports Development in schools. Consultants are bought in from other LAs e.g. most recent was to support planning and assessment of PE	Raise the profile of PE and the confidence of teachers and support workers in primary schools. In the first place to ensure that all children get their entitlement quality provisions	Improve the assessment and evaluation of PE – including an enhanced use of IT. Auditing provision had started and primary schools were asking the children themselves	A good school sports programme breaks down barriers to learning because it encourages children to come to school in the first place. It also helps for behaviour, motivation and concentration and obvious links between curriculum areas such as citizenship and SEAL. The LA and the PCT had recognised the importance of PE and supported it through its healthy schools programme

FIGURE 10.3 Key priorities for sport in primary schools

Most proud of

- Getting people together and making it happen. Now a large body of people in the authority know what is available.

- Creating courses and offering bespoke training, which is very focused for individual or clusters of schools.

- Reorganising primary swimming. It had always been one day per week in the past over a 10-week period. This was often seen by schools as quite disruptive over a long period of time and there were inconsistencies among the standards of training from different centres. The children who lacked confidence found this weekly programme quite easy to avoid, if they left their kit behind. Wendy initially emailed every primary school, with an alternative more concentrated programme being held over a 2-week block. The school response was very positive and it works much better. There have been some really magical stories about change in children's attitudes, as well as raising the numbers of children who can now swim besides improving their swimming. Funding was put in for transport and this also helped to persuade the children that swimming was important.

- Personal development. The post has enabled Wendy to move out of her own comfort zone and be challenged to try something new.

- Wendy felt that the work done with special schools has been important because it has had to be tailored for so many different specific needs. Particular challenges have risen because taxi cabs come to pick the children up at the end of the school day and therefore there has never been a tradition of after-school clubs. This has been largely turned round and a team went to Blackpool for a weekend for an national athletic competition.

- There have been good links built up with the PCT and they have helped to fund initiatives, such as the cycle paths.

Areas for development

- How to set up structures to reach the 'hard to reach'. Sadly, this might involve particular schools, as well as particular children.

- There is some really good partnership work taking place but it is heavily dependent on goodwill in schools and staff not being off sick.

- Sport England. The Sport Physical Activity Alliance (SPAA) recognise that these challenges are national ones and are bringing together anyone in the LA who is doing anything physical. They hope to sharpen up the provision and help managers to be more effective and efficient with different streams of funding and staffing. Their remit includes any group with sports involvement.

Barriers for learning

- The way in which schools value PE; in primary schools it is often last on the agenda, and literacy and numeracy are all important. This is reflected in initial teacher training (ITT), which is often as little as 6 hours over three, or even four, years. So student teachers only get small blocks of PE each year and this only really helps those who are already keen. It is difficult to provide a vision, skills and pedagogy in this small amount of time for those not interested in the first place.

Both Wendy's and Naseem's posts are insecure and heavily dependent on the politics of the local authority, as well as central and local government initiatives. They both facilitate services and streams of funding to primary schools, which would be virtually impossible for an individual primary teacher to do in every school in the LA. They also can support LAs in having a whole authority approach and having some sense of what goes on within the authority. They have, to some extent, replaced what 30 years ago would have been a local authority subject inspector on a fixed post. The funding streams ensure that funding is only gained if specific targets are worked for and gained.

The next LA post differs from this considerably, in the sense that this is a post that has grown from a small short-term project into a full-time post.

Annie: Study Support coordinator, covering ages 5 to 16

Figure 10.4 provides a quick guide to what is meant by Study Support in this LA. The activities can take place before and after school hours as well as during lunch-times.

Annie had decided to take early retirement from being employed as a senior teacher in a primary school, but, after 3 months, she found that she was getting bored and when this post was advertised she applied and was appointed. Initially, it was about looking at how the Lottery money was being spent on Study Support in primary, secondary and special schools. The money was allocated in line with the numbers of children on free school meals, which was seen as a method of targeting pupils who most needed Study Support. Initially funding had come out of the New Opportunities Funding (NOF) stream. This then became the Big Lottery Funding. Her initial task involved sorting out the administration of this, and for this she was employed on a temporary contract for 4 days per week.

Role

Between 2004 and 2006 there was one-quarter of a million pounds in funding and, from this, arose the job description:

- Providing schools with a vision of what Study Support involved.
- Supporting schools that were eligible for the funding so that they could create new activity clubs, both on and off the school premises.
- Setting up area packages in which schools could take part.
- Opening up the community for children so that they could visit museums, art galleries and take part in more unusual sports activities, such as canoeing, kayaking, sailing, and wall climbing.

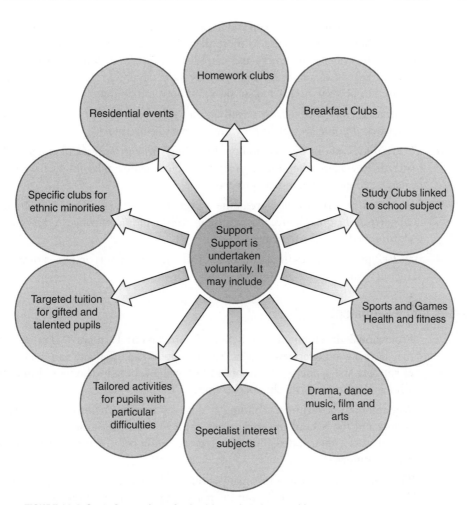

FIGURE 10.4 Study Support/out-of-school-hours learning: a guide

■ It involved being ready to think 'out of the box' and, although this was already happening to a small extent, the funding made it possible for children to do different things.

Most proud of

■ The Study Support itself – it does break barriers to learning and raise standards, but it is difficult to pinpoint the levels achieved. It is possible to look at the value added in terms of individual children, in particular to see the increased confidence they have, as well as watching them learning happily through the activities. However, it does need more tracking in individual children to see if there really is a transfer from behaviour, motivation and learning in the study centre environment to everyday school work. The Department for Children, Schools and Families (DCSF) is now looking at ways of doing this and as part of this process Annie has been asked to provide a personal record of achievement

(ROA) about what has done well and its impact. It has to fit in with the Children's Plan and help children aspire to more than they did before. The idea is to give children the wider experiences and confidence to make informed choices. The National Year of Reading, for example, involved targeting reluctant readers but you need to be very careful and subtle about how you do this.

- Homework clubs worked very well as they overcame the problems of doing homework at home, as well as providing access to computers.

- The awareness about the availability of funding was very successful and also the materials to evidence good local practice enabled schools who might have been hesitating about taking on new projects.

- It has been possible to measure some aspects of raised achievement, in both a qualitative and a quantitative way, through registers for attendance at the centres and improved school attendance.

- Box 10.2 provides an example of some of the Study Support activities over one academic year.

Areas for development

1. Professional development for School Improvement Partners (SIPs) so that they have a good overview of what Study Support can offer, and can then work to support and guide own schools and others. Eventually, she would like the schools to take on ownership of the work.

2. When central government funding is not ring fenced, such as the Standards Grants and the School Improvement Grants, it is left to the schools to spend and this is too open ended. There is no proper audit because the guidance given is not statutory.

3. There has been a growth of organisations, clubs and groups that are offering different activities to schools, but the marketing and quality assurance for these is very difficult, for both the schools and the organisations.

4. Sustainability – the Big Lottery money raised expectations and enabled clubs to be set up and everyone could see positive benefits. These now have to be sustained by funding from other sources and there is difficulty developing them. There are also issues when schools are not convinced or there are key staff changes and the clubs are stopped. This means that each year there is a need to raise awareness again; children are disadvantaged when they do not have access to Study Support.

5. Annie would like to have more involvement with those schools who are in special measures, through visiting and supporting and encouraging them to take up more activities.

6. Getting families to input more, and both pupils and parents doing activities that encourage respect for themselves, families and communities.

Box 10.2 Examples of some Study Support activities over 1 year: to enable, extend and enrich

Art/craft	Golf	Playground games
Athletics	Guitar	Quiet room
Aerobics	Healthy eating	Revision
Archery	ICT	Reading
Badminton	Instrumentals	Road safety
Basketball	Judo	Residential
Breakfast	Journalism	Sports
Board games	Ju-jitsu	Swimming
Cookery	Karate	Summer schools
Chess	Kick boxing	Skiing
Circus Skills	Languages	Tennis
Cycling	Leisure	Theatre
Dance	Library	T'ai chi
Drama	Literacy	Textiles
Design	Music	Tag rugby
Drumming	Museums	University outreach
Environment	Numeracy	Volleyball
Expressive arts	Needlework	Violin
Face painting	Newspapers	Wall climbing
Filming	Ocarina	Water sports
First aid	Orienteering	Yoga
Fencing	Pottery	Youth investigations
Gardening	Photography	Zoological visits

Barriers to learning

1. The whole ethos in activity clubs is that it is voluntary to take part; children are encouraged to do so and the clubs have to provide activities that the children are interested in or would like to become interested in. This is very different from the 8.00 am–6.00 pm provision, during which the child has no choice. Study Support does operate here, but there can be difficulties. One of the most popular activities has been judo for 50p per session.

2. More comprehensive provision to provide challenge to gifted and talented children.

3. Being able to move Year 6 children from Level 3 to Level 4 SATs.

4. Huge poverty and disadvantage in schools in highly deprived areas. Annie recognises that this is a postcode lottery, by which disadvantage, underachievement, poor punctuality and attendance produce communities in which children are more difficult to reach and more vulnerable – in particular, young carers, LAC, ethnic minorities and travellers, and, increasingly, recognition of male, white working-class pupils.

Annie was very confident about the quality of the provision made in this LA and felt that she had a good understanding of what was going on. The following interview illustrates how the same service can be very different, when the LA subcontracts to an agency – in this particular case to a commercial firm.

Jennifer: extended service link worker (ELW)

Background

Jennifer was finishing her degree when she found this post through the Jobcentre website. The job was with a commercial firm that was commissioned by the LA to coordinate schools to ensure that they were fulfilling the core offer for extended schools provision. The company was already running Adult and Family Learning and funding came from the Big Lottery through the LA. Jennifer had been really excited about it when she started in post.

Role

The service worked by separating the LA into three areas, so Jennifer was appointed as an ELW in just one of these areas and works with two other ELWs. She covers 17 primary and secondary schools and her initial role was to link with the 'contact person' in each school. In the majority of cases, this was the LM, and in one school the headteacher. The LA at this stage cut the salaries of LMs after a pay regrading and made all posts term time only. Many mentors were losing £3000 and one mentor in Jennifer's group had had a pay cut of £7000. This means that there was considerable resistance to working in the school holidays and after school hours.

The core offer for extended schools includes:

- A varied range of activities, including Study Support, sport and music clubs, combined with child care in primary schools
- Parenting and family support
- Swift and easy access to targeted and specialist services
- Community access to facilities including adult and family learning, ICT and sports grounds.

Most schools in Jennifer's LA provide their own breakfast, lunch-time and after-school provision so the bulk of the company's work is to cover the core offer in the school holidays. They do this by finding out what provision is wanted by the children. This is done using a questionnaire, so, before the Easter holidays, children were asked (through the questionnaire) what they would like. The result was three activities: bike riding, arts and crafts, and cooking. Jennifer's job was then to buy in the people and companies to cover the activities programme. This involved her networking with a large number of other public services, as well as private companies.

The company audits the provision and schools are encouraged to complete the questionnaire each term by getting £200 for the returned form. The last audit showed that there was full provision, but Jennifer pointed out that this is not a true picture because courses do not run if they are not taken up.

Most proud of

Jennifer is genuinely passionate about wanting to provide good core provision, but the post has not been what she expected. She is planning activities for the near future including a 'Love Music – Hate Racism' concert and a programme for the 'National Family Week'. And she has had the opportunity to undertake some professional development, which has included a Positive Parenting Programme (Triple P). She is now involved with working with families as a support worker. Families are referred to her company and the organisation is responding to this, although it is very challenging work.

Figure 10.5 supplies some of the reasons for Jennifer's frustration, and sometimes anger, about what was happening, and failure to provide a service that would interest and motivate children and young people in their leisure time. She was well aware of the need to ensure that children were motivated into positive activities and that this was likely to have a feedback in terms of their attitudes to school, learning and life generally.

Jennifer makes important points about the quality of provision made by her company and this is clearly a commissioning issue for the LA concerned. The company itself is also commissioning services and is involved in finding genuine means of auditing and reviewing quality assurance that the services provided. Annie also pointed out the difficulty of providing hard data over a period of time to provide evidence as to how effective the service was in terms of its initial remit. Annie's post, and the service provided, were much more tightly organised and she benefited from being within the LA, rather than outside it.

Summary

Table 10.2 summarises what barriers these educational professionals identified in terms of children's learning. Again, as with the TAs and LMs, parenting was identified as a factor, and, like the LMs in particular, the comments were made within a much more supportive context. Richard questioned government policy to encourage mothers of young children to go out to work, when the only work available to them was poorly paid. Several of those mentioned the more generic issues of poverty and disadvantage, but did see that schools could offer these children good educational outcomes. They saw that much of the work that they did provided strategies to raise barriers to learning, improve motivation and provide alternative activities to hanging about on the streets, and introduced children to new possibilities – including what was in their own community. Basically, they were engaged in widening experience, raising aspirations and providing opportunities.

There are too may organisations trying to do the same thing. They need better QA and this is not our company's role. This results in us not being sure about what we are commissioning. In some cases the money is virtually chucked away

Staff in this company are basically working for themselves. The teams within the company mirror the activities teams outside, where communication is poor and lacks overall leadership from the top. In this company there does not seem much investment in training project managers in basic leadership and management skills

Consultation with the children is the driving force, as it should be. But this largely involves tick sheets where only 10/12 different activities are offered. This is really done for ease of coordination by the company

The audit is faulty. It records full provision but does not identify the quality of provision, or whether it actually takes place. There is also pressure to include named 'targeted children' i.e. those likely to be in trouble, whether they attend or not

There can be issues about access to the schools during the holidays. It involves someone coming in during the holidays, additional payments etc. Caretakers are key here, but so also is the funding

FIGURE 10.5 Value for money?

TABLE 10.2 Barriers and strategies: a summary

BARRIERS	STRATEGIES
Attendance Nature of school itself – puts some parents and their children off attending because it does not reflect their lives, build on their known experiences	Procedures for persistent non-attenders: i. the carrot, carried out within the schools of rewards for attendance; learning mentors are largely responsible for these; ii. case work with individual children and families; iii. prosecution and fear of prosecution.

TABLE 10.2 (continued)

BARRIERS	STRATEGIES
Parenting, poverty and disadvantage Parents may not have the time to do many of the things the government seems to expect them to do.	Parenting programmes within secondary schools but also as part of adult education in the community, Sure Start, schools themselves. Employment of Family Case Workers to work with particular families. Ensuring that like all those interviewed in this section all those working as Educational Professionals know something about the data – poverty and health determinants for example that form part of the school community data base. This needs to be seen, as a factor, but not an excuse for not working at making a difference – the Star Fish theory again.
Resilience to life challenges/ absence of religion to support resilience.	Faith schools would see this as part of their faith remit as a matter of course. The Pastoral Support team, such as that in Chapter 9, would say that their multi-agency school based team did provide educative strategies for both parents and children to build up resilience – with and without religion.
Health i. Health determinants in specific areas very poor ii. Necessity for those in schools to identify specific health needs e.g. glasses ii. General knowledge about health issues iii. Low profile of PE	Encouraging children to wear glasses, provision of two pairs – one for school, one for home. Healthy school programme – committed to skilled-up primary workforce, programmes for certification for teachers. School Sports Partnership – raise profile and expertise in primary schools. Improved training in PE for student teachers. Study Support activities, where taking part is voluntary and in order to target specific children has to respond to their needs and provide really interesting and different activities from those already provided in school.
Dental problems	Good dental health service, starting with a pre-school programme working through the under-fives section, encouraging and showing children how to clean teeth. Healthy eating programmes within Sure Start provision, Children's Centres and Health Schools Programme. Forbidding junk food and drink to be sold in schools, inspecting lunch boxes (both very controversial)
The pressure to evidence data to show viability of initiatives – most outcomes take place over quite a period of time.	Self-evaluation forms, newer methods of auditing. Transparency and engagement with funding bodies hoping for easy solutions. Use of data from children themselves – school councils for example

11

Case Study: LA Integrated Working

Central Area Support Team is committed to working in an integrated manner together with other agencies and schools within the framework of 'The Children Plans', 'Change for Children' and promoting the five outcomes with which 'Every Child Matters' is concerned. These include:

Being healthy
Staying safe
Enjoying and achieving
Making a positive contribution
Social economic well-being.

(taken from the Guidelines for Operational Practice between CAST, schools and agencies)

Chapter overview

- To look at one way in which a local authority has worked to raise barriers to learning in schools through coordinating education, health and social care services into multi-agency teams

- Interviewing two members of one of the multi-agency teams involved at the operational end of this to gain some understanding of their perspective

- Interviewing two headteachers who are at the receiving end of the services.

Introduction

Local authorities have responded in many different ways to the statutory and non-statutory regulations and guidelines, which continue to come out from central government in response to the 'Every Child Matters' (ECM) agenda. This case study is just one example of how one LA re-organised its provision for children's services. Many more can be found through looking on LA websites directly or, more importantly, by talking and interviewing those who work in such services and are on their receiving end. This case study is an exemplar for finding out about operational aspects of multi-agency working, rather than a blueprint for best practice. The leadership team of the LA would certainly see themselves as part of an ever-changing service provision that is committed to providing the best possible services for their challenging area.

LA organisation of services

Well before the start of the new millennium, the LA, like most others, was looking for ways in which their services could be better organised to provided a more seamless approach to supporting children, families and schools. The re-organisation in 2001 of local NHS Community Trusts into Primary Care Trusts (PCTs) provided an opportunity to make the first steps towards achieving this. The NHS Community Trusts had been responsible for specific health services to children, such as clinics, school nursing, speech therapy and child guidance. This re-organisation of the local Community NHS services changed a provision that had been shared by two LAs to separate provision for each. The PCT for this particular authority had now become co-terminous in its services with the LA, although this was not true across the country. The existing senior executive officer, who had a portfolio that covered LA health services such as public health and also social care, then applied for, and was appointed to, the post of Chief Executive of the new PCT. This meant that her portfolio covered all primary health care and Social Services across the LA. At the time, this was seen as a radical and adventurous move, and it took several years longer to create the financial procedures to ensure that both NHS funding and LA funding were clearly accounted for.

Essentially, the coordination has been seen initially by the LA as an extension of their existing practice of putting together those operational workers who were employed in separate health (PCT and LA) and Social Services departments. The creation of a separate Director for Children and Family Services under the 2004 Education Act provided a further opportunity to pull the services already offered to the children and families together as much as possible. The strategic leadership became more formally coordinated and Figure 11.1 provides an exemplar of how, at the time of writing this book, this team was organised.

The Executive Director, who combined health and social care within the authority and who then became the Chief Executive for the PCT (NHS), became Executive Director of Well-being. Not necessarily in my view the most helpful of titles, so when you look at Figure 11.1 it may help to translate this into combined health and Social Services/care. The overview, as well as the leadership responsibilities, are very much broader than would ever have been possible in the past. It made it much easier for the authority to link this post in with the post of Executive Director for Children and Family Services. At the next level down, the responsibilities for Children's Integrated Services become more obvious, as indicated by the creation of eight Children and Family Services Managers.

The vital question of whether this will genuinely, in the long term, provide improved services remains to be seen. Certainly, the exemplar described below of

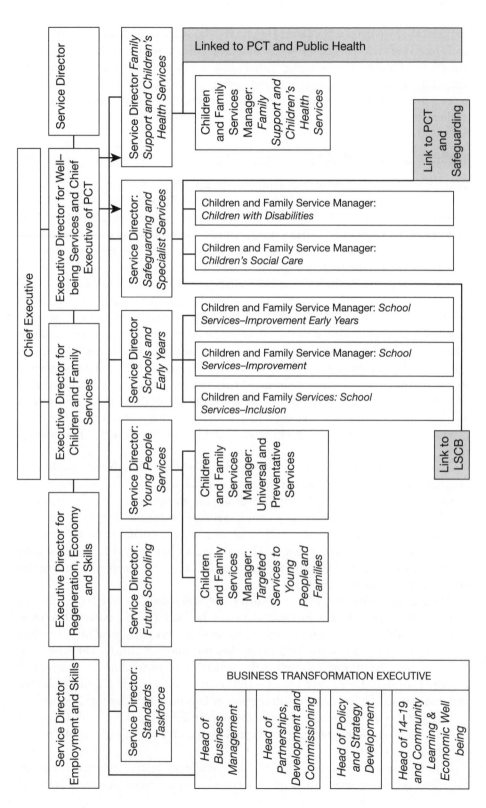

FIGURE 11.1 Exemplar of strategic organisation within the LA Department for Children, Families and Schools – Extended Leadership Team

one particular aspect of the work in relation to breaking down barriers to learning for children in schools is being well evaluated, and the authority is receiving visitors from all over the country to learn lessons from it.

Central Area Support Team (CAST)

The LA set up three sites offering commonly called-upon health, social care and support services in schools. The sites were positioned in the north, south and centre of the LA. The reasoning behind this was that the sites should be within reasonable distance of the schools that they served. The site being studied shared the same premises as a special school.

Sharing a building made meetings between different agencies more feasible and enabled important networking between different professionals to happen more frequently. Funding is complex and this was difficult to track from the interviews.

Currently the team on the central area site covered:

- Educational psychology
- Social work
- Sensory impairment service
- Specialist teachers for learning and access and inclusion (behaviour).

In all, this involved 23 operational workers on site, including a headteacher and the principal educational psychologist. Six operational managers were not on site.

Other off-site partnerships included SureStart, School Improvement, health visitors, school nurses, speech and language therapy, Social Services, Child and Adolescent Mental Health Services (CAMHS) and the Child Development Team. In addition, schools, through the schools service level agreements (SLAs), had access to additional support with specialist teachers and support assistants provided through special centres (special schools) in the authority. The SLAs are services run by the LA into which schools can buy.

Carol: educational social worker (ESW)

Carol spent 10 years in foster care herself and, during that time, had 11 different social workers. She was determined to try and make things better for other LAC and did a 3-year BA Honours degree in Social Work so that she could go into social work herself and make changes. When she finished her degree, she applied for this post and got it. She was particularly keen to work on the preventative side of social work and she saw this ESW post as being an important development in supporting children and families before a crisis took place. She believes that the creation of a number of ESWs over the authority is fairly unique. This use of the term ESW should not be confused with the post of education welfare officer, whose focus is generally on attendance.

Her role is a developing one and she is working with parents and children who are referred by schools, their GP and/or parents or carers. The referrals come because the children are identified as having social, emotional and/or behavioural difficulties – in addition, they may also have special needs. All of these issues are preventing them from learning and interfering with their general development. She covers 16 primary schools and two secondary schools. There are 5.5 ESWs across the LA but one post is currently vacant.

She meets with each school once a term for a planning and review meeting. This will involve the school Special Educational Needs Coordinator (SENCO), the headteacher, the learning mentor and representatives from the support team. This will include an educational psychologist, and an Access and Inclusion specialist (behaviour), as well as a learning support outreach worker. This termly meeting helps to channel referrals and everyone feels more ownership. According to the two headteachers I interviewed, the schools are much better informed than in the past and there are plenty of opportunities for feedback. The local authority has an agreed programme of need so that everyone follows the same procedures. Box 11.1 provides an example of the agreed proforma for the school-based planning and review meetings.

Figure 11.2 shows a tiered model, which triggers the involvement of the ESW, and Figure 11.3 shows the second-tier process for schools to access support from the ESW for young people whose needs are not critical. Referral to the ESW must involve issues at both home and school. The ESW cannot intervene if it is only the school, or only the carer, who has asked for the intervention. After the referral the ESW makes a visit to the child's home to complete an assessment. In the past, this would have been the role of the Child Guidance Service. The assessment forms used have been updated and matched more closely to the common assessment frameworks (CAFs). Only the family get a copy of this assessment form, because it is confidential, and the school gets a letter with the outcome of the meeting and the action and the implementation plan. This is reviewed (see Box 11.1) when strategies have been tried out; it takes about 3 months and is seen as a short-term intervention. There is a capacity issue here: Carol's case-load is 30+ cases and what should be a weekly session becomes drawn out to once or twice a month.

CAMHS is not an LA service, but any referral triggers a risk assessment for mental health issues, such as threats of suicide, threats of or actual self-harm. If this risk

Box 11.1 Agreed proforma for planning and review meetings

Agenda for termly planning and review meetings

- Apologies
- Feedback on past term's work between CAST and the school, e.g. educational psychologist, educational social worker or other area representative from appropriate agency, e.g. SureStart worker
- Feedback from school on impact of strategies
- Discussion of SEN school-related issues and negotiation of priorities
- Action plan for following term, including success criteria and personnel involved
- Items to be brought to operational group
- AOB
- Date of next meeting.

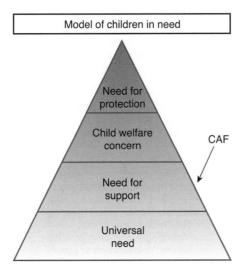

FIGURE 11.2 Tiered model of support

assessment shows that a child has urgent and critical social and emotional needs then they are moved into the third tier of the model.

The ESWs have a number of different strategies that they can put into place at the second tier of the model. These include:

1. Running specific parenting courses when there are gaps in existing provision. These have turned out to be parenting issues for parents/carers who have children with special needs. Some parents need one-to-one support before they are ready for parenting courses and some may never be at the stage when they are confident enough to work with other carers in a group. Other courses cover topics such as autistic spectrum disorder (ASD), Attention Deficit Hyperactivity Disorder (ADHD) and anger management. The anger management course involves two sessions on parents' own anger and two at looking at children's anger.

2. Individual work with child on issues such as self-esteem and bereavement. Bereavement, here, is seen in its widest context of loss associated with parental separation, divorce, deaths in the family, rehousing, moving into new areas and/ or a different country. In the past, the team had been able to draw in specialists on domestic violence and play therapists to work with children, but the funding has been withdrawn from both of these areas. ESWs have also started to work with small groups of children on social and emotional aspects of their lives. This is proving popular with the children and is effective as a strategy.

3. There has been a growth in the number of children identified with ASD and ADHD. This has resulted in the creation of two specific pathways and, again, the identification and referral has to be multi-agency. This has produced a core group of specialists, as well as other professionals and others feeding into it

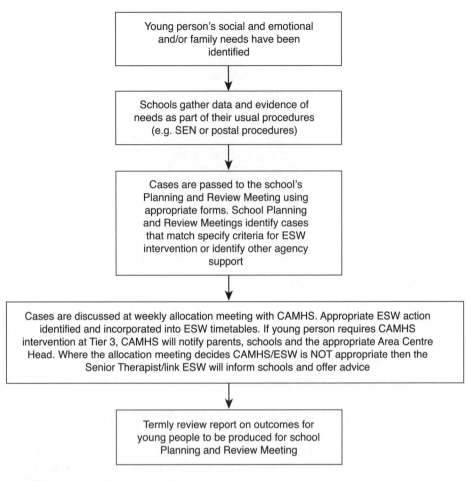

FIGURE 11.3 Tier 2 process for schools to access support from the ESW for young people whose needs are not critical. If CAMHS become involved then the child moves up on to the third tier of the pyramid, i.e. a child with a welfare concern

as appropriate. For ADHD there is a special formal assessment that provides a developmental history interview for the assessment of ADHD. The LA has produced this itself and it has also invested in two teachers for ASD plus an Early Years family support worker. Details of all of the meetings and assessments go on the child's file and form part of the initial process. Strategies tried are recommended by the educational psychologist. There is an overall wish to avoid the use of drugs to treat ADHD, but, in severe cases, they are sometimes prescribed to provide a 'window of opportunity' to try and get the strategies off the ground. Box 11.2 provides an example of a difficult behaviour matrix, taken from this development history proforma.

4.   The ESWs do not have statutory powers, but feed into the statutory process by helping to support SENCOs in writing statements and often holding

Box 11.2 Difficult behaviour matrix

The following is a list of difficult behaviours that children with ADHD often display. Consider each behaviour with the parent and add any comments if appropriate.

DIFFICULTY	YES/NO	COMMENTS
Sleep disturbance		
Tics		
Avoids school or work		
Anxiety		
Cries or laughs too easily		
Exhibits excessive unhappiness		
Has temper tantrums		
Is negativistic or defiant		
Teases or bullies		
Lies, cheats or steals		
Too physically aggressive		
Swears in inappropriate situations		
Engages in inappropriate sexual behaviour		
Destroys own or other people's property		
Has difficulty following instructions		
Time-keeping		
Controlling impulses, anger, hurt feelings, etc.		

---

responsibility for completing the CAFs. As they have visited the child's home they can provide more of an overall picture. The support given to schools may increase, as it is likely that schools will have greater involvement in completing the CAFs and will need support. Social Services are now asking that any child referred to them should already have a CAF. This can be problematic, as completing a CAF requires a multi-agency meeting and this can be difficult to organise quickly. The school planning and review meeting does ensure good coordination of CAFs.

5. The LA has been very proactive in identifying the process for the use of a CAF. They define it as a process for:

    ■ Recognising the signs that a child may have unmet needs.
    ■ Completing a common assessment – guidance on who should do what, what areas should be assessed and how, and how to respond to the child's needs.
    ■ Recording and, with consent, sharing information.

- They also make it clear that everyone who provides services to, or comes into contact with, children and young people should:
  - Be able to recognise and respond to the key signs of need;
  - Know the basics of the CAF process;
  - Know how to have a common assessment completed or how to complete one themselves.

It is made clear that if more than one practitioner is involved, one of them must take the lead. This is to ensure that support is coordinated, streamlined, effectively delivered and regularly reviewed.

The Children's Workforce Development Council (CWDC) website provides some useful factsheets and guidance about the contents of the CAF and how it should be completed. These are, at the time of writing, regularly updated.

Most proud of

1. Establishing professional relationships that can result in making a difference to a child and their family. For example, a mother came into the borough with two children under six and had learning difficulties herself. One of the children was referred (by the school) as having behaviour that was 'off the wall' and was identified with both ASD and ADHD, for example being able to eat only white food. Carol's role involved building up a trusting relationship with the parent and signposting as much support as possible. Now the parent is active in the borough as a parent volunteer and the child in one of the borough's very small number of special schools.

2. Parenting course provision. ESW's can provide a different slant and expertise, and the courses have a good take-up. Some parents come back for more.

3. Working in a service that is really preventative and in many cases the work does stop crisis intervention. She also likes the way the team works, believing that it has real advantages for everyone and feeds in to the effectiveness of the reviews.

Areas for development

1. More staffing is needed and more cases could be taken up. This would also enable more than one professional social worker in each team. It can be professionally isolating working by yourself and difficult to keep up with new developments in the professional social work field. The main strategy to avoid this is for social workers to meet up together.

2. Line management can be confusing because the ESWs have a dual role and, like CAMHS, feed into other agencies. There is also a real risk that success data can be double accounted and this needs to have more clarity in order to evaluate the effectiveness of the services provided to children in breaking down barriers to learning in its widest sense.

Barriers to learning

1. Parenting – many of the parents with whom Carol works have not experienced the importance of learning themselves and pass on their own low expectations and aspirations of schooling to their own children. This can become a self-fulfilling prophecy.

2. Staffing – such as LMs 'who are brilliant', but there are not enough to go around. This is particularly important because the emotional aspect of children's lives has a huge impact on their learning.

3. When talking with children they seem very concerned about exam/SATs pressures.

Paul: principal educational psychologist

Paul is a member of the Central Area Operational Managers group and works in the CAST team as the principal educational psychologist. The LA have the equivalent of eight full-time educational psychologists of whom 3.9 are based in the central team. Paul was appointed over 4 years ago from another LA, where he was working in a multi-agency team.

Traditionally, educational psychologists are associated with working in an LA from child guidance clinics, where they carry out a wide range of strategies to enhance children's learning. This is usually after a referral from the school, and often marks the despair of the school with a particular child, as well as a reluctance to exclude them from school. Educational psychologists usually go in to schools, colleges, nurseries and special units to observe children in their formal learning setting and report back. This traditional role included helping teachers and support workers in schools to look at some of the factors that might be affecting a child's learning. They were often solely responsible for reports needed for special educational places, court proceedings and children's panels. As part of this role they worked with teachers, parents and other educational professionals.

The interview with Paul was very much about how this traditional role has changed and developed through the process of multi-agency working. Generally, over the whole country, working practices for educational psychologists are becoming more variable and this has caused some concern from the Association of Educational Psychologists (AEP). Paul himself and the two headteachers who were interviewed in relation to this team were extremely enthusiastic about the improved working practices it had produced, but Paul could understand the concern of the AEP.

When he first arrived in the authority, the CAST team was in the process of being created. As was discussed in Chapter 1, many of the fundamental features of change were taking place. Professionals felt uncertain about how 'the team' would work and were not necessarily committed or convinced that it would improve the service to children. A small number left so that they could return to work in a more familiar and traditional setting. This meant that consultations could take place about how the new setting should develop, what those working there believed should happen to improve the service, and ways in which their own expertise might be developed. The change in working practices led to vacancies and new appointments could be made 'with like-minded people' and the team reformed. It was important that joint working was seen not just as co-location, by which professionals such as ESW and psychologists would continue to work in their professional silos, but as something much more radical and dynamic.

Paul felt strongly that professionals, particularly those who had gone through many years of professional education, had vested interests in keeping their traditional role. Services could end up working against each other and providing poor support for children. The example he gave provides a good question mark over the literature that looks at professional identity within specific silos (see Chapter 1). Traditionally, educational psychologists had been used at the end of process, when several other specialists had worked with a child. Other specialists felt threatened and it was possible to find services working against each other to keep a sense of their specialist professional identity. 'We've tried everything and now the Ed. Psy goes in and says we should . . . What does he know about teaching 30 children?' The vision for the support team is that if a child is in crisis then the team should work round the child and use their skills and knowledge collectively. This reinforces the ECM agenda of having a holistic view of the child and having a support team made up of different expertise can provide a variety of perspectives and knowledge. The pooling of this means there is a much greater chance of working something through than with a number of people operating as individuals within their own silo.

Case study 1: demonstrating the effectiveness of the 'team' approach in breaking barriers to learning

Early on in the creation of the team, Paul felt it was important to be able to demonstrate how the team could work successfully in practice and gave an example from a local school where the headteacher, whom I had already interviewed, had had very little time for the support services the school had bought in to help in the past. Using the new procedures, the school called in the 'team's' support for a Year 6 child who was extremely disaffected. Both his attendance and attainment were poor. His disruptive behaviour was to flatly refuse to do what he was asked to do. If he did not want to do it, he would say so and not do it. The team met in the school to review the child's case (sees Figures 11.2 and 11.3), and, as a result of this meeting, a specialist support teacher (SST) from the CAST team came in to the school. The importance about this meeting was that it involved several professionals who contributed their perspectives to the strategy and would be involved in providing evidence for the next meeting. The ESW, for example, would visit the home and be able to provide information. The SST found, not surprisingly, that one reason that the child refused to do the work was he often could not do it and more importantly felt that he would never be able to do it. She worked with the child to encourage a 'can do' attitude. She also felt that the child might be dyslexic and asked the educational psychologist to assess him. At the same time, the ESW visited the home, which was chaotic. The worker identified parenting issues, including quite severe substance abuse. As a result of this, the child was taken into care formally by a member of the extended family.

This placement provided an 'intervention window of opportunity' for both the child and the team and in his new situation he improved significantly. He became compliant with the behaviour expected in the classroom, he understood that reading was about learning and that he could do it. However, the boy was not the only one to learn. The school moved from being sceptical and critical about the slow and ineffective service they had got in the past, became confident about what could be offered and started to report learning difficulties much earlier. This, in turn, made it possible for the team – including its school members – to make a difference much earlier and more effectively. It established a successful model for both the school and the team, and demonstrated that the change in both working practices and attitudes had been very positive.

Case study 2: establishing a pastoral support team

This was a product/programme that was developed for children who were at risk of permanent exclusion. Again, it involved drawing together information from different individuals involved with the child.

Paul is a strong believer in Kelly's personal construct theory (PCT) that all behaviour is purposeful and if you want to know why a child is doing something you need to ask them. This sounds so obvious that it is sad that only relatively recently has there been concern about the 'pupil voice' and mechanisms put in place to 'hear' it. The same is just as true for the individual voice of the child. He gave, as an example, a child who had been referred by both school and parent for stealing in school. A member of the team went into school and found that the child was stealing solely for attention. She always got caught, nothing stolen was worth anything (paper clips, for example) and she was quite ready to give it up as soon as she was found out. The strategy recommended to the school was that the child was engaged in 'notice me' behaviour, which linked with the PCT view that unmet needs, even in early infancy, still impact on an individual years later. The example is that when a baby's basic needs, such as food, water and physical safety, are not met then this results in frustration. The teacher arranged a daily time to 'notice' the child. She was low key on the child's stealing, inviting her quietly to return items taken, but gave attention to her in other ways. The stealing stopped. PCT challenges the moral dilemma about stealing being a sin and wrong, and moved into looking at the purpose of the behaviour. Importantly, the approach worked on most occasions.

Another advantage of working in a genuine team of professionals is the opportunity for professional development. This includes actually running team meetings so that it is not always the operational manager who is expected to run the meetings, but all members of the team. This avoids team members feeling that this has to be part of the role of the senior manager; instead they will see it as a role for a CAST member. This also applies for professional expertise when shared. It raises confidence as well as increasing the capacity of the team. Like the ESWs (see above) the educational psychologists do meet regularly as a team in order to ensure that their professional experience in their trained area is updated. This should help to appease the professional associations involved, who express concerns that multi-agency teams will lead to loss of professional identity.

Pathways for ASD and ADHD

These have been developed in response to the rise in numbers of referrals from both schools and parents. At one time they would seek a statement from the community paediatrician, who would interview the parent and make a decision based on this interview. The paediatricians found the increase in referrals meant that they did not have the capacity to do this any longer and requested assessments from the educational psychologists. It was obvious to the support teams that there needed to be a clear pathway for such referrals. The pathways were drawn up, starting with the need for all referrals to go to the planning and review meeting (see Figure 11.3). This meant that the learning behaviours had to be common to both home and school. Once the meeting had taken place, the strategies could be taken up by any member of the CAST team in school. This meant that all CAST members needed to be skilled up to work the strategies. This has happened and the whole team is now 'specialist'. It has resulted in a much more informed approach to looking at both ASD and ADHD, and in different professional expertise feeding into other professions; for example, the educational psychologist, with a clear understanding of the syndrome, learns from the ESW the skills of interviewing and vice versa.

Developing a pathway for cognitive behaviour therapy (CBT)

This is developing and has involved bringing in the Access and Inclusion team and also putting on 10-week courses for LMs.

Team evaluation

The team has been very successfully reviewed through the Joint Area Review (JAR) and through separate reviews such as those carried out by Ofsted on the schools it serves. The LA had a critical review of their work and the team came out very positively. Both Carol and Paul felt that some of the key reasons for the team's success were:

■ Good communication strategies.

- Avoidance of hierarchical structures, and the willingness of all team members to see themselves as members of a 'team'. The differing pay structures complicated this, but this team was a genuine team of equal professionals who were working together to support children.

- A willingness from each professional to try out new and different ideas that were outside their own silos.

- A desire to work towards being recognised as a Hub of Excellence for Education Services. This would involve an expansion of multi-agency work to include Social Services and health services.

There is a temptation to look at success stories of individual children and undervalue the difference it makes to the other children in their class and/or year group. One troubled and disruptive child in a primary classroom and on the school playground can frighten others, divert teaching and learning and prove a model to other children for ineffective learning strategies. Success does not come quickly, easily or cheaply. The overall value for money (VFM), when it does come, cannot be measured as audits are done just on the one child, and not on all the other children and adults affected by him/her. Nor can it be done on the future. The prison figures shown in Figure 2.1 show only too clearly how very expensive it can be for the community when it goes very wrong, never mind the cost to the individual. For this reason Boxes 11.3–11.5 are included to show how long it can take for a successful outcome and how time-consuming it can be.

The two headteachers who were interviewed in relation to the service were amazingly positive. Both were experienced headteachers, in challenging schools, who used the service a great deal. They spoke of the improvement since re-organisation, the professional approach and response to their concerns, and, perhaps most importantly, the effectiveness of the service provision in raising barriers for learning for individual children.

Box 11.3 Programme plan of support for Pupil L

PROGRAMME
PLAN OF SUPPORT
For

PUPIL L.

Of

Primary School

Start Date:	Mid Term Review:	Final Review:
12.12.08	26.2.09	25.04.09

PERSON INVITED TO ATTEND	PERSON PRESENT AT MEETING (✓)
EP	✓
Outreach Teacher	✓
Learning Mentor	✓
Mark X. (Father)	✓
Karen X. (mother)	✓
ESW	
Teacher	✓
Outreach Manager	✓
Head teacher	✓
Key stage co-ordinator	
Pupil L.	L.'s views brought to meeting

Pupil Details

Name	D.O.B	Year
L.	17.3.01	3

Address

Daytime Telephone Number:
****

Home Telephone Number:

Lives with:

Karen and Mark X.
K. (10 years)
C. (4 years)

Special Consideration (disability/looked after child etc)

Box 11.3 (continued)

Key Worker   School Key Members of Staff

Irene R (CT)
Jackie E (TA)

Stage of S.E.N. Code of Practice
Statement

Outline background details, nature of difficulty and cause for concern:

L. has been a pupil at St. A's since November 2007. His behaviour has been a cause for concern from the beginning. Mum and Dad report that his behaviour at home is also causing difficulties. L. has attended 3 schools (St. B's and a school in Flint)

L. does not respond to direction from an adult. He chooses what he wants to do and refuses to comply with wishes from an adult. L. can be openly defiant.

When upset L. can become violent and will throw objects, pick up sticks to threaten people or destroy property.

L. is unable to communicate his feelings except using visual aids although he has good vocabulary and is articulate. When he is upset, L. has begun to make grunting noises and scream. L. has physically assaulted members of staff and hurt other children. On occasions he has also used inappropriate language. When L. feels anxious he can become very withdrawn and will physically curl up.

L.'s outbursts are unpredictable with no discernable triggers and frequently it is difficult to calm him down.

He requires skilful verbal prompting to stay on task and is very easily distracted.

Identify Strengths:

L. has a good general knowledge and loves science based activities (e.g. collecting moths and spiders). He likes construction activities and has an excellent spatial ability which enables him to make amazing models. He enjoys cooking and is good at maths, enjoying problem solving activities. He is articulate and will engage in conversation with adults and children. L. also likes art and craft activities.

Behaviour we would like to see:

For L. to take responsibility for his actions and make amends for any upset caused.

School would like L. to be able to accept direction from adults to enable him to access the curriculum.

For L. to be able to articulate his feelings and learn strategies to help him calm himself down and be in control of his actions.

For L. to be taught alongside his peers in the classroom. (in the long term)

Learning needs:

It is difficult to make a proper assessment of L.'s learning needs but schools feels that he is of average/above average intelligence. L. does not enjoy literacy based activities and finds handwriting difficult. However, he can articulate imaginative stories using good vocabulary but cannot record these in writing. Staff find it difficult to engage L. in reading activities.

Identify Motivating Factors for Change (why would the behaviour change?)

L. would like to behave better at school and at home and knows that his parents think he behaves badly.

Box 11.3 (continued)

WHAT ARE THE TARGETS?	STRATEGIES/ACTION TO BE EMPLOYED INCLUDING REWARDS AND SANCTIONS	WHO WILL DELIVER THE STRATEGIES/ACTION?	HOW WILL PROGRESS BE MEASURED AND CELEBRATED?
Aim: To follow a timetable of activities selected by an adult.			
Target: To select from a choice of 3 adult selected activities once a day. (if he does not choose to do what is on the timetable)	Reward: a sticker on a special chart or book. (This is to be shared with Mum and Dad so praise can be given at home) (Need to decide when in the day the choice is to be made). Sanction: sad face sticker	Mrs E (TA) Mrs R (T) Mr M (HT) Mrs C (LM) Mr N (Deputy Head)	Sticker chart – weekly monitoring Once an agreed number of stickers have been awarded then L. will be able to have a special reward that has been negotiated with him
Aim: To verbalise emotions and feelings. Target: To select the appropriate feelings card or puppet and say how the puppet is feeling as he gives the card to the adult.	Select feelings card in morning and after lunch. Reward: sticker on chart or book Sanction: Adult expresses disappointment	Mrs E Mrs R	Noted by TAs in daily log. Reviewed at next meeting.

Box 11.3 (continued)

WHAT ARE THE TARGETS?	STRATEGIES/ACTION TO BE EMPLOYED INCLUDING REWARDS AND SANCTIONS	WHO WILL DELIVER THE STRATEGIES/ ACTION?	HOW WILL PROGRESS BE MEASURED AND CELEBRATED?
Aim: For L. to take responsibility for his actions and make amends for any upset caused.			
Target: For L. to work with his TA in tidying up or mending things that he has broken.	Allow time for L. to calm down following an incident.	Mrs E Mrs R	TAs will note on how many occasions L. joins in tidying up.
	TA to begin to pick up /mend items and talking to L. about how it is good to do this and encourage him to join in. Reward: sticker on chart or book		Sticker chart – weekly monitoring Once an agreed number of stickers have been awarded then L. will be able to have a special reward that has been negotiated with him
	Sanction: Adult expresses disappointment and gives sad face sticker		

Box 11.3 (continued)

PUPIL TARGETS

Positive Handling

When physical intervention is necessary, staff will complete the appropriate form.

Positive Handling will be implemented only in the following circumstances.

If L. is in danger of injuring himself

If L. is in danger of injuring other staff or children

If he is causing serious damage to property

Records maintained by Mr M (in liaison with Mrs R and Mrs E)

Young Person's Comments

L. likes school 6/10

He does not think that his Mum and Dad think he behaves well 1/10

L. does not like playing with other children 1/10

He feels that he is as clever as other children 10/10

L. feels that his parents are proud of him but would like to behave better at home 10/10

He would like to behave better at school 7/10

Signature

Parental Views

Mum and Dad report that they feel L. is making some progress now and is a lot more positive. He seems quite happy and is beginning to share things now at home.

Box 11.4 Pastoral Support Programme – Mid term review

PASTORAL SUPPORT PROGRAMME

MID TERM REVIEW

For

Pupil L.

Of

Year 3

Start Date:	Mid Term Review:	Final Review:
12.12.08	26.2.09	25.04.09

PERSON INVITED TO ATTEND	PERSON PRESENT AT MEETING (A)
EP	✓
Outreach Teacher	✓
Learning Mentor	✓
Mark X. (Father)	✓
Karen X. (mother)	✓
ESW	✓
Teacher	✓
Outreach Manager	✓

Box 11.4 (continued)

WHAT WERE THE TARGETS?	HOW WERE THE STRATEGIES/ACTION TO EMPLOYED INCLUDING REWARDS AND SANCTIONS	WHO DELIVERED THE STRATEGIES/ACTION?	WHAT WAS THE PROGRESS? HOW WAS IT MEASURED AND CELEBRATED?
Aim: To follow a timetable of activities selected by an adult.	Reward: a sticker on a special chart or book. (This is to be shared with Mum and Dad so praise can be given at home) (Need to decide when in the day the choice is to be made.) Sanction: sad face sticker	Mrs E (TA) Mrs H (CT) Mr M (HT) Mrs C (LM) Mr N (Deputy Head)	L. understands and follows his timetable most mornings. On 9/10 occasions he will comply with the choices on his timetable. When L. does not comply, he can easily be 'brought round' by reading a book or using other distraction/descalation techniques. The timetable will now become part of usual practice.
Target: To select from a choice of 3 adult selected activities once a day. (if he does not choose to do what is on the timetable) Aim: To verbalise emotions and feelings	Select feelings card in morning and after lunch. Reward: sticker on chart or book Sanction: Adult expresses disappointment	Mrs E Mrs R	Although L. will use his rainbow to scale how he is feeling (1–10), he has not engaged in any work to help discuss his own feelings using puppets, cards etc. He will talk about the feelings of others in books etc.

Box 11.4 (continued)

WHAT WERE THE TARGETS?	HOW WERE THE STRATEGIES/ ACTION TO EMPLOYED INCLUDING REWARDS AND SANCTIONS	WHO DELIVERED THE STRATEGIES/ACTION?	WHAT WAS THE PROGRESS? HOW WAS IT MEASURED AND CELEBRATED?
Target: To select the appropriate feelings card or puppet and say how the puppet is feeling as he gives the card to the adult.			
Aim: For L. to take responsibility for his actions and make amends for any upset caused.	Allow time for L. to calm down following an incident. TA to begin to pick up/mend items and talking to L. about how it is good to do this and encourage him to join in.	Mrs E Mrs R	This has also been difficult to work on although L.'s outbursts that result in damage to property have decreased greatly. Following an outburst, L. does not want to speak about the incident, seeming to blank it out. He has behaved in an embarrassed or sheepish manner following outbursts. L. is more unsettled and prone to outbursts before holiday time. This may be due to less structured leisure time as opposed to a timetabled school day.
	Reward: sticker on chart or book Sanction: Adult expresses disappointment and gives sad face sticker		
Target: For L. to work with his TA in tidying up or mending things that he has broken.			

Box 11.4 (continued)

Identify strengths and progress made since start of programme:

L. seems happy in school and gives good eye contact to the people he works with. He is very bright and often smiles and laughs. He interacts well with others on the playground and will come in when the whistle blows. He especially likes trading football cards with other children. L. likes to work on the computer. Other pupils have come to work with L. during 'golden time' activities. L. has had good reports from an after school club that he attends. At home, Mum and Dad have reported some improvement. Although L. still has major outbursts, they tend to be less frequent.

What behaviour needs to change?

L. continues to have very violent outbursts when he will throw objects, punch, kick and damage property. (approximately 70% of these outbursts are predictable)

L. is anxious when he enters his classroom even if only for a few minutes. He has said that he is not going into class in September.

When playing, L. always has a violent end to his play with characters getting killed or hurt.

L. can be very stubborn and refuse to do things.

Behaviour we would like to see:

L. working with other pupils in preparation for going into class in September.

L. beginning to recognise and discuss his emotions.

To take some responsibility for his actions and have a responsibility within school.

Learning needs:

It is important to continue to give L. learning opportunities parallel to those of his classmates. This will enable L. to understand his learning in class in year 4.

Identify Motivating Factors for Change (why would the behaviour change?):

L. would like to behave better at school and at home and knows that his parents think he behaves badly.

Box 11.4 (continued)

WHAT ARE THE NEW TARGETS?	STRATEGIES/ACTION TO BE EMPLOYED INCLUDING REWARDS AND SANCTIONS	WHO WILL DELIVER THE STRATEGIES/ ACTION?	HOW WILL PROGRESS BE MEASURED AND CELEBRATED?
For L. to work on a joint activity with a group of children to achieve a common goal.	L. to choose a group of 4/5 children from his class to work on a structured activity for about 1 hour per week. Initially, the activity may be one of L.'s choice then should move to be a project agreed with others. Praise and stickers for the group for completing task.	Mrs E Mrs R Log to be kept of how L. works in the group situation.	L. able to share his success with others (parents/other adults in school/class?)
For L. to recognise a variety of feelings and possibly begin to express his own feelings.	Feelings of others to be discussed with L. using stories and Transporters computer programme.	Mrs E Mrs R	Discussions with L. to be recorded in log and reviewed at next meeting
For L. to take responsibility for his actions and make amends for any upset caused.	Following an outburst, a staff member who has not witnessed it should enter the room and encourage L. to sort things out. L. will have a responsibility to carry out around school for initially one occasion per week Reward: sticker on chart or book Sanction: Adult expresses disappointment and gives sad face sticker	Mrs E Mrs R Mr M Mrs C Mr N	TAs will note on how many occasions L. joins in tidying up. Sticker chart – weekly monitoring Once an agreed number of stickers have been awarded then L. will be able to have a special reward that has been negotiated with him

Box 11.4 (continued)

Positive Handling

When physical intervention is necessary, staff will complete the appropriate form.

Positive Handling will be implemented only in the following circumstances.

If L. is in danger of injuring himself

If L. is in danger of injuring other staff or children

If he is causing serious damage to property

Records maintained by Mr M (in liaison with Mrs R and Mrs E)

Young Person's Comments

L. has said that he will not go into class in September.

He does not like to go home following an outburst.

L.'s views about his behaviour should be sought for the final review.

Signature

Parental Views

Mark and Karen are still concerned about the number and severity of outbursts L. has at home.

L. will be taken to his GP to investigate the possibility of food allergies as it has been noted at home and school that L.'s behaviour often deteriorates after having eaten certain foods.

Signature

Box 11.5 Pastoral Support Programme – Final review

PASTORAL SUPPORT PROGRAMME

FINAL REVIEW

For

Pupil L.

Of
Year 3

Start Date:	Mid Term Review:	Final Review:
12.12.08	26.2.09	25.04.09

PERSONS/AGENCIES INVITED TO ATTEND	PERSON PRESENT AT MEETING (A)
EP	apologies
Outreach Teacher	✓
Learning Mentor	✓
Mark X. (Father)	✓
Karen X. (mother)	✓
ESW	✓
Teacher	✓
Outreach Manager	✓
Head teacher	✓
Key stage co-ordinator	✓

Box 11.5 (continued)

REVIEW OF PUPIL TARGETS

WHAT WERE THE TARGETS?	HOW EFFECTIVE WERE THE STRATEGIES/ACTION EMPLOYED?	WHO DELIVERED THE STRATEGIES/ ACTION?	HOW HAS THE BEHAVIOUR IMPROVED?	WHAT WAS THE PROGRESS? HOW WAS IT MEASURED AND CELEBRATED?
Aim: To follow a timetable of activities selected by an adult. Target: To select from a choice of 3 adult selected activities once a day. (if he does not choose to do what is on the timetable)	Strategies employed worked very well. L. has a sticker badge which he enjoys showing to people including his Mum and Dad.	Mrs E (TA) Mrs R (CT) Mr M (HT) Mrs C (LM) Mr N (Deputy head)	L. now follows his timetable on most occasions. When he is less happy to follow it, staff can negotiate with him for a positive outcome.	Excellent progress with this target. The consensus was that this target had been achieved.
Aim: To verbalise emotions and feelings Target: To select the appropriate feelings card or puppet and say how the puppet is feeling as he gives the card to the adult.	Staff felt that asking L. how he felt twice a day was a little artificial and L. did not always engage, therefore this target was less successful. L. made a happy and sad face puppet and does still use his rainbow feelings gauge – it is often a 10 now meaning happy.	Mrs E Mrs R	L. still doesn't like to say how he is feeling. He has demonstrated through his actions that he obviously feels happier in school and does not have as many angry outbursts.	Although the target has not been achieved, it was felt that as L. is so much happier in school that telling staff how he felt was not so important.

Box 11.5 (continued)

WHAT WERE THE TARGETS?	HOW EFFECTIVE WERE THE STRATEGIES/ACTION EMPLOYED?	WHO DELIVERED THE STRATEGIES/ ACTION?	HOW HAS THE BEHAVIOUR IMPROVED?	WHAT WAS THE PROGRESS? HOW WAS IT MEASURED AND CELEBRATED?
Aim: For L. to take responsibility for his actions and make amends for any upset caused. Target: For L. to work with his TA in tidying up or mending things that he has broken.	It has not been appropriate for L. to engage in this activity since before Christmas as he has not broken any equipment or trashed any rooms.	Mrs E Mrs R	L. will help to tidy up at the end of the day.	L. enjoys the praise and attention he receives from his positive actions.

Box 11.5 (continued)

Outcome ☐ (please tick one)

Significantly improved behaviour ☐
Improved behaviour ☐
Slight improvement in behaviour ☐
No improvement in behaviour ☐
Behaviour deteriorated ☐

Exclusions (complete if relevant) N/A

Fixed term exclusion ☐ number of occasions ☐ number of days ☐
Permanent exclusion ☐

Young Person's Comments

L.'s comments will be gathered by Mrs E and Mrs R and compared to the scaling
activity when the PSP first began.
Staff working with L. feel that he is very proud of his behaviour now.

Signature

Parental Views

Mark and Karen are really happy with L.'s progress. They feel things are looking more
promising now and L. is getting his work done. They have also noticed a difference
in his behaviour at home. L. likes to tell what he has done at school to his Mum, Dad,
Nan and Grandad.

Signature

Identify strengths and progress made since start of programme:

L. has made incredible progress since the start of the PSP but the meeting felt
that the continued structure of the PSP would improve things further and help L.'s
transition into year 4 run smoothly.

Why do we want the behaviour to change? (agree a common purpose):

To enable L. to integrate as much as possible with his peers in class and other times
during the school day.

Behaviour we would like to see:

For L. to take part in a timetabled activity in class every day.

For L. to feel more comfortable in expressing emotion.

Box 11.5 (continued)

Learning needs:

It is important to continue to give L. learning opportunities parallel to those of his classmates. This will enable L. to understand his learning in class in year 4.

Identify Motivating Factors for Change (why would the behaviour change?)
L. is enjoying the attention he receives from his positive actions. He has made friends and received awards in assembly. He feels very proud and wants this to continue.

Box 11.5 (continued)

PUPIL TARGETS

WHAT ARE THE NEW TARGETS?	STRATEGIES/ACTION TO BE EMPLOYED INCLUDING REWARDS AND SANCTIONS	WHO WILL DELIVER THE STRATEGIES/ ACTION?	HOW WILL WE KNOW THE BEHAVIOUR HAS IMPROVED?	HOW WILL PROGRESS BE MEASURED AND CELEBRATED?
For L. to take part in a timetabled activity in class every day.	L. will be rewarded in line with the other children in the class for good work and behaviour.	Mrs E Mrs R	L. will willingly go into class every day for an adult selected activity.	L. will receive stickers to put on his badge when he joins in with the planned activities.
For L. to feel more comfortable in expressing emotion.	L. will work through a programme based on the SEALS activities that will give him the vocabulary needed to express himself and a better understanding of the range of feelings we have.	Mrs E Mrs R Mrs B	L. is approachable and open. He has positive body language.	As above.

These targets will be reviewed at a meeting on 10th July at 10.30

12

Public Services: Police and Fire

Relationships with the schools are key to breaking down barriers to learning.

(Carol, primary school liaison officer)

Chapter overview

In this chapter, we look, in particular, at the changing role of the police in primary schools. Two interviews took place with school liaison officers (SLOs) – one based in a secondary school with a number of primary schools, the other working as a primary school liaison officer (PSLO). We also hear from a fire officer about his work in schools.

Safer Schools Partnerships

The media at different times have made great play about police officers stationed in schools, with headlines such as '400 officers patrol schools to curb truancy and violence'. It is made worse in the USA, of course, because the school patrol officers are armed. Certainly, the most alarming thing I have read was in the *New York Times*, 2 years ago. Bob Herbert recorded the arrest of a 6-year-old after she threw a tantrum in her kindergarten class. After 20 minutes of 'uncontrollable behaviour' the police were called and eventually she was pulled from under the table and handcuffed. There was a problem – the handcuffs were too large. Having experienced arresting a child before, the police were not thrown by this – they handcuffed Desre'e by her biceps. Later, she was charged with battery on a school official (a felony) and two misdemeanours, finger printed and a mugshot was taken.

This attitude fits very clearly into the construct of children as threats (Chapter 4). The journalist who covered the story pointed out that once you adopt 'the mindset that ordinary childhood misbehaviour is criminal behaviour it's easy to start seeing young children as somehow monstrous'.

Happily, this chapter is not about that, although some of the initial UK documentation in 2002 focused on behaviour in schools, rather than some of the wider issues that all three of those interviewed discussed. The 2008 DfES and Home Office guidance on Safer Schools Partnerships made it clear that the focus was on early intervention and prevention: 'The schemes encourage the police, children and young people to build up good relationships, trust and mutual respect.'

Primary schools have long been involved with the emergency services: police, fire and accident. Their role is a preventative one and they have brought in people from the emergency services to talk and work with children. The Safer Partnerships Programme formalises this. Healthy Schools, which we examined briefly in Chapter 10, is the preventative end of sickness and hospital admissions; along these lines, the fire and police service are, ironically, trying to prevent children having any contact with them outside of their preventative work.

Table 12.1 shows how this is seen at policy level and is taken from the Safer Schools Partnership guidance. It is breath-taking in its remit, and is far too broad and unfocused. The interviews provide the practical example of three of those people who are actually working at an operational level. There is an acknowledgement by all three of the difficulty involved in demonstrating the outcomes required over a relatively short period of time. Many of the aspects cover the work by other agencies, so it is also virtually impossible to provide the specific evidence for value for money (VFM). Attendance as we have already seen is a remit taken on by practically all of those interviewed, in one way or another. Figure 12.1 provides a more manageable job sheet and is also taken from the Partnership guidance.

Under the Safer School Partnerships, schools that are in areas with high levels of street crime are targeted. The formal statements are very much about working in partnerships with teachers in both primary and secondary schools, and also working with education services and related agencies. The officers I spoke with were mostly involved with the learning mentors in the primary schools, rather than the teachers. The intention of the partnerships is that the work in schools will help the police to 'identify, support and work with young people who are victims or offenders, as well as those at high risk of victimisation, offending and social exclusion'. As Figure 2.1 showed very clearly, those who have high truancy rates and low literacy and numeracy skills are far more likely to be excluded and to offend.

Matt: police officer

Matt works full-time as a police officer and in the school term times he is based at a secondary school. He has responsibility for this school, along with 12 primary schools, some of which are feeders for the secondary school, but the majority are not.

Prior to joining the police, Matt was an engineer with the Regional Travel Company for several years and left to train for the police. In this previous role, he had worked locally to the school for over 15 years, crossing the LA boundaries, which are more confined than the police ones.

When the post was advertised, there was difficulty recruiting for it and it remained unfilled for 2 years, partly because it was linking school hours and police hours and made for long working days, weekends and evenings. In the school holidays he works his regular beat. The LA pay 50 per cent of his salary. There are also specific risks involved; for example, police get called into other areas when extra help is needed.

TABLE 12.1 Links between 'Every Child Matters', Safe School Partnerships and the ECM joint area review inspection

ECM OUTCOMES	SSP QUALITY STANDARDS	ECM – JOINT AREA REVIEW OVERLAP
Be healthy	Promote healthy lifestyles Address drug and alcohol misuse Identify those at risk of offending, neglect or abuse	Under 16 conception rate Extent of participation in PE/exercise Drug-related mental health and behaviour problems Proportion of young people who consider they have been given sufficient guidance on health issues The health needs of young people with learning difficulties/disabilities are addressed
Stay safe	Ensure staff are CRB checked and at least one is child protection trained Comply with Health and Safety legislation Ensure child protection concerns are picked up and passed on as appropriate To promote antidiscriminatory behaviour and prevent bullying To reduce young people's experience of, and involvement in, crime and anti-social behaviour To steer young people away from involvement in criminal gangs	Secure recording and sharing of information on young people at risk of harm Targeted services for highlighting truancy Incidents of young people being killed or injured as a result of road traffic accidents Proportion of young people being bullied or discriminated against Young people's perceptions of safety within school Percentage of young people who have been victims Support for victims of crime/bullying Clear policies are developed on bullying
Enjoy and achieve	To promote young people's attendance at school To ensure young people are in full-time education, training or employment To help young people make full and constructive use of their leisure time To provide positive and accessible recreational activities for young people	Targeted specialist support for difficult to manage young people Re-integration into mainstream or work for excluded young people Percentage of half-days missed through absence Proportion of pupils permanently excluded Students receiving fixed term exclusions Proportion of schools in which behaviour is satisfactory or better and the proportion where it is good or better Proportion of pupils achieving the relevant level at the end of each key stage Identification of young people subjected to domestic violence within the home

TABLE 12.1 (continued)

ECM OUTCOMES	SSP QUALITY STANDARDS	ECM – JOINT AREA REVIEW OVERLAP
Make a positive contribution	To ensure young people are fully involved in the design and development of Safer School partnership activities	Identify young people at risk of anti-social behaviour
		Provide access to a range of activities to deter young people from anti-social behaviour
	To reduce the experience of bullying and anti-social behaviour (ASB) of young people in the Safer School Partnership's neighbourhood	Young people who have offended/at risk of offending are provided with a range of activities and support to assist with a law abiding life – raise self-esteem
	To provide opportunities for young people to contribute to the local community through active citizenship	Mentoring and support is provided for young people
		The extent to which young people contribute to key decisions effecting their lives
		The proportion of young people offending
		The proportion of young people re-offending
		The extend of bullying and discrimination by young people
		Young people initiate/manage organised activities in schools and voluntary organisations
Achieve economic well-being	To promote the engagement of young people in education	Measure how many young people leave school and engage in further education, employment or training
	To assist in the preparation of the young person for further education, training and employment	Young people are helped to prepare for working life – self-confidence, team working and enterprise
	To ensure young people involved in Safer School Partnerships are linked into further support where required	Needs are addressed before problems become intractable
		Services work together in a coordinated way
		Young people, parents and carers are involved in identifying their needs and designing services

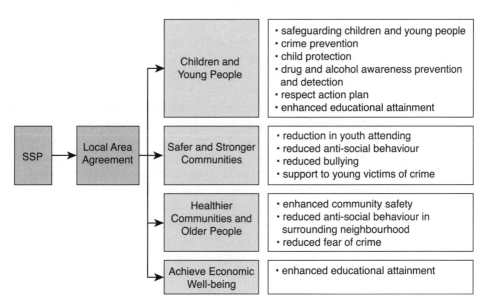

FIGURE 12.1 Aims and ECM

He has to ensure that if there are raids, he does not cover them in the area covered by the school. There are difficult barriers anyway to break down with the pupils, and he has to work hard to get rid of them before he can do anything worthwhile in terms of prevention. If he is seen involved with local raids he – and his family – are at increased risk.

He has found that he has some significant barriers to break down when working even with the youngest primary children, many of whom come from homes in which there is deep suspicion of anyone wearing a uniform. When visiting the reception class, for example, he will talk about the uniform, taking off his tie and jacket and giving children the opportunity to try them on and link with things that they may have in their role play corner. Clearly, for this to be successful the school also needs to be working on preparing children for such visits, as well as consolidating and developing their work afterwards.

He visits each primary school twice per term and has spent much of his 18 months in this post building up relationships with LMs based in the schools. He sees the LMs as the key link for the work he is doing. When in primary schools, he gives talks on the obvious areas such as stranger danger, bullying and anti-social behaviour. He also gets referrals about specific children who are deemed likely to fall 'into the net of policy'. This seems a rather nice catch-all phrase to describe those children who are likely to be known to the police in years to come. Recently, he dealt with a primary child who had been making 999 calls using his mobile phone. He came out to the school and spoke to two classes about the risks involved in doing this and the calls stopped. One of the things that did occur to me during the interview was that I wondered how much LMs and teachers were aware of what the officers could provide and whether there were other areas that could have been explored. There was also an issue with linking the partnership messages with the primary curriculum. Inputs on all of the issues are best done as part of a coordinated programme rather than as one-off inputs, and this requires much closer partnership and primary expertise than that which exists in this authority at the moment. These practical aspects are not acknowledged in the guidance.

The police are building up a skills force in terms of their work in schools, and Matt will call in a colleague to do some of the personal, social and health education (PSHE) work that he has been asked to cover. This colleague will work on topics, such as 'hate', and this nearly always finishes up with children saying that they hate the police; following this, Matt himself does the work simply because such statements have been made. He finds that anti-police attitudes vary from school to school and may remain a hidden, rather than overt, cultural norm when children are in school. When they are out of the school building and on the streets it then becomes overt. Children who are happy to talk to him in school are less likely to do this outside school. Now, when police are in training, they have to spend time in schools and it is seen as a more general part of police work than it used to be.

Most proud of

■ Breaking individual barriers, so that he is seen as an individual and not just Matrix (police tackling gang-related crime) within the department.

■ Ensuring that schools are safer as a direct result of his presence. Teachers have told him this.

Areas for development

The police need to have a greater presence in primary schools. In his patch, Matt sees particular difficulties with disaffected Year 5 and 6 pupils, as well as the increased use of drugs and alcohol among primary children generally.

Collette: primary school liaison officer

Collette left school with no qualifications and did not have any particular interests so she went through a number of different jobs that did not require any qualifications. Eventually, she decided to do a degree as a mature student.

When she left university, she knew she wanted to work with children, but definitely not as a teacher. Initially, she became a sessional supervisor for the probation office, working in bail hostels and supervising community service. Then she moved into being a sessional worker in the Youth Offending Team (YOT). This involved reparation work for under-17s, restorative justice, and teaching on a PSHE type programme called 'Jo Blagg'. This was a commonly used programme across the country and was rather like an older version of Circle Time. It involved bring up certain moral issues for discussion and drama. The impact of 'Blagg' on challenging and reducing offences by young people was formally evaluated and is similar to programmes within the social and emotional aspects of learning (SEAL) materials.

After this, she moved into the Youth Inclusion Unit, which was targeted at the 50 children and young people most likely to offend. The level of involvement varied, depending on the young person. It included those who were excluded from school, but she felt that it was probably less strict that the pupil referral units (PRUs). The PRUs are focused much more on getting the youngster back into school, and included youngsters who were involved with the Intensive Surveillance and Supervision Programme (ISSP). Involvement in this programme would arise as a result of part of a court order, with 25 hours allocated to YOT and then some young people were referred to the Youth Inclusion Programme (YIP), to cover education, where they would undergo testing to cover basic literacy, numeracy and computers. Permission to play pool in these circumstances became a bargaining tool.

Collette, like others interviewed, was unhappy about using this sort of behavioural carrot. She felt that it created a dilemma because pool play was being used to bribe youngsters into doing something educational. But, basically, there was just not much for youngsters to do in this situation. The YIP was open at night for those attending mainstream schools, but who were felt to be at risk of offending.

All of this provided important experience for Collette in developing the skills associated with restorative justice and general preventative programmes. This sessional work helped to get her into more secure work as a police community support officer (PCSO), and from there into the role of a PSLO.

Initially, the post involved working with materials that were created by the Suzy Lamplugh Trust. This Trust (Live Life Safe) aims to provide practical support and personal safety guidance for everyone. The website covers its work and provides details about training. This includes 'practical support and personal safety guidance as well as developing skills and strategies for avoiding violence and aggression'. The materials provided for the programme included a 20-question quiz, with open-ended questions, such as 'what would you do if . . . ?'. All of the PCSOs got copies of the questionnaire and the idea was to give it to primary pupils. Collette decided to do it differently and turned it into a presentation. This impressed her sergeant, and then his line manager, and this helped to get her into the post of PSLO. She had also found the missdorothy.com website to be useful. This website is aimed at providing activities 'to advance the education of people under 16 to relieve sickness, disability, poverty, cruelty and hardship'. It includes information on SEAL, downloads of songs, extension lesson and character cards. These are directed at raising confidence, self-esteem, emotional literacy and safety.

Role

Like Matt (who worked in a different LA), she worked 9 am to 5 pm (as a PLSO) during the school term time and in the school holidays returned to shift work as a PCSO. Her role covered 15 primary schools and initially she visited each school and spoke with each primary headteacher: all, except two, were very supportive. Now she finds that she works with the LMs.

Initially, she had not realised the importance of LMs, but, from working with them, and from her experience with primary pupils, she decided to change the type of presentations for different age groups. She felt that it was useful that she had come from a family of teachers and so understood the way in which the system was organised, the language used and the ethos of primary schools. One of the things this helped her with was to link the Safer Partnership objectives with the school's PSHE curriculum programme, and any other aspects of the curriculum that the teachers identified. This covered anti-social behaviour, criminal damage and experimenting with different types of drugs. For example, she got Year 6 pupils to design a poster on anti-social behaviour and the winning child from each school got an Argos voucher for £10. The poster was put into strategic places around the city and provided the opportunity to show what a Year 6 child felt about his own behaviour.

Collette felt that the relationships with the schools were key to breaking down barriers, but there are sometimes differences over issues such as safeguarding. For example, in one school a child had a very erratically shaved head and demonstrated other indicators of neglect; the headteacher was unwilling to report this until the Behaviour and Education Support Teams (BEST) team also identified it. Collette feels that good leadership is essential in putting measures into place and has been very grateful to one of the headteachers, and several of the LMs, who have looked at the presentations and helped her to improve them and try out other activities to hit the required targets. It has also provided a good opportunity to discuss other presentation issues, such as 'Death by PowerPoint', and varying the types of input and activities that can be offered.

Now that Collette has been in post longer, she uses a variety of these strategies and has included additional ones that she has discovered and tried out. She has also found and used materials from other relevant agencies, such as Kidscape (bullying), *Child Exploitation and Online Protection* Centre (CEOP – web safety) and NSPCC (Hector's World). Using these as starting points, she has experimented with activities that reinforce the teaching message after she has left the school. These include posters for Hallowe'en (Year 3), acrostic poetry on web safety for Year 4s, word search on criminal damage for Year 5s, and posters on anti-social behaviour for Year 6s. Drama and role play have been used with Crime Scene Investigation (CSI) equipment to look at subjects such as the theft of motor vehicles. Also, visits to see the mounted police, training dogs, helicopters, airports and the police museum have been provided. This involves taking fifteen children at a time; the school provides the transport, which, in Colette's authority, is a mini-bus that is shared by five schools.

Most of the schools are very supportive and she has been given a wide brief and welcomed. They have a 'can do' culture. There is a genuine wish to build bridges and make links between their children and the local police. This is particularly important because often the teachers do not live in these areas themselves and recognise that they do not have a first-hand knowledge of the local community. There are issues on the police side too, when the role of the PCSOs has been seen just as a step before becoming a police officer. It can also be used as a means of gaining experience, but actually you do need some experience as a criterion for doing the job in the first place.

The ECM agenda is an important element in this and links with the Safety in Schools initiative. The police and fire service are now committed to working together at an official level.

Most proud of

1. Building up relationships with children who have been identified as troublemakers and fairly useless members of society (nicknamed 'scrots'). This seems to be linked with parents who are third- and fourth-generation unemployed and basically anyone who just 'doesn't fit'. Collette feels that they can relate to her, even when she is in uniform. The children do tell her things and seem to trust her. This trust has to be built up over time. It is a different relationship and is particularly rewarding when links are made with those who are at risk of disaffection.

2. Interprofessional relationships are easier than they used to be. Here, dealings in school now tend to be with either LMs (on whole-school issues) or class teachers (on specific issues and children). The other support staff, such as TAs, tend to be pulled out of the presentation and children's activities if she is in the classroom and used in other classrooms.

3. Willingness of headteachers and LMs to be honest about how the programme is going, allowing some experimentation and ability to build up strong relationships.

4. Being challenged to try out things, such as being live on local radio, answering questions from children about drugs, weapons and street safety.

Areas for development

1. Relationships with her police colleagues can be difficult because they tend to think that spending so much of your time in primary schools is an easy ride. Ironically, she has found that older police officers are more supportive as they have seen similar initiatives in the past.

2. Wider understanding of the role of police in primary schools, what is involved and why it was set up.

Barriers to learning

1. Challenges for everyone involved about knowing ways in which children learn most effectively.

2. Outside influences, such as financial deprivation, domestic violence, drug abuse and English as an additional language (EAL).

3. Challenges of interagency working. Most of the initiatives are working, but there is still a great reluctant to bring in Social Services. Police can over-ride this with a police protection order (PPO), which does mean that children can be removed into a place of safety but Social Services can then return them; for example, a Year 2 girl, who was regularly in a local park until very late at night by herself, but was not seen by the local Social Services as in need of safeguarding because the child was clean and not bruised.

Carl: fire officer

Carl works as a fire liaison officer and covers one secondary school and five feeder primary schools. Carl does this in his own time, but does get paid for 7 hours per week. He feels that he needs to know more about children and young people, despite having four children of his own. Therefore, he is spending time working voluntarily in a school, which he feels is the key to getting the safety messages across in a non-judgemental way and avoiding conflict. The main issues with the primary school children are vehicle fires, rubbish fires and physical acts against fire officers. This is usually with small groups of youth, but, increasingly, older primary children are becoming involved, and certainly there are children of all primary ages who are standing by and watching. It sometimes seems as if the force is having to deal with feral children and young people. The incidents vary at different times of the year.

The service does have performance indicators about the success of raising issues in school, but he often feels outside his comfort zone. He gets support from the schools, but would welcome workshops and training courses to become more effective.

Findings

1. The barriers to learning here are linked to trying to support children so that they feel they are part of community and have a vested interest in it. This is part of the real message of community cohesion – in which firefighters and police officers are often on the frontline outside schools.

2. None of those interviewed had been given any real support in how to present the central government messages of safer partnerships. There were materials available, but only Collette had realised that these would need interpreting in terms of local community needs and the ages, interests and motivation of the children. She had also identified the importance of linking the message with other curriculum areas and researching into other related materials that could be used.

3. Collette also recognised what others interviewed had identified regarding differences in interpretation of safeguarding in terms of individual children, and instances when the school, and/or visiting professionals, felt that there was a safeguarding issue. This was across local authorities and may be linked. A foster parent, who was also interviewed, but not included here, told me that this was due to a shortage of places of safety for children, in both the short and long term. The Baby P incident in 2008 triggered increased numbers going into care and also a massive fostering campaign.

4. The current relationship with primary schools for both Matt and Carl seemed very piecemeal and heavily dependent on their own understanding of how schools worked, as well as their experience as parents. There is a real danger that presentations and visits can be seen by both school staff and the children as one-off entertainments or even a means of 'filling time' while teaching staff are moved into other areas.

5. Carl was very honest about his lack of confidence regarding the work in schools that he is expected to do and the need for professional development. It is likely that many others who go into schools also feel like this, or may not be aware that what they do is not as effective as it should be. Really, anyone coming into schools should have support and guidance about presentations and activities, so that the intended learning is more effectively and professionally supported.

13

Charity, Consultants and Volunteers

The school has made me think I've got a future and this has shown my own children that you can go for something and get it. And because I have gained qualifications and play a role in the school and bring up six children, others like me have confidence that they can do this as well.

(Tola, parent volunteer)

Chapter overview

In this chapter we just touch on the very traditional role of parent volunteers, but also look at some of the other organisations and personnel who are involved in primary schools. The involvement of the third sector, quangos and private consultants has also changed over the past 5 years and, indeed, will continue to change. The chapter covers interviews with a person who works for a major charity (third sector), a Primary Care Trust (PCT) Children's Champion (quango) and as a private consultant. Three of those interviewed were also governors in primary schools. As all were very busy people, and school governorship is both time-consuming and unpaid, this represents a real commitment to the sector.

Parent volunteers

Most of the teaching assistants (TAs) and some of the learning mentors (LMs) who were interviewed had started off their work in schools by becoming parent volunteers, and, in one case, one person was actually asked to volunteer because her child was being 'badly behaved' (her words!). Through this, the one-time volunteers themselves realised, sometimes for the first time, how much they enjoyed working with children. Certainly, that was my own experience. Schools identified a valuable resource, and when it suited both parties, were willing to pay when an opportunity for employment rose, although not all parent volunteers wanted or needed this.

Maddie: parent helper

Maddie became involved when her own child started school and the school was asking for parent volunteers. She was working in full-time employment, but felt that she should volunteer as it would be useful for her own development. Maddie was an IT specialist and, initially, on visits to the school, noticed that very little IT was used, so this became her focus and she visited two other schools to find out more about IT in primary schools. Four years later, Maddie is still a parent volunteer and has used her IT expertise to make a significant change in the way in which children are introduced to technology in this school.

The school is in an area where a lot of parent volunteers have professional qualifications and Maddie met up with an ICT teacher from a secondary school, who was also a parent volunteer. The class teacher was very enthusiastic about the idea of focusing on technology and this has led to the establishment of an ICT circus every Friday afternoon. It provided access to new technology for the very youngest children in school and would not have happened without the parent volunteers. The school is a large and popular three-form entry school and two of the teachers have Planning, Preparation, Assessment (PPA) time on a Friday afternoon and it is then that the parents and the other teacher run the ICT circus for all three Year 1 classes.

Currently this involves the use of digital cameras, voice recorders, LEAPs, keyboards, microscopes, videos, etc. After each session, the parents and teacher talk over what has happened and plan for the next week. It is very tightly organised and parents are working alongside the teacher. In some cases they may have more technical expertise than the teacher, but this particular teacher is happy and enthusiastic about this.

Most proud of

1. The growing confidence of the children in the use of technology.
2. Several successful entries to the British Educational Communications and Technology Agency (BECTA), which have won additional technology for the school. This has included two Apple computers and a set of digital cameras.
3. Coming first in a BECTA competition, which was focussed on creativity in digital media.
4. Extending the range of learning in different ways, for example incorporating literacy and numeracy creatively. Maddie felt that it was important that the IT did not just replace paper and pencil – rather it was used to provide children with different ways of tackling and developing literacy and numeracy skills, and it should take their learning further. As an example, she explained that rather than just recording an event in a book they could use their IT skills to take photos and comment on them. Doing so involves very young children in their own assessment and provides opportunities for them to discuss how their work could be improved.
5. She is really pleased that her child goes to a school where the learning ethos has enabled this to happen.

Areas for development

Maddie does not feel that there are any areas for development at the moment because there is a good handful of willing and helpful parents.

Barriers to learning

She does think that there are barriers to learning for children, created by the restrictions of the National Curriculum targets. ICT can help children to learn in lots of different ways, but, because of constraints on the primary timetable, it cannot be as integrated as it should be. It would be really good to be able to broaden the ICT circus across the school as an initial strategy for increased integration of ICT in the timetable.

She also felt that learning support workers in school needed to be IT competent and enthusiastic, because, however good the class teacher may be, if this isn't reinforced by the support worker, the essential work done by the TA cannot build on the high quality of the teaching and learning. BECTA, itself, looks to the Training and Development Agency (TDA) to provide the training for TAs, along with the support, and it records that new TAs receive induction for literacy and numeracy, including some ICT in learning and teaching. However, looking at the TDA materials (112 pages) in the *Guidance on Introductory Training for Teaching Assistants and School Support Staff* it is difficult to find this ICT induction for primary school support staff. The actual primary induction materials on the TDA website do provide a short module on ICT for primary staff, but it does not require either the support workers or their trainer to have any more understanding or skill than what is on the PowerPoint provided. There is far more guidance for the foundation stage and for secondary support staff.

Here we have a highly skilled and enthusiastic parent, in a school with similar parent volunteers, who has added considerably to the quality of the curriculum for children. It raises an interesting question about the postcode lottery of parent helpers and thence on those likely to be employed by the school through the parent helper route. Maddie also raised key issues about the expertise of support workers in being able to develop the curriculum if they do not have the necessary expertise to start with. The government programme of support was limited to small-scale literacy and numeracy initiatives and linked closely with meeting SATs targets. And as we have seen above the potential of IT has been virtually ignored within the development of the NLF and NNF and now the National Strategies. This may be partly linked with the gap between those at the Web 1 level who devise the strategies based on the subject knowledge and those IT experts who are well into teaching potential with Web 2 technologies, but lack the primary subject knowledge in maths and English.

Tola: parent helper

Tola left school with no qualifications and initially worked with disabled adults, then at a hostel for battered women and children. She had six children and, through the school, got interested in family literacy when the school ran courses for parents. This was about basic skills in English and maths. Since then Tola has done many other courses in the LA Family Learning Programme (FLP). She feels that the school experience and the FLP have changed her life and those of her family. The healthy cooking course, for example, had resulted in her family now making all of their own food.

Eventually, after doing a lot of volunteer work at the school, Tola was offered a welfare assistant's job. She explained that it was difficult to separate the volunteer and paid parts of the role because she spends so much time in school.

As a parent volunteer, Tola works as part of the school breakfast club team and brings children from several homes to the breakfast club, to ensure that they get up for school and get something to eat. This is an everyday commitment. She has her own volunteer timetable, with a parent/toddlers group on a Monday, at which she works alongside the parent mentor. She goes into classes for reading, copying arts activities, small group work and spelling – in fact anything she is asked to do. Then she does organisational activities, such as stocktaking and meeting guests. At the time of the interview she was banding books for the school library. After school she runs the Boccia club – a form of indoor bowling.

Tola is most proud of the relationships she has with the children. They call her by her first name and this makes it a different type of relationship from the relationship they have with teachers and TAs; for example, when a Year 5 girl came to her that morning to tell her that she was having pains, she listened to what the child was saying and discussed it. At home time she told the girl's mother, whom she knew well, and the mum then knew that she needed to get her daughter ready for her periods. Another child, who was mute in the classroom, started to talk to Tola and Tola started to call her Smiley because she always had such a lovely smile. Now this child is beginning to talk a little in the classroom. She is proud that the children see her as someone to trust. She is also a parent governor and finds this interesting, as it provides another way of supporting the school and being able to represent the views of parents. Being a parent volunteer had given her the confidence to do this and she has encouraged other parents to stand as governors as well.

Tola is also proud of passing all the courses she has taken, and is now waiting for funding for Level 4 courses. This is harder to get because it is at the higher level. She would also like to do courses on special needs, as she has just been identified with dyslexia herself and this has helped her to understand the difficulties children have. Money for volunteers to do courses such as this and the Level 4 NVQ is just not available.

The inspirational quote from Tola at the start of this chapter on how parent volunteering had given her – and her children – a future is something I did not expect to find and raises important issues about higher-level funding for courses beyond basic skills courses. Tola and her family do have a very real future as she is now involved in plans to open her own Youth Club because she sees it as something needed in the area and it will provide her with a challenge for fundraising. She has already identified a building for the club and she wants it to cover both young people and older people in the community.

She identified the constant changes that the government makes in primary schools as a real barrier to children's learning because they are not always what children need. Through spending so much time in classrooms, she also sees that some children do not understand what is being taught for a lot of different reasons; their experienced curriculum is interfering with their learning. She has just completed a counselling course and part of this involved being able to read the body language of children.

Maddie and Tola: summary

These two parent volunteers worked in schools with two very different catchment areas and both have worked in the school for several years. The relationship between themselves and the schools has been mutually beneficial and in both cases provided an expertise that the school could use. Both were in schools which were ready to try things out and this is also reflected in the very positive responses from TAs and learning mentors, who had worked in schools were the ethos was conducive to new challenges, trying things out and developing both adults and children.

Rob: private consultant working with primary children

Rob started out working with a large rural county council in their training department, and part of his remit was to bring a 'training eye' to education and explore links between schools and businesses. During this time he became a governor of a primary school as the community element of his role as a training centre manager.

He then set up as a private consultant and took on different contracts in both the public and private sector. His initial remit as a private consultant with the local Children's Services Department was to create projects involving schools and 'Business in the Community'. It involves a number of employers engaging in business and education together, and would now be seen as meeting the economic well-being strand of the ECM agenda. It was also about brokering sustainable links between schools and employers. Initially, it was secondary school based because employers were looking at their potential recruitment. Now it involves primary children and the initial programme has expanded to several other parts of the country.

Other primary projects have included:

1. A primary-aged version of *Dragon's Den*, based on the TV programme. The latest version of this has been a project to reverse the Dragon's Den procedures. This is to let the children be the Dragons and then bring in business people to bid, either for a particular project or for something the schools might buy from them, for example a calendar.

2. Junior Workwise was developed to encourage businesses to work in schools, generally after the Year 6 SATs. A package was created and trialled with two primary teachers, and was aimed at getting employers to work with primary schools. It involved encouraging them to recognise that primary-aged children and their parents formed an important part of the local community, including the potential workforce. Rob also sees this as an important means of raising aspirations for primary children.

3. Involving local employers in other ways. For example, the Regional Rail Company and Starbucks Coffee Company were persuaded to run an art competition, which had two prizes for under-12s and two for those aged 12 plus. It could be any form of art related to the environment. It resulted in 260

entries and was judged by local artists. The work appeared on the local arts website and the winning entries were exhibited in Starbucks coffee shops over the region.

4.   Rob has also written and established a motivational programme with a series of strategies to go through using business managers as role models. The business people were trained to work with primary children and this training helped to provide the structure and framework to the relationship.

5.   'My Community' project. In seven schools in part of the outer sprawl of the city, children had to come up with ways of describing their community in song, dance and art. The regional radio station was persuaded to invest some money in each of the schools and this enabled the purchase of radio station equipment. This was also used as a means of improving communication skills through having a school radio station and was very successful in involving parents; for example, 85 had showed up for the community theatre to demonstrate children's work.

Rob sees that his work gives him the opportunity of watching youngsters realise that they can bring something to the world and that they can have a part in it. A lot of youngsters he sees come from unemployed families, who have few, if any, aspirations and have low self-esteem. So, seeing their art in a local art gallery, in a coffee shop and on a website gives both them and their parents a pride in what they have done and its public recognition. For children who had never done anything successfully in school it provides an opportunity to 'walk on air' and let their parents and carers do the same.

As an independent consultant, Rob has been able to take ideas and packages into many parts of the country and he would like to see all primary schools being involved with initiatives like this, bringing business and local employers into schools and taking children into working environments. He finds the lack of aspiration in some senior managers depressing, as well as preventing children gaining new experiences. He is aware that health and safety are a real issue in a litigious society and also with regard to the safeguarding requirements, but he has seen how when primary schools do become involved, the project really takes off.

Anna: PCT Children's Champion

Anna is also a school governor, but the interview covered her other work as a Children's Champion in the local PCT. She is a retired primary headteacher and, prior to retiring, she decided to extend the volunteer work she had just begun in a local hospital. When she had mentioned this, she discovered the world of the quango and non-executive directors. Another retired colleague had been on a PCT board and told her how much she enjoyed her work with the PCT. It had sounded quite exciting and she had applied for and got a post as a result of an advertisement in the local paper. She was formally appointed to start about 6 months before she retired.

The board of a PCT technically runs it and sets the strategic agenda. The non-executives are appointed through the NHS wing of the Appointments Board and receive some remuneration. In Anna's case it was £7000 per year and involved a commitment of 2 days per month. The non-executive chair received considerably more. Anna replaced a non-executive, who had just died, and was appointed as a PCT

Children's Champion about 6 months after she started with the PCT. The role was to be the chief spokesperson on the Board for Children, attend meetings especially related to children, and go for specialist training. There was some confusion generally about the role of Champion in PCTs and this included that for other Champions, such as those for Older Persons, Mental Health and Dental Health. However, the influence over strategic or operational work seemed to vary between different PCTs.

Anna was most proud of being able to use her lifetime experience in the primary sector to speak up for children at PCT Board meetings. In particular, she felt that she gave a voice to primary and nursery children, who she felt were key change agents in health promotion 'pester power'. In the early days when health promotion was on the agenda it often seemed to be aimed at secondary pupils and Anna felt that she had helped to change this. She could give easy examples from her experience of how initiatives could be enhanced and extended for younger children. Basically, it linked education with health prior to the Integrated Services agenda. She also set up a network of Children's Champions in the region. This enabled her to find out what was happening in different PCTs.

However, Anna felt that perhaps she was not the best person to ask about this work, because she came off the PCT after 4 years, as she did not feel that non-executives in this particular PCT had much influence on policy, strategies or operational aspects – it was a bit like being an item on a checklist, waiting to be ticked off. If at one year into the appointment I had asked her about this she would have said that the non-executive role of the Children's Champion gave greater informed emphasis on the Board for the role of schools – particularly on what was not possible for them to do, as well as what was. A countrywide network of such Champions could provide strong pressure group; in particular for stronger links between the PCT and Social Services. There were many links on paper, but, in fact, when she had wanted information that was held by someone in Social Services, it was virtually impossible to get hold of either the key person or a colleague. She also felt that, in view of local and national publicity about safeguarding children, it was important that the wider messages of the ECM agenda were not lost.

Anna felt that there had been some breakdown of silos between professionals in all areas who work with children and who have responsibility for them. Although there are issues about lack of specific knowledge and skills between different areas. There was evidence that more professional courses were including wider issues about Integrated Children's Services, but some courses were just too short, for example the 1-year course for graduates who train to be teachers. This was effectively only 9 months and could only give very little time to other professional areas. She was also concerned about the political imperative to evaluate new initiatives as being very successful as soon as they were in place. She compared this to planting a potato on Monday and then digging it up on Friday to see how it was growing. This also led to sanitised case studies on multi-agency working and Integrated Children's Services that were virtually worthless, distorted the challenges in this area, and failed to examine strategies based on operational experience.

Pat: team leader and family support worker with a national charity

Before she was 30, Pat had spent time travelling and doing a lot of different jobs. She then decided to settle down a bit, did the Certificate of Qualification in Social Work (CQSW) and went to work in the North East as a generic social worker. After a few years she moved back to the Midlands, where she spent 19 years as a social worker and then, later, became a team manager. By this time, social work had changed considerably and there were family support workers, who did much of the operational work that the trained social worker used to do. She talked about the huge increase in paperwork since she had first trained as a social worker, but suggested that the increase in bureaucracy could be seen positively because it prevented a general drift, had review stages and implemented timescales.

After working with the LA for this long, she felt in need of a change and came as a job share to work for this charity. The charity was very much focused around families and had developed new models of working with them, based on Family Group Meetings/Conferences (FGMs). This concept came from New Zealand, where the Maori people had pushed for more family involvement. It placed the emphasis back on families and in New Zealand there were no care orders without an FGM. The FGM service is expanding in this charity and the team leader's role is changing.

The charity had a contract with the council, to expand its FGM service as mentioned in the 2004 green paper. The 'Public Law outline' changes care proceedings and FGMs were seen as part of the layers to support families. Practice varied from among different LAs and was covered by the Social Services wing of the authority.

Pat is involved with three projects – Family Group Meetings, Family Support, and Contact Service. She supervises seven family support workers, which involves allocating work, conducting informal case discussions and the budgeting involved. Her line manager runs the whole centre and consolidates the budget arrangements. Workers are employed by the charity, but work for the LA, so they basically form another arm of the LA. The family support workers mainly have attained NVQ3s and have a wide variety of experience of other life skills, such as youth work. The charity does not have a waiting list for its family support work, because the numbers are negotiated with the LA. This results in no formal waiting list. Obviously, if there were more staff it would be possible to work with more families.

She felt that the charity has an advantage as a voluntary agency because it appears to many as less threatening and the workers can spend more time with the family. At the moment of interview, the FGM involved the family, the family worker and the LA worker, but this was in the process of change. The workers looked at the presenting issues, what the family wanted and what the Family Support Worker needed to do. The case study (see later in chapter) shows how successfully this can work.

Poverty was a major issue and, recently, one of the youth groups had made an animated cartoon video with the BBC, in which they discussed what it was like to be poor from their perspective.

The family support worker assists with managing a routine such as getting children to school – if you have five young children then this is hard work. It provides an opportunity to set boundaries and routines for daily life, and provides an individualised parenting programme, as well as giving an opportunity to be involved with a group programme. The parenting programme is heavily into developing self-esteem and confidence, and it mainly works through with mothers.

Joint working with the local authority and other agencies can be very successful and creates a real 'feel good factor'. It moves people on to other supporting agencies that are available for them in the community, such as those dealing with domestic violence, substance misuse, benefits help, pregnancy, etc. Those working have to be very non-judgemental and able to build up self-esteem through sharing conversations. They can then refer people on to more generic parenting programmes, such as the Webster-Stratton one. The charity has two workers who are trained in running this programme and it was held within the family centre. They have a list of contacts with both primary and secondary schools and hold sessions in school with children and young people.

Pat said that they help to remove barriers to learning through helping families with routines, making clear boundaries for the children, getting them up and ready in the morning, providing support and advice, and liaising with other agencies and within the family itself. It is a mixed individualised approach with the child(ren) and parent(s)/carer(s).

This section of the charity has two groups of children with whom they work: the 'Be Smart' group, between the ages of 11 and 15, and the 'Schools Out Group', between the ages of 7 and 11. The 11–15 group have recently had inputs on sexual health, healthy eating, and safety with the community police officer. The young children have had work on healthy schools, cleaning teeth, etc. Pat acknowledged that they had to be very careful that it is not what they get in school because the children do not want this. There are generally ten or eleven children and young people in these groups, and transport is provided for the younger age range. There are both paid workers and volunteers involved, who all undergo a proper training programme and, in addition, have to go through the Criminal Records Bureau (CRB) disclosure process. The whole set-up is run by the Children's Service Manager and there are full- and part-time staff, as well as sessional staff. These sessional staff receive in-service training.

The charity also has a Contact Service, which involves children linking with a parent or parents under supervision. It is generally very prescriptive and informed by court proceedings. Records are kept to feed into future custody proceedings.

Other wings of the charity in other places have these and/or other projects. There are Keeping Children Safe projects, which are targeted at those at risk of sexual exploitation, a Leading Care Team, and a fostering service for children with disabilities. The success of the charity is largely because it has a long history with troubled families. It is seen differently from agencies in the state sector and it seems to be able to give more time and support.

Pat felt that they had some great success stories, as it was a skilful and hardworking team. She firmly believed that those working for the charity needed to see the work as vocational in order to provide the appropriate support for families.

The following case study is an example of the work the charity does to raise barriers to learning – it is quite genuine and written by a parent who had been supported by the charity. See also Figure 13.1 for further details on raising barriers to learning, which were mentioned during the interview.

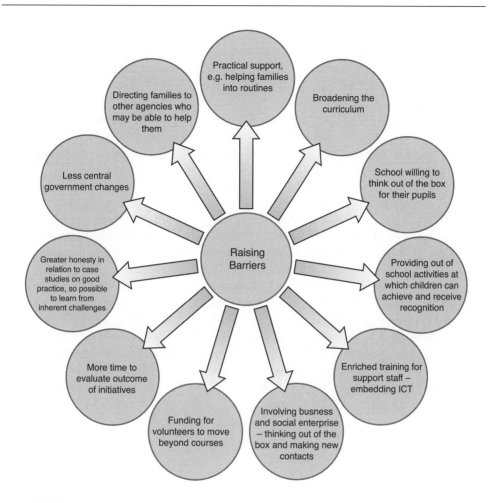

FIGURE 13.1 Raising barriers to learning

Before the charity was involved, I was, and still have been, under Social Services for 10 years. I had help only a few times from them. Me and my kids were put on the Child Protection register for nearly 2 years and I still never got much help. My kids were classed as 'children in need' after that. A few years passed and things got worse. Then they were placed back on the register just a year ago because of an incident that happened. And then up until just under a year ago the charity were involved: (1) because my house was a tip, I could say worse but I won't, and (2) it took Social Services to get me the help, only because they came out to my house and saw the way I was living.

So when X from the charity came out and looked around my house, that is when my help started with the charity. I was sent a 2 weeks, every day, course, when I had someone come out to me to see if I had done what they had set for me to do. I even done more work because I wasn't willing for Social Services to take my other kids off me. For 2 weeks of daily visits I had to do tasks they set out for me, which was a bit upsetting for me when I thought I hadn't done enough just to prove that I could do some. X came and took photos of my house, well I'd say dump, because that's what it was. So when I finally got it like a home my landlord decided to come in and turn it upside down. I did break down at one point but the charity were very helpful and understanding when I was feeling very low. They were more helpful than Social Services. X was made my family support worker who works for the charity. She is very understanding and she made me want to live my life again. She helps me so much it's like having a big sister around. Being honest, if it wasn't for her and the help from the charity I'd be in the gutter now. I would have had my other kids taken off me and I don't know where I would be.

I owe my life to them from the bottom of my heart and if I could do anything to improve my life I would work for the charity, only because I've had the experience with my home being the way it was and the problems I've had with problem kids and the way social workers are.

At the end of the day if it wasn't for the help from the charity I wouldn't be where I am today. So if you ever get offered help from them don't turn it down, always let them help you because if you don't take their help there's no one else, believe me, I know.

CHAPTER

14

Believe in Children

The title for this final chapter is taken from Barnardo's and it reflects the views of the vast majority of those who were interviewed about their work for this book. They did 'believe in the potential of every child and young person, no matter who they are, what they have done or what they have been through'.

Chapter overview

The purpose of this chapter is to bring together some of points made in this book to enable readers to:

- Look at the evidence within the book and compare it with what they can see in schools. This needs to include their own experience as pupils as well as their current evidence
- Use the interviews to make links between how educational professionals saw their roles and how this linked with what has been written about improving educational outcomes
- Inform and improve current practice in whatever role they may be in as an educational professional.

This book has looked at two different sides of the same coin. It has used the literature to see the place of the wider school network in making a difference in children's lives. The first section was very much about the need for this wider school workforce to gather data from many different fields, then interpret this evidence, and use it for planning and informing strategies for raising barriers to learning and improving individual educational outcomes. In the second section, we looked at some examples of current practice. Those who are actively involved in this wider workforce were asked to explain how they do it. The workforce remodelling programme has opened the way for making a real change in children's lives and the purpose of a text such as this one is to show both how the literature can inform practice and how practice can inform the literature.

Overview of the literature: identification of barriers and strategies

Part 1

Chapter 1 provided an overview of the Wider Children's Workforce and the ways in which the government presents this. It also touched on the Integrated Qualifications Framework, which is still, at the time of writing, being developed in greater detail. The initial 'Every Child Matters' (ECM) documentation required a much more integrated workforce and, clearly, induction training and continuing professional development (CPD) form an important part of this. The current evidence from some of the documentation, for example that for looking at induction for teaching assistants (TAs) in primary ICT, looks very lightweight and does not recognise that simply knowing how IT is important and its safeguarding aspects does not skill up those who are not confident in their own use of it. This was just one example within the chapter, but this was repeated during the interviews by those who raised training needs. Levels of current training were raised and comparisons made between the intensive full-time training involved in becoming an NNEB-trained nursery nurse and the vocational Levels 3 and 4. The current system is a starting point, but many good practice schools already supplement this by their own training.

1. *Differential performance in schools.* This looked at some of the data collected on potential barriers to learning within neighbourhoods and for specific groups. It raised the danger of seeing these as fixed, so that a child once labelled in some way as deficient by postcode or stereotyping would have a mental ceiling put on their outcomes from school. This labelling can also be related to schools, for example, 'Bog standard primary school is in a challenging area'. Individuals working in schools labelled in this way, or feeling personally challenged by specific children, need support in both understanding the data and avoiding using it to write off children. The data currently available needs a critical eye cast over it and although league tables and contextual data provide a carrot-and-stick approach, individuals and teams working within the system can be helped by a greater understanding of them.

2. *Tackling poverty.* This moved beyond the 'vulnerable' groups in school as identified in the past by psychologists and sociologists and currently by the media, Ofsted and politicians. Again, this chapter illustrated the need to question some of our concepts about poverty in the UK and to avoid stereotyping children whose family situations frequently put them in and out of the poverty definition. It also questioned the practical usefulness of the term 'inclusion' to describe everyone, yet funding only specially identified groups.

3. *Learning and concepts of childhood.* This chapter looked at traditional ideas of learning, including some such as Gardner's multiple intelligences. Through these, some of the current strategies that are used for breaking down barriers to learning were examined, which draw on these traditional ideas. It also suggested that educational professionals should stand back and look at the construct of childhood, which implicitly defines the determinants for an effective learner. It

also looked at the need to examine differing views about childhood provided by the media, politicians, economists and Social Services. Anyone who works with children knows that fixed views about children are less than helpful when trying to lift barriers to learning.

4. *Identifying and lifting hidden curriculum barriers for children*. Most schools are well aware of the different types of curriculum presented to children within and outside their walls. In this chapter we moved from areas such as the official and observed curriculum into the hidden and experienced curriculum of the timetable, school toilets, design, noise, lighting, furniture and space.

5. *Challenges for primary schools*. This looked at some of the complexities involved in breaking barriers to learning through technology, neuroscience and greater scientific evidence about learning and brain care. This chapter also looked at the changing social climate in which we work and the potential provided by increased school and agency support for learners.

Part 2

Asking the workers

In this section we asked those actually working with children to describe their work, what they felt most proud of and what they felt needed developing. They were then asked what they felt were barriers to learning and what sort of strategies could be used to lift these barriers. Chapters 7, 8, 10, 12 and 13 provided an overview of these barriers and strategies. Chapters 9 and 11 provided two case studies, which looked at fairly imaginative and creative strategies developed in Chapter 9 by a small group of schools and in Chapter 11 by a local authority working closely with a Primary Care Trust.

Some surprises

1. The huge number of people who were involved in supporting children's learning in primary schools. A significant number of these were involved in off-site activities, for example the Study Support Services. Each person whom I interviewed had a number of other contacts who they thought would be useful for such a book. Consequently, I am very much aware of many of the other educational professionals who help to break down barriers to learning who could have been included as well. The reader might like to fill some of the gaps.

2. The fantastic amount of good will involved. Nearly all those I interviewed, particularly those who were working directly with children all the time, were regularly working hours well over their allocated time. And this was because not only did they believe they were making a difference to children's lives, but they could actually see it and give me examples.

3. The varied streams of funding which are used to pay operational workers and as a direct result of this:

- The time spent by primary heads and operational managers within different organisations, looking for funding, managing it, evidencing VFM, and often for reasons well outside their control having to repeat this with different funding streams. There were linked issues with how VFM could be identified with hard evidence outcomes and also when several different agencies were involved the danger of double or even treble accounting.

- Huge variations between schools and LAs about the amount of money available, often as a direct result of ring-fenced government funding.

- Salaries and conditions of service – one particular anomaly which struck out for those employed directly by schools was how many were not paid for school holidays. Other factors included the numbers of those on temporary contracts and those being paid through more than one funding stream. This is in the process of changing, but variation between schools will continue as heads and their governing bodies have to use their most expense resources – salaries – to balance budgets.

4. The increased awareness by those involved of the complexity of some children's lives and the consequent need to involve other skilled professionals to work with individual family members or the whole family. These included parent mentors, Family Learning Services, Family Support Workers and Educational Social Workers. Parenting came out as a key issue and was accompanied by a number of parenting courses.

5. The links between the research and data collections were explicitly made by some of those interviewed. In nearly all cases there was a degree of understanding from Educational Professionals about the complexities and challenges of many of the children's lives. The hard data behind this was less well known. This included very easily digestible neighbourhood statistics from the government's statistics site as well as more complex research evidence from bodies such as the Sutton and Rowntree Trusts, the Child Poverty Action Group and charities such as Barnado's.

6. So many of those interviewed mentioned that the formal curriculum itself was a barrier to learning. This covered content overload as well as prescribed methods of teaching, which assumed all learners responded in the same way. It takes considerable courage for a school, particularly those who appear low down in the league tables, to move towards a more holistic approach. This is true even when government documentation urges schools to be creative.

7. Parenting was seen as needing support and it was recognised that often those most in need of this help needed one-to-one support before they felt confident to join a group. The Team Leader and Family Support Worker who worked for a charity provided an example of a woman who had been helped by the charity and it illustrates how isolated many parents feel.

8. Poverty was mentioned surprisingly rarely as a barrier to learning, although the evidence from the literature indicates that it is a major factor in educational outcomes.

9.   The huge number of acronyms in use by differently trained professionals, some having the same abbreviation for two very different things e.g. PCT. Hopefully more integrated training will encourage the development of greater shared professional language.

And what did not surprise

The gender and race bias within the workforce. The vast majority of those interviewed were women and only schools with a significant percentage of ethnic minority children either employed or bought from their LA ethnic minority workers.

The overall message was from those working 'on the shop floor' was that there were some clear reasons why some children had barriers to learning, but were really optimistic about ways in which they could make a difference to lives. The Star Fish theory (see Chapter 9) is alive and well in our primary schools today.

Bibliography

Introduction

Bartholomew, J. (2006) *The Welfare State We're In*, London: Politico.

Central Advisory Council for Education (1967) *Children and their Primary Schools*, London: HMSO. (Commonly known as the Plowden Report.) Also available online at www.dg.dial.pipex.com/documents/plowden.shtm.

DfES (1999a) Guidance for Learning Mentors, London: DfES.

DfES (1999b) The National Curriculum, London: DfES.

DfES (2003) Excellence and Enjoyment, London: DfES.

Hughes, P. (2008) *Principles of Primary Education*, London: Routledge.

Hughes, P. (2009) 'Breaking Barriers to Learning', Chapter 7 in Warren, S. (ed.) *An Introduction to Education Studies*, London: Continuum.

Shuayb, M. and O'Donnell, S. (2009) 'Aims and Values in Primary Education: England and Other Countries', in Cambridge Primary Review, *Towards a New Primary Curriculum*, Cambridge: University of Cambridge.

TDA (2006) *Raising Standards and Tackling Workload: A National Agreement*, London: TDA

Theme 6 (2009) 'Settings and Professionals', in Cambridge Primary Review, *Towards a New Primary Curriculum*, Cambridge: University of Cambridge.

Tymms, P. and Merrell, C. (2009) 'Standards and Quality in English Primary Schools Over Time: The National Evidence', in Cambridge Primary Review, *Towards a New Primary Curriculum*, Cambridge: University of Cambridge.

Whetton, C., Ruddock, G. and Twist, L. (2009) 'Standards in English Primary Education: The International Evidence', in Cambridge Primary Review, *Towards a New Primary Curriculum*, Cambridge: University of Cambridge.

Wood, M. (2009) 'Listening to Pupils' Voices', Chapter 10 in Warren, S. (ed.) *An Introduction to Education Studies*, London: Continuum.

Chapter 1: The Wider Children's Workforce in Primary Schools

Brighouse, T. (2006) *Essential Pieces: The Jigsaw of a Successful School*, London: RM.

Brott, P. and Kajs, L. (2001) 'Developing the Professional Identity of First-Year Teachers Through a "Working Alliance" '. Available from www.alt-teachercert.org/Working%20Alliance.html.

Burgess, H. (2008) Primary Workforce Management and Reform. Primary Review Research Survey 6/4, Cambridge: University of Cambridge Faculty of Education.

CWDC (2009) Functional Map of the Children and Young People's Workforce in England: the foundation of a coherent workforce. Leeds: CWDC. Also available from www.childrensworkforce.org.uk/assets/0000/0365/Functional_map.pdf.

DCSF (2007) Building Brighter Futures: Next Steps for the Children's Workforce, London: DFCS.

DCSF (2008) 2020 Children and Young People's Workforce Strategy, London: DFCS.

DCSF (2009) The Children's Plan. One Step Onwards, London: DFCS.

DfES (2003) Every Child Matters, London: TSO.

DfES (2004) Every Child Matters: Change for Children, London: TSO.

DfES (2005) Common Core of Skills and Knowledge for the Children's Workforce, London: DfES.

Friedson, E. (1994) *Professionalism Reborn: Theory, Prophecy and Policy*. Oxford: Polity Press.

Hughes, P. (2008) *Principles of Primary Education*. London: Fulton/Routledge.

Ofsted (2005) Remodelling the School Workforce, London: NOS. Also available at www.ofsted.gov.uk/publications/2596.

Ofsted (2007) Reforming and Developing the School Workforce. London: NOS. Also available at www.ofsted.gov.uk/publications/070020.

Ofsted (2008) The Deployment, Training and Development of the Wider School Workforce, London: Ofsted.

Smith, A. (2002) *The Brain's Behind It*. Stafford: Network Educational Press.

TDA (2006) Raising Standards and Tackling Workload: A National Agreement, London: TDA.

TDA (2008) Guidance on Introductory Training for Teaching Assistants and School Support Staff. Available from the TDA website.

TDA (2009) The Integrated Qualifications Framework, London: TDA.

TES (2009) 'Young Breed of "Stepford heads" Threaten Staff Wellbeing, Delegates Told', *TES*, 17 April.

Walton, A. (2009) 'Support Staff as Professionals' in Walton, A. and Goddard, G. (eds) *Supporting Every Child*, Exeter: Learning Matters.

www.cwdcouncil.org.uk/ – Website for all of those working with children and young people. It has specific pages for those working in the children's workforce, employers, local authorities, training provides, parents and carers, and children and young people themselves; also a surprisingly large 'postcard' section, covering the bulk of its online resources.

www.iqf.org.uk – For information regarding the Integrated Qualifications Framework (IQF).

www.mirandanet.ac.uk – For information regarding braided learning and professional social development.

www.tda.gov.uk/remodeling/nationalagreement.aspx

www.tda.gov.uk/support.aspx – For TDA information about support staff.

Chapter 2: Setting the Scene: Differential Performance in Primary Schools

Ainscow, M., Conteh, J., Dyson, A. and Gallanaugh, F. (2008) 'Children in Primary Education: Demography, Culture, Diversity and Inclusion', *Primary Education Review* 5/1. Cambridge: University of Cambridge.

an Ghaill, M. (1994) *Making of Men*, Milton Keynes: Open University Press.

Barker, I. (2008) 'Challenging Education Stereotypes: Class', in *TES*, 23 May.

Bartholomew, J. (2006) *The Welfare State We're In*, London: Politico.

Bernstein, B. (1975) *Class, Codes and Control*, London: Routledge.

Blakemore, S. and Frith, U. (2006) *The Learning Brain: Lessons for Education*, Oxford: Blackwell.

Blanden, J., Gregg, P., and Machin, S. (2005) *Intergenerational Mobility in Europe and North America*, Princeton: Princeton University.

Bourdieu, Pierre (1984) *Distinction: A Social Critique of the Judgement of Taste*, London: Routledge.

Central Advisory Council for Education (1967) *Children and their Primary Schools*, London: HMSO. (Commonly known as the Plowden Report.) Also available online at www.dg.dial.pipex.com/documents/plowden.shtm.

Claxton, G. (2002) *Building Learning Power*, Bristol: TLO

Crompton, R. (1998) *Class and Stratification*, Cambridge: Polity.

DfES (2003) 'Youth Study Survey: Activities and Experiences of 16 Years Olds: England and Wales 2002'. Available from www.dcsf.gov.uk/rsgateway/DB/SFR/s000382.

Donaldson, M. (1986) *Children's Minds*, London: Harper.

Douglas, J.W.B. (1964) *The Home and the School*, London: McGibbon & Kee.

Dweck, C.S. (1999) *Self Theories: Their Role in Motivation, Personality and Development*, Philadelphia: Psychology Press.

Gove, M. (2008) *A Failed Generation: Educational Inequality under Labour.*

Hughes, P. (1990) *Gender Issues in the Primary School*, Leamington: Scholastic.

Hughes, P. (2008) *Principles of Primary Education*, London: Fulton.

Illich, I. (1995) *Deschooling Society*, London: Marian Boyars.

Jones, T. (1993) *Britain's Ethnic Minorities*, London: Policy Studies Institute.

Kendall, S., Straw, S., Jones, M., Springate, I., and Grayson, H. (2008) *Narrowing the Gap in Outcomes for Vulnerable Groups: A Review of the Research Evidence*, Slough: NFER.

Kent County Council (undated) *Boys Can Do Better* Kent: KCC. Also available from www.literacytrust.org.uk/database/boys/Kentcasestudies/pdf.

Magadi, M. and Middleton, S. (2007) *Severe Child Poverty in the UK*, London: Save the Children Fund.

National Council for School Leadership (NCSL) (2008) 'Seizing Success', NCSL Annual Leadership Conference, June 2008, Birmingham.

Ofsted (2007) *Raising Standards, Improving Lives*, London: Ofsted.

Robinson, K. (2006) 'Schools Kill Creativity'. Available from www.ted.com/index.php/talks/ken_robinson_says_schools_kill_creativity.html.

Rose, S. Lewontin, R. and. Kamin, L. (1987) *Not in Our Genes: Biology, Ideology and Human Nature*, London: Penguin.

Rosenthal, R., and Jacobson, L. (1968) *Pygmalion in the Classroom*, New York: Rinehart and Winston.

Sharp, R. and Green, A. (1975) *Education and Social Control*, London: Routledge.

Shuayb, M. and O'Donnell, S. (2008) 'Aims and Values in Primary Education: England and Other Countries', in Cambridge Primary Review, *Towards a New Primary Curriculum*, Cambridge: University of Cambridge.

Smith, N. and Middleton, S. (2007) *A Review of Poverty Dynamics Research in the UK*, York: Joseph Rowntree Foundation.

Swann Committee (1985) *Education for All: Report of the Committee of Enquiry into the Education of Children from Ethnic Minority Groups*, London: HMSO.

TDA (2008) 'Guidance on Introductory Training for Teaching Assistants and School Support Staff'. Available from the TDA website.

Willis, P. (1978) *Learning to Labour*, London: Ashgate.

www.bbc.co.uk/whereilive

www.cypnow.co.uk/news/ByDiscipline/Health/login/873128/ – Children and Young People, now a newspaper archive covering social care, health, education, child care and early years, youth work, youth justice, and advice and guidance.

www.direct.gov.uk – Local services.

www.jrf.org.uk/centenary/

www.jrf.org.uk/knowledge/findings/socialpolicy/pdf/2041.pdf

www.literacytrust.org.uk/talktoyourbaby/discussionpaper.pdf

www.myneighbourhood.info – Local information, search by postcode, street, neighbourhood or on interactive map.

http://neighbourhood.statistics.gov.uk

www.nfer.ac.uk/research-areas/childrens-services/narrowing-the-gap

http://reactor-core.org/deschooling.html

www.statistics.gov.uk/about/data/classifications/current/

www.suttontrust.com/index.asp

www.ted.com/index.php/themes/top_10_tedtalks.html

www.tinyurl.com/2qcvog – Scotland, Northern Ireland, Wales.

www.ukaerialphotos.com – To buy aerial photo of a UK neighbourhood as it looks today or back as far as 1947.

www.neighbourhood.statistics.gov.uk – Know your neighbourhood.

Chapter 3: Tackling Poverty: From Beveridge to 'Every Child Matters'

Bartholomew, J. (2006) *The Welfare State We're In*, London: Politico.

Boyce, T. Robertson, R. and Dixon, A. (2008) *Kicking Bad Habits*, London: King's Fund.

Cabinet Office (2001) Preventing Social Exclusion: Report by the Social Exclusion Unit, London: Cabinet Office.

Cameron, D., Fryer-Smith, E., Harvey, P. and Wallace, E. (2008) *Practitioners' Perspectives on Child Poverty*, Nottingham: DCSF.

Cassen, R. and Kingdome, G. (2007) *Tackling Low Educational Achievement*, York: Rowntree Foundation.

CPAG (2009) *Poverty in the UK: A Summary of Facts and Figures*, London: CPAG.

DCSF (2005) *The Children's Plan: Building Brighter Futures*, Norwich: TSO.

DCSF (2009) *Children and Young People's Plan Guidance*, Norwich: TSO.

Castell, S. and Thompson, J. (2007) *Understanding Attitudes to Poverty in the UK*, London: Joseph Rowntree Foundation.

DfES, DH (2003) *Every Child Matters: Change for Children*, Nottingham: DfES.

DfES, HO, DH (2003) *Every Child Matters*, Nottingham: DfES.

DfES, HO, DH (2004) *ECM: Change for Children in Health Services*, Nottingham: DfES.

DfES, HO, DH (2004) *ECM: Change for Children in Schools*, Nottingham: DfES.

DfES, HO, DH (2004) *ECM: Next Steps*, Nottingham: DfES.

DfES, HO, DH (2006) *Working Together to Safeguard Children*, London: TSO.

Horton, C. (2009) 'More Children Taken into Care following Baby P', *Guardian*, 8 May.

Hughes, P. (2008) *Principles of Primary Education*, London: Fulton.

Laming, A. (2003) Victoria Climbie Inquiry Report, Nottingham: DfES.

Lowe, R. (2005) *The Welfare State in Britain since 1945*, Basingstoke: Palgrave Macmillan.

Maslow, A. (2000) 'Hierarchy of Basic Needs', in Carlson, N., Buskits, W. and Martin, N. (eds) *Psychology: The Science of Behaviour*, London: Pearson.

Naidoo, J. and Wills, J. (2009) *Health Promotion*, 3rd edn, Oxford: Baillière Tindall.

Smith, N. and Middleton, S. (2007) *A Review of Poverty Dynamics Research in the UK*, York: Joseph Rowntree Foundation.

Social Exclusion Unit (2001) *Preventing Social Exclusion: A Report by the Social Exclusion Unit*, London: Social Exclusion Unit, available at www.socialexclusion.gov.uk.

www.everychildmatters.gov.uk

www.barnardos.org.uk/childpoverty – Careful and well researched evidence regarding the extent of child poverty in the UK.

www.cwdcouncil.org.uk/caf – Useful and readable fact sheets and guidance on topics such as the CAF and Schools.

www.everychildmatters.gov.uk/IG00079/ – Regularly updated list of Chairs of Local Safeguarding Boards.

www.kingsfund.org.uk

www.sochealth.co.uk/history/beveridge.htm – The Executive Summary of the Report.

www.teachers.tv – This website is also excellent at covering growing issues about the ECM agenda as it relates to schools.

www.whois.com

Chapter 4: Learning and Concepts of Childhood

Alexander, R. (2008) *Emerging Perspectives on Childhood*, Cambridge: University of Cambridge Faculty of Education.

Bandura, A. (1977) *Social Learning Theory*, New Jersey: Prentice Hall.

Barron, I., Holmes, R., MacLure, M. and Runswick-Cole, K. (2008) *Primary Schools and Other Agencies*. Primary Review Research Survey 8/2, Cambridge: University of Cambridge Faculty of Education.

Boxall, M. (2002) *Nurture Groups in Schools: Principles and Practice*, London: Paul Chapman

Bruce, T. and Meggitt, C. (2005) *Child Care and Education*, Oxford: Hodder & Stoughton.

Central Advisory Council for Education (1967) *Children and their Primary Schools*, London: HMSO. (Commonly known as the Plowden Report.) Also available online at www.dg.dial.pipex.com/documents/plowden.shtm.

Canter, L. and Canter, M. (1992) *Assertive Discipline* (updated in 1996, 2001, 2002, 2005) Santa Monica, CE: Lee Canter Associates.

CPAG (2009) *Child Wellbeing and Child Poverty: Where the UK Stands in the European Table*, London: CPAG.

Cunningham, H. (2006) *The Invention of Childhood*, London: BBC Books.

DfEE (1998) *The National Literacy Strategy*, 1st edn, Nottingham: DfEE Publications.

DfEE (1998) *The National Numeracy Framework*, 1st edn, Nottingham: DfEE Publications.

Fetsco, T. and McClure, J. (2004) *Educational Psychology: An Integrated Approach to Classrooms Decisions*, Boston: Allyn & Bacon.

Gardner, H. (1993) *Frames of Mind: Theory of Multiple Intelligences*, London: Fontana.

Hughes, P. (2008) *Principles of Primary Education*, London: Fulton/Routledge.

Jones, P., Moss, D., Tomlinson, P. and Welch, S. (2008) *Childhood: Services and Provision for Children*, London: Pearson.

Kolb, D. (1984) *Experimental Learning: Experience as a Source of Learning and Development*. New Jersey: Prentice Hall.

National Research Council (2001) *How People Learn*. Washington: National Academy Press. Also available as an e-book.

Palmer, S. (2006) *Toxic Childhood*, London: Orion Books.

Reitemeier, B. (2008) 'Making Childhood Better', Childhood, Well-being and Primary Education Conference, 17 March, London.

Robb, J. and Letts, H. (2003) *Creating Motivated Kids*, London: Hodder.

TLRP (2007) *Neuroscience and Education*, London: Institute of Education.

Chapter 5: Identifying and Lifting Hidden Curriculum Barriers for Children

Hickton Madeley Architects (2008) Exemplar Studies for the Provision of New Build Primary Schools, Telford.

James, C. (1968) *Young Lives at Stake*, Glasgow: Collins.

Knight, G. and Noyes, J. (1999) 'Children's Behaviour and the Design of School Furniture', *Ergonomics*, 42, pp. 747–60.

Meighan, R. and Siraj-Blatchford, I. (1997) *A Sociology of Educating*, London: Cassell.

Pollard, A. (2002) *Reflective Teaching*. London: Continuum.

Pollard, A. and Tann, S. (1994) *Reflective Teaching in the Primary School*, London: Cassell.

Pricewaterhouse Coopers LLP (2007) *Evaluation of Building Schools for the Future*, London: DCSF.

Raveaud, M. (2005) 'Hares, Tortoises and the Social Construction of the Pupil: Differentiated Learning in French and English Primary Schools', *British Educational Research Journal*, 31(4), 459–79.

Sousa, D. (2009) *How the Brain Learns: Management Strategies for Every Classroom*, London: Sage.

Suknandan, L. and Lee, B. (2004) *Streaming, Setting and Grouping by Ability*, Slough: NFER.

Teaching and Learning Research Programme (2004) *Personalised Learning*, London: ESRC. Also available from the TLRP website.

Wall, K., Dockrell, J. and Peacey, N. (2007) *Primary Schools: The Built Environment*. Primary Review Research Survey 6/1, Cambridge: University of Cambridge Faculty of Education.

Willis, J. and Ross, T. (2002) *Doctor Xargle's Book of Earthlets*, London: Andersen Press.

Woolner, P., Hall, E., Higgins, S., McCaughey, C. and Wall, K. (2007) 'A Sound Foundation? What We Know about the Impact of Environments on Learning and the Implications for the Building Schools for the Future', *Oxford Review of Education*, 33(1), pp. 47–70.

Chapter 6: Change and Challenges for Primary Schools

Bartholomew, J. (2006) *The Welfare State We're In*, London: Politico.

Batmanghelidj, F. (2003) *Your Body's Many Cries for Water*, Manchester: Tagman Press. (There have been very controversial responses to this book, and it should be treated with caution.)

Bellisle, F. (2004) 'Effects of Diet on Behaviour and Cognition in Children', *British Journal of Nutrition*, 92 (Suppl 2), S227–32.

Blakemore, S. and Frith, U. (2007) *The Learning Brain: Lessons for Education*, Oxford: Blackwell.

Chambers, M., Powell, G. and Claxton, G. (2004) *Building 101 Ways to Learning Power*, Bristol: TLO.

Claxton, G. (2005) *Building Learning Power*, Bristol: TLO.

Cooke, L. (2007) *Moving Minds*. DVD (www.movingminds.org.uk).

Corrie, C. (2003) *Becoming Emotionally Intelligent*, Stafford: Network Educational Press.

Curran, A. (2008) *The Little Book of Big Stuff about the Brain: The True Story of Your Amazing Brain*, Carmarthen: Crown Publishing.

DCSF (2005) *Social and Emotional Aspects of Learning: Improving Behaviour, Improving Learning*, London: DCSF.

De Bono, E. (2000) *Six Thinking Hats*, London: Penguin.

Dennison, P. and G. (undated) Edu-Kinesthetics Inc. Available online at www.braingym.co.uk. (Also, Dennison can be seen on YouTube, with Jeremy Paxman, defending Edu-Kinesthetics.)

Drucker, P. (2003) *The New Realities*, New York: Harper and Row.

Dryden, G. and Vos, J. (2005) *The New Learning Revolution*, Stafford: Network Educational Press. (Also available online.)

Goldacre, B. (2008) *Bad Science*, London: Fourth Estate.

Goswami, U. and Bryant, P. (2007) *Children's Cognitive Development and Learning*, Primary Review Research Survey 2/1a, Cambridge: University of Cambridge Faculty of Education.

Greenhalgh, P. (2002) *Reaching out to All Learners*, Stafford: Network Continuum Education.

Hannaford, C. (2005) *Smart Moves: Why Learning is Not All in Your Head*, Arlington, VA: Great Ocean Publishers.

Hughes, P. (2008) *Principles of Primary Education*, London: Fulton.

Laurillard, Diane (undated) 'Digital technologies and their role in achieving our educational ambitions', Inaugural Lecture, London: Institute of Education.

Mezirow, J. (2005) 'The Transtheoretical Model of the Stages of Change and the Phases of Transformative Learning', *Journal of Transformative Education*, 3(4), 394–415.

NRC (2000) *How People Learn: Brain, Mind, Experience and School*, Washington, DC: National Academics Press. Available online at www.nap.edu/catalog.php?record_id=9853.

Palmer, S. (2006) *Toxic Childhood*, London: Orion.

Palmer, S. (2007) *Detoxing Childhood: What Parents Need to Know to Raise Happy, Successful Children*, London: Orion.

Richardson, W. (2008) *Blogs, Wikis, Podcasts and Other Powerful Web Tools for Classrooms*, 2nd edn, London: Sage.

Robb, J. and Letts, H. (1997) *Creating Kids Who Can Concentrate: Proven Strategies for Beating ADD without Drugs*, London: Hodder & Stoughton.

Rose, J. (2009) *The Primary Review*, London: DCSF.

Smith, A. and Call, N. (2000) *The ALPS Approach*, Stafford: NEP.

Sousa, D. (2004) *How the Brain Learns to Read*, London: Sage.

Sousa, D. (2006) *How the Special Needs Brain Learns*, London: Sage.

Sousa, D. (2007) *How the Brain Learns Mathematics*, London: Sage.

Sousa, D. (2009) *How the Brain Influences Behaviour: Management Strategies for Every Classroom*, London: Sage.

TLRP (2007) *Neuroscience and Education*, London: Institute of Education.

Yelland, N. (2006) *Shift to the Future: Rethinking Learning with New Technologies in Education*, Abingdon: Routledge.

www.bristol.ac.uk/education/enterprise/elli – Information about the Effective Longlife Learning Inventory (ELLI).

www.childhoodbereavementnetwork.org.uk/documents/ParticipationGuidelines.pdf

www.durhamtrial.org/

www.guardian.co.uk/commentisfree/2008/mar/29/5/

Chapter 7: Teaching Assistants

Campbell, A. and Fairbairn, G. (eds) (2005) *Working with Support in the Classroom*, London: Paul Chapman Publishing.

DfEE (1997) Learning Support Assistants, London: HMSO.

Fox, G. (1998) *A Handbook for Learning Support Assistants*, London: David Fulton Publishers.

Hall, W. (2004) 'Inclusion – Special Needs', in Bold, C. (ed) *Supporting Teaching and Learning*, London: David Fulton Publishers.

National Teacher Research Panel (2006) The Active Engagement of Teaching Assistants in Teaching and Learning. Contact e-mail: Langley.infants.school@plymouth.gov.uk

Ofsted (2002) Teaching Assistants in Primary Schools: An Evaluation of the Quality and Impact of their Work, London: Ofsted.

Ofsted (2008) The Deployment Training and Development of the Wider School Workforce, London: Ofsted.

QCA (2000) A Language in Common: Assessing English as an Additional Language, London: QCA.

Smith, P., Whitby, K., and Sharp, C. (2004) The Employment and Deployment of Teaching Assistants, LGA research report 5/04, Slough: NFER.

TES (2008) 'Heads are "Failing to Support Assistants", TES, 7 November.

Walton, A. (2009) 'Support Staff as Professionals', in Walton, A. and Goddard, G. (eds) Supporting Every Child, Exeter: Learning Matters.

Warnock Report (1978) Report of the Committee of Enquiry into the Education of Handicapped children and Young People, London: HMSO (www.dg.dial.pipex.com)

www.continyou.org.uk/ – ContinYou aims to 'open up opportunities for learning that will help people to change their lives, improving the well-being of individuals, families and communities'.

www.tda.gov.uk – Comprehensive section on how the TDA see the role of teaching assistants.

Chapter 8: Mentors

DfES (2001) Guidance for Learning Mentors, London: DfES.

DfES (2003) Excellence and Enjoyment, Nottingham: DfES.

Hobson, A. and Kington, A. (2002) Evaluation of Excellence in Cities Primary Extension. Available from www.nfer.ac.uk/research/eic.asp.

Hughes, P. (2005) 'Learning Mentors', Chapter 4 in Campbell, A. and Fairbairn, G. (eds) Working with Support in the Classroom, London: Paul Chapman.

Liverpool Excellence Partnership (2003) Learning Mentor Training, 3rd edn, London: DfES.

Maslow, A. (1962) Towards a Psychology of Being, New York, NY: Nostrand.

www.tda.gov.uk/support.aspx – This covers the TDA view of roles, standards, qualification options and progression routes for support staff in schools.

www.cwdcouncil.org.uk/ – A website for all of those working with children and young people. It has specific pages for those working in the children's workforce, employers, local authorities, training provides, parents and carers, and children and young people themselves.

www.liv.ac.uk/educational-opportunities/primary – Liverpool University Centre for Life Long Learning – Professor Fluffy.

www.andrelleducation.co.uk – The Big Write Project.

www.dcsf.gov.uk/strategy/children'splan – Children's Plans.

Chapter 9: 'An Exceptional Pastoral Care Team': A Case Study

Jones, P., Moss, D., Tomlinson, P. and Welch, S. (2008) Childhood: Services and Provision for Children, Harlow: Pearson/Educational.

Chapter 10: Attendance, Health and Study Support

DCSF (2007) Extended Schools: Building on Experience, Nottingham: DCSF.

DfES (2006) Study Support: A National Framework for Extending Learning Opportunities, Nottingham: DfES.

TDA (revised 2008) Professional Standards for Qualified Teacher Status and Requirements for Initial Teacher Training, London: TDA.

www.biglotteryfund.org.uk/

www.everychildmatters.gov.uk/ete/extendedschools/

www.healthyschools.gov.uk/Resources/ – For case studies, resources on healthy schools and related areas.

Chapter 11: Case Study: Local Authority Integrated Working

Graham, P. (2004) Cognitive Behaviour Therapy for Children and Families, Cambridge: Cambridge University Press.

Hughes, P. (2009) 'Breaking Barriers to Learning', in Warren, S. (ed) An Introduction to Education Studies, London: Continuum.

Kelly, G. (1991) *The Psychology of Personal Constructs*, London: Routledge.

Maslow, A. (2000) 'Hierarchy of Basic Needs', in Carlson, N., Buskits, W. and Martin, N. (eds) *Psychology: The Science of Behaviour*, London: Pearson.

www.aep.org.uk/ - Website for the Professional Association of Educational Psychologists.

www.bps.org.uk/careers/what-do-psychologists-do/areas/educational.cfm

Note: LA websites generally include information on integrated services working.

Chapter 12: Public Services – Police and Fire

Anon. (2006) 'Over 400 Officers Patrol School to Curb Truancy and Violence', *Daily Mail*, 27 October.

DfES and HO (2008) Safer School Partnerships, Nottingham: DfES and HO.

Graef, R. (2001) Why Restorative Justice? Repairing the Harm Caused by Crime, London: Calouste Gulbenian Foundation.

Herbert, B. (2007) '6-Year-Olds under Arrest', *New York Times*, 9 April.

Hughes J (2003) 'Blagg! An Evaluation of a Drama Based Offending Behaviour Workshop', Manchester University Centre for Applied Theatre Research. Available from www.tipp.org.uk/tipp/index.php?page=research.

www.suzylamplugh.org/index.asp

www.teachernet.gov.uk/teachers/issue22/primary/features/Rightingwrongs/

www.transformingconflict.org/Restorative_Approaches_and_Practices.htm

Chapter 13: Charity, Consultants and Volunteers

TDA (2007) Primary Induction ICT. (Available as a PowerPoint file from the TDA website.)

TDA (2008) Guidance on Introductory Training for Teaching Assistants and School Support Staff'. (Available from the TDA website.)

Webster-Stratton, C. (2006) *The Incredible Years*, London: Incredible Years Publishing.

Webster-Stratton, C. and Mostyn, D. (1999) *How to Promote Children's Social and Emotional Competence*, London: Incredible Years Publishing.

Chapter 14: 'Believe in Children'

www.barnardos.org.uk/who_we_are.htm

Index